A
Voice
in the
Wilderness

A
Voice
in the
Wilderness

LORAN W. HELM

Compiled and Edited by Jon L. Cullum

EVANGEL VOICE PUBLICATIONS, INC.

Parker, Indiana 47368

First Printing, August, 1973 - 5,500 Copies
Second Printing, September, 1974 - 20,000 Copies
Third Printing, March, 1977 - 16,000 Copies

EVANGEL VOICE PUBLICATIONS, INC., Parker City, Indiana 47368

Printed in the United States of America by:
Harmony Press, Inc., Bourbon, Indiana 46504
(Formerly Country Print Shop)

Preface

As adequately as words can convey, I wish to express my deep thanksgiving to each one who has sustained us in prayer and petitioned the Throne that this humble pilgrimage might be shared wholly and entirely for the glory of God. I have hoped to not overlook a single person who, through the months and years, has assisted us in our calling to declare the message of the Kingdom of God to all the precious churches of Jesus Christ throughout the world. (It is important to review that wherever two persons gather together who have experienced the New Birth, who love Jesus with all their hearts, and are obeying the Holy Spirit —they are the true Church of God.) To each of these in the Body of Christ around the world, I greet you in the matchless name of our risen and soon-coming Lord.

I only wish it were possible for me to relate how glorious it has been to walk with God over these years; but I sense the acute inadequacy of a single volume to even approach the wonder of it. It has been my constant prayer that, in spite of our human limitations, the Holy Spirit will be sensed within every paragraph and through every phase. It is my hope, as well, that each of you will consider these pages not simply a book, but rather a personal conversation between the two of us.

Though it has been my sincere longing that I not offend one person or create a single moment of misunderstanding, I recognize that the testimony of God's servants has almost always been received with difficulty, especially by religious leaders. My words to the professed church may sound severe to some ears, but, by God's grace and the cleansing power of the abiding Holy Spirit, I can attest that they flow from a heart which is broken with love for every living person, and for the true Church of Jesus Christ.

Try to bear with me, please, when I speak of the Lord "telling" me something or of the Holy Spirit "speaking" to me. God has very rarely communicated Himself to me in an audible voice, but, for over forty years, He has made His will known to me by the operation of His gifts within me. It is only by His grace and mercy that I would know anything at all, let alone be capable of discerning His sacred voice. Whenever these terms of "speaking" or "telling" are used, simply recall that God did not audibly tell me something, but He revealed it to the inner man by His Spirit.

Upon occasion I have included words, phrases, and even entire paragraphs in the **boldface type.** By means of this, I have sought to alert dear ones to the special importance of that particular section. Generally the words or phrases will be very simple and unauspicious; yet, they contain a seed of eternal truth which God has revealed to me only after years of walking with Him. If we could but grasp one or two of these tiny gems of divine reality, it would be worth more than gold to a true follower of the meek and lowly Jesus.

To my son-in-law, Jon Cullum, I wish to voice my appreciation for his labor of love in compiling and editing the materials of this book. Since he has lived and traveled with me for nearly four years, he is aware that God works through me more extensively by means of the spoken word. He has, therefore, maintained the sharing in the first person throughout.

I want very much to express whole-hearted appreciation for what my faithful wife, my precious parents, and my dear family have meant to me and my ministry through almost four decades. What an encouragement it is to have many of my own children, nephews, nieces, and my own brothers and their companions who would drive hundreds of miles to be with this limited and unworthy servant in services wherever the Holy Spirit would send me.

I would like to acknowledge the assistance of Virginia Yoder in transcribing many messages, from which a number of our experiences were taken, and also make mention of Geneva Walker's contribution in transcribing related materials. To Rev. and Mrs. Wesley Bullis, for their invaluable insights and suggestions, I express my deep appreciation. Likewise, I wish to thank Terry Hogue for his dedicated assistance.

I should especially wish to express gratitude to Vera Wagner for her many hours of unflagging devotion to the typing of this manuscript, from the very beginning to its completion. I also owe an unusual debt of thanksgiving to Artley Cullum, Tom Harman, and the entire staff of the Country Print Shop for how they have been used of the Lord to help us these past ten years.

The man primarily responsible for this book getting under-way is Comer Tankersley, a precious man who Jesus wonder-fully saved and transformed on our first journey to Israel in 1969. He has been the only person who said to me, "If you need money to print this book, I will simply borrow it." On the basis of this loving and gracious confidence, I felt led of Jesus to have my son-in-law begin the research and preparation of this volume.

I know that I am a needy person before the Lord. Because of this, wherever I might have come short of God's will, or whenever I might have disappointed or failed precious ones, I ask forgiveness, for I desire to be holy unto God at all times. I am aware that I have prayed too little and won too few to Jesus. I need so much more of God's holy love, which is the only true evidence of Christianity.

I trust this book, through the Holy Spirit, will lift your heart, awaken a determination to press toward the cross, and inspire you to God's perfect will, as you seek first, not the plans of noble men, but the glorious Kingdom of God.

A trusting servant of Jesus,
Loran W. Helm,
Parker, Indiana,
April 17, 1973.

LORAN W. HELM

Foreword
by Mary Webster

Before I was to speak, I saw him! In fact, you couldn't miss him! Seated on the aisle, he just stood out among the rest of the audience—a very unusual, well-dressed distinguished looking man with the "smile of God" upon his face. Everything about him seemed to say: this man is different! I thought: "Melchizedek—no beginning—no end."

When we bowed our heads for the opening prayer, the Lord revealed to me that I was not the one to bring the message, but that I was simply to introduce this brother and he would speak. It was so strange trying to introduce someone whose name I didn't know; so I simply related what had been revealed to me, then called on "Melchizedek" to tell us what God had laid on his heart. Later, I learned his name was not Melchizedek, but Loran Helm.

It was evident why God had chosen to use Brother Loran that morning, for people were really blessed.

Later, I told him he must be a very lonely Christian, for few people had gone as far in their walk with Jesus as he had. Not everyone could share the heights and depths he knew, for they had not surrendered to Jesus in the same degree. He only smiled.

During a retreat in which he was a leader, I watched this beautifully "free spirit" nearly breaking his wings trying to fly inside a cocoon of the framework, boundaries, and constraints of a structural organization. It led me to suggest to him that it might prove more redemptive for him and others if he dropped the "cocoon", which bound him like a straight-jacket, and soared the heights with Jesus, free to do His bidding.

As you read this book, you will find yourself soaring also—or, at least, desiring to go to Jesus and get the wings to try!

There's a Voice in the Wilderness Crying

There's a voice in the wilderness crying,
A call from the ways untrod:
Prepare in the desert a highway,
A highway for our God!
The valleys shall be exalted,
The lofty hills brought low;
Make straight all the crooked places,
Where the Lord our God may go!

O Zion that bringest good tidings,
Get thee up to the heights and sing!
Proclaim to a desolate people
The coming of their King:
Like the flowers of the field they perish,
The works of men decay,
The power and pomp of nations
Shall pass like a dream away.

But the word of our God endureth,
The arm of the Lord is strong;
He stands in the midst of nations,
And He will right the wrong:
He shall feed His flock like a shepherd,
And fold the lambs to His breast;
In pastures of peace He'll lead them,
And give to the weary rest.

There's a voice in the wilderness crying,
A call from the way untrod:
Prepare in the desert a highway,
A highway for our God!
The valleys shall be exalted,
The lofty hills brought low;
Make straight all the crooked places,
Where the Lord our God may go!

—James L. Milligan

Used by permission of A. Lewis Milligan, from "The Book of Hymns," Abingdon Press, Nashville, Tennessee, 1966

Testimonials

I am deeply indebted to Rev. Wesley Bullis, my present pastor, and to Rev. Robert Boggs, my former pastor, for writing the following letters describing briefly our relationship with them over the years. I can attest that these two servants of God love Jesus with all their hearts and desire to be directed daily by the Holy Spirit.

"I am confident that one of the most sensitive professional relationships existing anywhere must exist where a retired pastor or an evangelist is a member of a local congregation. The relationship of that person with the pastor is a very delicate professional relationship. It can be a source of rich fellowship or a source of irritation and distress.

"For eight years I have served in the United Methodist Church of Parker, Indiana, of which Rev. Loran Helm is a member.

"Brother Loran Helm and I have the most congenial relationship. He is never condemnatory of our denomination or the local church. He is always concerned, supportive, interested, and in prayer for the best interest and effectiveness of the church, for its pastor, and family. He never intrudes, but only participates as invited or as he is made to feel free and welcome. I am never uneasy when he is in the service or other activities, but always encouraged and strengthened.

"Our fellowship has been a source of great personal strength to me and an encouragement to press on in my ministry and in my commitment to Jesus Christ. Brother Loran is also appreciated and loved by my entire family.

Wesley M. Bullis, Minister"

"Friends,

"I count it a high privilege to have had the privilege of pastoring Parker United Methodist Church for four wonderful years, 1959 to 1963. Rev. Loran Helm, whose pilgrimage with Jesus is the subject of this book, was a member of the church. Much of the time he was out in evangelism wherever the Lord sent him, but the times he was in Parker were very encouraging occasions to the parsonage family. The Lord sent him to us, it seemed, just when we needed him most. Sometimes I felt the need of a lift and encouragement. At times, one of the children needed a healing touch from the Lord. Always it was a tremendous help to have him in the congregation on Sunday. His prayer power seemed to bring Heaven closer and make it easier to preach.

"As you will discover, this is more than a book about a man, be that man ever so filled with the Spirit of Jesus, of wisdom, of brotherly affection, and all the Christian graces you could name. This book is about Jesus, the all-sufficient Saviour and all-loving Lord; about what He can and will do with a life truly yielded to him!

"God richly bless you as you pursue this adventure with Jesus our Lord.

So gratefully,

Robert Boggs, Jr."

I have discovered in my walk with God that Satan opposes only that which God is truly leading. Therefore, I include the following precious words written by my dear companion, for I believe they may help dispel the doubt and unbelief which Satan will attempt to place in each person who reads this humble pilgrimage. It is only by the mercies of God, the continual help of Jesus, that she would be able to say these things. I include them only to glorify God, who alone has made all things possible.

"It has been a great joy and pleasure to be walking hand in hand with a true man of God for over forty years. There has never been any doubt in my mind concerning his walk with God, for it has always been unwavering and completely consistent at home and abroad.

"Prayer has always been a very real and daily part of our life, and Loran has spent many, many hours in prayer through the years. When we left all plans of earth to wait upon God's plans, my husband lived a life of read-

12

ing the Word and praying—always striving for God's perfect will. He had no thought then of starting any new church, nor does he have now. His whole life's desire is to do God's will and love everybody in the world.

"I am happy to say that listening to my husband preach for all these years is still exciting and lifting. The Holy Spirit-led services are always refreshing and convicting to the heart. It is wonderful to listen with the knowledge that the message is coming through a life that is being lived in the same manner in which it is being preached.

"I am so thankful that all of our dear children believe the Lord is leading their father, because they have seen it working consistently through the years at home. This does not mean life has been easy, for it has been a continual pressing forward.

"When carnal men have spoken out such untruthful things about us, it has grieved our daughters and our loved ones very much. Anyone who really makes an effort to know my husband and watch his life could not make the many damaging statements we have heard and be a true follower of Jesus.

"I am happy to say that the dear Lord has always sustained and undergirded us through the hard places. He causes us to love all people everywhere, especially those trying to discredit my husband's ministry. Praise the Lord for the marvelous grace God gives us at all times and under all circumstances. I desire to be true and faithful to the high calling of God in Christ Jesus.

"This book gives only the very briefest account of God's leading through the years, for His sweet guidances have been a continual day by day experience and have never failed. I can truthfully say that in these forty years, my husband has never wavered or turned to look back at any time or under any situation.

"I am speaking as a wife who has lived closely for many years with the author of this book. I rejoice in the leading of the Lord, and over the continued faithfulness of Loran's life. Right now my heart is stirred and witnesses to the truth of these feeble words I have tried to write conveying my love and appreciation for my dear husband and for his life of obedience and trust in God.

Florence M. Helm"

Contents

1 "WHY DON'T MEN OBEY GOD?"

Pulling the front door shut of the lovely home which Jesus had provided us, I started to turn toward the car where my dear wife was waiting to accompany me to a restaurant. At that moment God spoke within me: "Someone is near death!" The burden was severe. "Honey," I told my wife, getting into the car, "the Holy Spirit is revealing to me that one of my family is close to death. I must call out to God for them." As we drove toward the highway, I prayed and prayed, but the revelation became so intense that I finally said, "We can't go any farther. We will have to go back home and intercede with God for this dear one in peril."

A fine meal now forgotten, I returned to my prayer room and cried out to God, "Oh, God deliver, deliver, deliver! Lord, undertake! Jesus, we need you badly!" I pled and prayed for two or three hours before I began to get relief.

The following day my parents were called to officiate at a funeral in Cromwell, Indiana, several miles north; but my mother awoke that morning with an unusual feeling upon her. When she started to get dressed for the journey she would almost lose her breath. The burden was so strong that finally she said, "Eldon, I am not supposed to go to that funeral."

My father was surprised: "But Mother, they're expecting us. They're all expecting you." They had pastored in this community years before and had many friends there.

"I can't help it," she insisted. "It takes my breath to talk about it." So my father made the trip alone.

On the way home, he began to round the bend at Big Lake in a 1959 two-door Ford, when a man in a large Hudson, outweighing my father's car by about a thousand pounds, swerved over into the left-hand lane and hit him head-on. The impact drove the engine back into the driver's compartment a little, injuring him.

If Mother had been in the car, it would surely have killed her; but Dad was always an exceptionally strong man. He had more power in his arms at the age of seventy than many men have at the age of fifty. This enormous strength spared him from worse injury or death, because he simply braced his arms against the impact and bent the steering wheel down. As it was, the wheel dealt him an awful blow, and left its impression in his chest for some time. A few ribs were hurt and the muscles were badly bruised. One of our dear friends who saw Dad's car following the accident remarked, "How did he ever get out of there alive?"

I answered him, "God's mercy spared him."

The doctor prescribed a strong pain medication, which Dad took Sunday, Monday, and Tuesday. By Wednesday the pain pills had lost their effectiveness and nothing would diminish his suffering. He told me, "These pills don't do me any good now, Son. I don't know whether I can stand much more pain."

At that, I dropped to my knees beside his chair, laid my hand across my father's arm, and began to pray: "Oh, God, my Dad is hurting so badly, and nothing seems to stop this pain. Would you, dear Father, in the matchless name of Jesus, now remove this suffering for your glory and honor?" The power of God came down into his body and I sensed it. "Did you feel that?" I asked my dad.

"Ohhh, yes!" he answered. "That feels so much better!" He got up from his chair, took his cane in hand, and began to move about. To God's glory, he never again had pain from that injury.

It was the Lord who had heard and answered prayer. He

18

had revealed the burden of this accident the day before it occurred. His message to me just as I turned to leave our home was: "Some of your loved ones are about to leave home now." I praise Him for His faithfulness.

I praise the Lord that I was born of parents who feared God, who loved God and taught me of Jesus. My earliest recollection is of my mother talking and singing to me of Jesus. She would hold me in her arms and sing, "Oh, yes, there is power in Jesus' blood to wash and make me clean."

I came from a line of people who loved God. On my father's side of the family, my great, great-grandfather helped build the little Methodist church at Windsor about 115 to 120 years ago. He was a very faithful man, a very humble man.

His son, my great-grandfather, walked to Sunday morning and evening services, to prayer meeting and evangelistic services, and not a short distance either. Rev. Eddie Greenwald said to me years ago, "I think perhaps your great-grandfather didn't miss a service in thirty to thirty-five years." My mother remembers going up the church steps when she was a little girl the age of eight to ten hearing her mother say, "Well, we will have a good meeting tonight: Uncle Jerry is here." He was only an humble farmer, but he loved Jesus.

The home of my mother's folks, Loran and Elizabeth Dickson, had always been the home of visiting ministers. Regardless of their church affiliation, they were welcome at my grandfather's table, and also at his father's table. Rev. Gilmore, the first man I recognized as a man of God, had a deep appreciation for my mother's parents. He told me years later when he was not well and I was taking him to a medical clinic, "Loran, your grandmother, Elizabeth Dickson, lived for others. The epitaph on her tombstone could read: 'She lived for others.' "

I was born in Muncie, Indiana, February 3, 1916, the first son of Alvin Eldon Helm and Mary Rosetta Helm. We re-

19

mained there only a short time before moving a few miles southeast to the small village of Windsor, where we lived in what Dad and Mother called "the little red house."

It is in the village of Windsor that I really first remember prayer, remember church, remember the preaching. The Lord has somehow permitted me to recall definite experiences from an early age. I can remember well the buildings which stood across the street from our home when I was less than three years old. You would wonder how a boy could recollect when he was so small, but I see them now just like a picture. Standing in his place of business in one of those old buildings is a man they called "one-armed Dudley." Over to the east I can see Mary West sitting on her porch. Those buildings were torn down to build the new Christian Church, dedicated in 1920.

Most vividly I recall sitting in church near the front listening to Rev. Gilmore preach. Following one Sunday morning service I remember very well my father coming home and asking my mother, "Mary, why didn't men and women obey God in church today?" And she answered, "I don't know." Upon another Sunday I can hear my father again saying, "Mary, why didn't men obey the Lord this morning in church?" And my mother replied, "Eldon, I just don't know what to say."

Each time my father asked, "Why didn't men obey God?", it was getting inside of me until I began to wonder myself: why aren't men obedient? Why aren't they humbling themselves? This question pierced my heart. Somehow God allowed my little four to five-year-old heart to hear that question deep in the interior life and hold on to it.

In the last few years God has revealed to me that the seriousness and the urgency of obeying the Holy Spirit is not getting into the hearts of many people, even into those who have been in the church for fifty years. God has made known to me that very few in either the ministry or the laity have perceived the mystery or the absolute necessity of

20

truly obeying God. Few have grasped the message that we must do what God reveals rather than what we desire, what we arrange, or what we plan. Surely it is a miracle that the seriousness of obeying God took root in my heart at such a young age.

I believe my hearing God's call to obedience as a child was because of the Holy Ghost falling upon me as I was born. It is of such consequence that I hesitate to speak of it; but my mother tells me that the Holy Spirit fell upon both of us as I came into this world. She did not relate this to me until May 1956, when I was forty years of age.

I had taken Mother to Rev. L. M.'s church in Kokomo, where God had led me for revival services, and after returning home the second night of services we were enjoying the sweet fellowship in the Lord. The presence of Jesus was to be sensed all around, and Mother said to me, "Son, I have had the most wonderful rest in the last two nights that I have had in two months."

I replied, "Mother, it is because of the precious presence of the Holy Spirit."

She nodded her agreement, for the Spirit of God was then falling so sweetly upon us. She then said, "This is the way I felt, Son, when you were born."

I was stunned. "Mother!"

"Yes, Loran," she continued, "the Holy Spirit fell upon me when you were born, just as you came from my body. I thought that all mothers experienced this with each child, until I had borne five more sons and never felt that Presence again."

"Mother!" I managed to say again. "This is so sacred! It is so serious!" This knowledge of God's Spirit falling upon me at birth brought me, as it were, with my face to the floor beseeching God that I would be faithful to Jesus. I was crying out in my heart not to fail God as men have in the past over women, over money; through prayerlessness, faithlessness, trustlessness; by disobedience, resentment, strife, or

21

analyzation. If you read the Bible carefully, you will observe that almost all men failed God; they came short of His will. I prayed, "Oh, Lord, deliver me that I may never grieve Thy Holy Spirit!"

Through my mother and father, God taught me the urgency of obedience, and made me aware that men seldom consistently obey God. In my early background God was preparing me to see that men should obey the Lord and strive to do His will, for Jesus said in Luke 13: "Strive to enter in at the strait gate: for many I say unto you, will seek to enter in, and shall not be able."

So, you see, it isn't by accident that I have been striving to obey God. It isn't by chance that I heard at this early age the command: "Obey God; obey the Holy Spirit; do what God wants you to do." It is because the Lord has been dealing with me. It is because of my heritage. It is because of the gift God gave us in Jesus Christ that He laid it deep in my heart—placed it deep in the interior life (and the Holy Spirit operates within me as I tell you this)—to obey what the Holy Spirit wants me to do. Praise God!

These thirty years and more of walking with God seem but a few days, because the delight of all living is to walk with God, to trust Him, to wait upon Him (and when I say that, I feel the power of God coming through my body and up into my arms). Of course, my path has not always been easy, but it has been wonderful and glorious. I have not looked to the difficulties, I have looked to Jesus. I have not proceeded according to the patterns of the earth, I have endeavored to follow God's Word and the revelation of His Spirit. It is God who has brought us to victory. It is God who has given us daily strength. He is the One who has given all things that we have experienced in this sacred walk with Jesus Christ. Praise be unto His name forever.

2 MY FATHER

I believe God has had His hand on my father and mother since they were born. Although I can only acquaint you with a tiny portion of how God has worked with my parents and spared them, by His kindness, I do have on record some of the events as they have told them to me. If it had not been for God's faithfulness, I would not be here to share with you this walk with Jesus. It is truly only by God's grace that we have come this far.

Dad never tired of telling me how God miraculously spared him from death when he was but a youngster:

"Daddy and Uncle Pete were going for gravel one day," he recalls, "and you might remember the old gravel wagons—they were long, heavy-bedded constructions with huge wheels. One sat up pretty high in them.

"Well, I was sitting between Dad and Uncle Pete, and since I was only two-and-a-half to three years old, Daddy told his brother, 'Now Pete, I want you to take care of Eldon.' So he was trying to hold on to me as we jolted along.

"Suddenly, with the big team pulling hard against that heavy load of gravel, the wheel came off on the right-hand side. The wagon dropped fast and hit the ground with such a jolt that Uncle Pete was hurled into the fence. I must have been thrown forward directly under the horses, because the first thing Pete remembers seeing when he stopped moving was the freshly-shod hoof of the huge mare coming down right on my head. Of course, the horse was excited and nervous because of the accident. That hoof would have crushed my head like a mallet."

23

"But quicker than lightning," Uncle Pete told me, "faster than I have ever moved, my hand shot out, grabbed hold of Eldon's foot, and pulled him out of the way just as the mare's hoof came down." He told me a number of times that something far beyond him helped him to get Dad out of there. Granddad had always chided Uncle Pete for being slow and poky, but he never teased him again after that day. Dad was spared only through the mercies of the Lord.

About a year or two later my father experienced another miraculous deliverance from death, this time through prayer. When the large work horse he was riding stumbled, Dad suffered a severe fall on his neck and back. At first there didn't appear to be any permanent injury, but the next day he experienced difficulty in walking. At evening time, while helping his father feed the pigs, his legs buckled under him. Unable to get up, he was carried to the house by his father.

Dr. Chenoweth took much time in examining him, I understand, concluding that Dad had a creeping paralysis as a result of his fall. He informed my grandfather William and grandmother Esther Helm that their sixth child possibly might get better, but could get worse; and Dad's condition worsened. He began to lose the use of one part of his body and then of another. Soon he wasn't able to talk, and then he couldn't swallow. Though they kept him alive by injecting food and medicine into him, hardly a muscle of his body moved. Even his eyelids were lifeless. Only his breathing continued, slow and shallow. Three doctors said that he could not live.

But Dad had an aunt, his mother's sister, who lived fourteen miles away in Muncie. Aunt Zelpe lived close to God: she talked with God. One day she appeared at the farmhouse door. "The Holy Spirit has revealed to me," she told William and Esther, "that if I come and pray for Eldon's healing, he will live. William, would you have any objection if I pray for your son?"

24

Grandfather replied. "No—Dr. Chenoweth and the other doctors have given him up. He is at the edge of death now." So I am told that Aunt Zelpe moved into the Helm household, spending most of her waking hours by my father's bedside. This was to be her vigil of intercessory prayer for days to come: an assignment she had never before attempted and was never called to repeat for anyone else in her lifetime. It is said that she would rub my father's frail body and pray until she would collapse to the floor in exhaustion. But in spite of her ministrations, his condition worsened. His flesh was hardly noticeable against the protruding frame of his skeleton.

Uncle Pete shared with me fifty years later that on three occasions they called the family around my father's bedside: "If you want to see Eldon alive," they said, "you'll have to hurry, because it won't be long and he will be gone." Yet he lived on, even when it became too painful to continue injecting him with food and medicine.

One morning God revealed to Aunt Zelpe that the boy would be healed if his mother would yield her heart to Jesus. She was thrilled with the revelation and tried to speak with her sister concerning her soul. But Esther seemed to sense something of the nature of Zelpe's purpose and managed to avoid her for some time. She would see her sister coming and go another way through the house. Finally, Aunt Zelpe confronted her at the door leading into the hallway. "Now Esther," she said, "do you want this boy to live?"

Of course, my grandmother was perturbed by this question and replied, "Why yes, Zelpe, you know I do."

"Well," her sister said kindly but firmly, "you must give your life to Jesus so I can pray and have faith for this baby to be raised up." Immediately Grandmother Esther dropped to her knees and asked Jesus to forgive her and come into her heart. Praying through to victory, she was converted and became so happy, she shouted nearly all over the house. Esther was just a little woman, a short Dutch woman, but she was unable to contain the joy she experienced in Jesus that day. I have heard it said that whenever there was a cottage prayer meeting, my grandmother was often heard to shout for joy in Jesus.

Since her sister had fulfilled her part in God's leading, Zelpe returned to her intercession with renewed strength. Each day she would pray for a specific part of my father's body to receive help. She would first tell the family how she was going to pray, and God would answer according to her prayer. On the third morning she announced, "Eldon will call for something to eat within the next twenty-four hours. I'm going to pray for his appetite and his voice to return." All day she prayed. Then that afternoon, a wonderful miracle took place—my father, who hadn't been able to speak or swallow for many days, whispered, "I would like some crackers and tea."

My grandparents were beside themselves with joy! Since there was no tea in the house and not a cracker was to be found either, William told Uncle Pete to saddle old Clyde (the same horse Dad was riding when he fell) and ride as fast as possible the two miles into Windsor for tea and crackers. Later that night, Grandfather was holding my daddy in his arms, thankfully feeding him crackers and tea.

People came from around that area to see the boy who was a living miracle. As a very little girl, my mother can recall standing between the carriage wheels when her grandmother and grandfather Dickson said, "We have just returned from seeing a little boy who was raised up from the edge of death by a life of trust and faith in Jesus." She later reminisced, "Little did I know that that young boy would grow up to become my husband, the father of our six sons."

God spoke a prophecy through Aunt Zelpe at the time of this miraculous healing. She declared: "This young man is going to be a man of God; and his faith, or that of his seed, will circle the globe." We are believing God to someday see this fulfilled, by His grace and only for His glory.

26

3 NARROW ESCAPES FROM DEATH

It seemed that Satan was determined my father would not fulfill the place to which God had appointed him. Dad once told me:

"I was about six years old, or I might have been seven, when I nearly missed death again. It was out near our schoolhouse, which stood in the woods, and all around were saplings—tall, slender saplings. We boys would climb up high in them, grab the top and jump down. They would just swing you to the ground and let you down real easy. It was good sport.

"Well, one day Daddy had left Uncle Pete to work back in the creek bottom and my brother, another boy, and I were sent to help. While we were there, I thought I would show this other boy how we would swing from the saplings. There were some tall, young trees there; so I started up one of them. Of course, I didn't know one tree from another. I didn't realize that I was climbing up a white sycamore that wouldn't bend.

"I remember yet how I took hold of the top of the tree with my hands, my feet on the lower limb, and just swung out into the air. I was already looking forward to the exciting glide and easy touch to the ground some twenty feet below. But instead, when I swung out, the top of that little tree broke off and down I came. I hit the ground hard on my neck, my head, and my back, just missing a fallen log by inches. It could have broken my back or just plain killed me. By God's grace, it only stunned me. After a few minutes I was able to get up and walk around.

"Pete didn't think I was going to be worth much for work, however, and he said, 'Now you go to the house and ask Addie (my older sister) how soon she will have dinner ready for us." So I headed for the house. I can remember going up through the fields, then stopping about halfway and returning to the creek. 'What did you come back for?' Pete asked.

"I said, 'Where was I going?'

" 'I told you to go tell Addie to get dinner,' he answered. "Why didn't I know it?" I replied. But Pete urged me, 'You go ask Addie how soon she will have dinner.' So I turned and again made my way through the fields to the house. Going in I asked Addie when she was going to have dinner. (Now this is what she told me afterwards. I knew nothing about it at the time because I didn't know what I was doing.) She told me the time dinner should be ready.

"Then I went into the room where my other sister, Flo, was and asked her the same question: 'When are we going to have dinner?' And she answered me. Pretty soon I was out with Addie again asking, 'When are we going to have dinner?' Then I was back to Flo with the same question.

"It wasn't long before they recognized that I was out of my head and didn't know what I was saying. They became pretty alarmed and had me lie down fast. That was around ten in the morning. I never came to my senses until about four in the afternoon. It is a miracle that my mind worked well afterward, let alone that I wasn't killed on the log at the bottom of that sycamore tree."

When he was about twelve to fourteen, Dad had another close brush with death. For some reason he and his brother were left alone on a Sunday afternoon, and, as boys do when they are alone, they thought they would do something exciting. They decided to go to the creek and skate.

"It was bitter cold," Dad relates, "but George and I had on warm clothes and our half-soled felt boots. We didn't have regular ice-skates, but you could slide on your boots almost as well as you could on real skates. We were having a time skidding up and down that creek on our boots.

"There was one sharp bend in the creek where the

water had rushed fast enough to keep washing the bottom deeper and deeper. It must have been a couple feet or more over my head. I didn't think about it, but, of course, the ice would be thinner where the water was moving faster. As I was skating around that bend, the ice gave way under me. Before I knew it I was clear to the bottom underneath the ice in freezing water.

"Here I had on heavy winter clothing and those big felt boots. As soon as I hit the water my clothes were soaking wet, and I weighed an awful lot more than normal. With current as swift as that was there, and as heavy as I was with all that water-logged clothing, one would have expected me to be swept downstream. By all rights, I should have died a prisoner under the ice.

"But, by a miracle of God, I managed to come back up right where the ice had broken. Think of that! If I would have been swept just a short distance down stream, I never would have been able to find the hole in the ice even if I could have fought the current. It was a marvel, I know.

"Somehow George managed to get a long stick to me while I hung onto the ice. It's not easy to get out of a hole in the ice. The sides generally keep breaking away and, more often than not, someone else gets dragged into the water before the whole thing is over. But he managed to haul me out. As soon as I hit that cold air, my clothes were frozen stiff as a poker. That was a very close call with death."

Upon another occasion, Dad was home alone with Uncle Pete. As Pete cleaned his 32-caliber pistol, he was snapping the hammer, unaware that a cartridge was in the cylinder. Dad happened to be walking past him when the pistol discharged with a tremendous bang. It frightened them both nearly to pieces. The bullet shot behind my dad and splintered the casing across the room. My father stated, "If it had been a little sooner, he would have shot a hole right through me." The incident was not mentioned by either of them until much later. Dad's parents never knew how close he came to death that time.

The horse and buggy era was not without its own peculiar type of dangers, as well. Dad told me:

"I was out riding around in a rig with two other young men when three fellows in another buggy came up beside us. Ray Pond, the one driving our rig, thought he would just let our horse out to keep them from going around us. He nudged the horse and it took off. When our horse began to run faster, the other driver said, 'Oh no, Wendy! (that was Ray's nickname)—you will never see the day that you can outrun me!' And he urged his horse into a run to pass us.

"About that time our horse made a sudden jump, which startled all of us. I mean, it made a tremendous lurch! When it jumped, it tore loose the belly band, and the two buggy shafts flew up into the air. There we were with our horse running madly off and the buggy shafts flying up and then smacking down on the horse's back. The more they slammed, the harder it galloped.

"Now unless you have been in one of those frail little rigs with the horse running out of control, you can't imagine what is was like. That horse wasn't just running a race; he was madly out of control and running berserk. If we had hit a rough road or come to a sharp turn, we wouldn't have had a chance. Getting thrown from an open rig at that speed would have meant permanent, crippling injury, or death, one or the other. It was only a miracle that we got him stopped. We all could have been killed."

Death continued to stalk my father on the Fourth of July, just before he started courting my mother. At the age of eighteen he was helping extract pipe from abandoned oil wells. A block and tackle was being used to exert the force necessary to pull the pipe from the ground. In order to begin the process of extracting the pipe from one of the oil derricks, Dad was on the platform helping to pull the huge pulley block into the top of the derrick and fix it securely. This large block weighed over two hundred pounds. Connected by ropes to this was a second pulley block weighing some one-hundred-fifty pounds in itself.

30

As this apparatus was being hoisted to the top by a big horse team, it became entangled or lodged in some manner that was unsatisfactory. The boss yelled, "Grab that bottom block, Eldon, to keep her from going up too far." When my Dad grabbed that lower pulley block as it started up past him, it simply lifted him right off the platform, leaving him several feet in the air, his feet dangling.

Just at that moment, high in the top of the derrick, the rope supporting Dad and the pulley blocks suddenly broke. Dad fell to the oil-soaked platform below with a two hundred pound weight hurtling from the top of the derrick onto his head!

By a miracle of Jesus, when his feet hit the oily platform, he skidded sideways just a little. That huge block came crashing into the wood less than two inches from his body, nearly grazing his head. Just a little closer and that heavy block would have crushed him. Once again, God had spared my father.

1923—A. E. Helm with his first Standard Oil gasoline truck.

1925—A. E. Helm with three of his sons: Richard, Warren, and Terrance.

4 MY MOTHER

My mother's childhood was so sweet, I understand. She lived across from her Grandfather and Grandmother Dickson and, oh, how they did love her. She looks back and remembers, "It was love always. I wasn't pampered. It just seemed that what they said, I believed."

Often her folks would be gone and would leave her at Grandpa and Grandma Dickson's. When she began to be sleepy, she would go up to her grandfather and say, "Pap, this pillow is getting heavy." Then he would get up, fix the pillow on the round of the rocker and rock her to sleep.

"They lived what they preached," Mother has told me. "Grandpa was an old Civil War veteran, leaving his family to go help free the precious slaves. The only things Grandmother had when he went to war were her cows, her chickens, and what she could raise. The only money she had she earned by knitting socks or stockings for other people. Her folks, the Butlers, came through as pioneers from Virginia in an old ox cart. Grandmother was about three years old when they arrived· here in Indiana. They were truly godly people."

Loran O. Dickson, my mother's father, grew up in his father's blacksmith and wood shop. He was a skilled mechanic and could make almost anything in iron or wood, but everything had to be just right. He would work on one job all day to make sure it was absolutely correct, even if he made only fifty cents on it. He was not one to put work out merely to make money, but a man to do the job accurately and precisely.

I remember waking early in the mornings to the sound of my Grandfather Dickson pounding on his anvil. I would ask my mother if I could go down and watch him work, and sometimes she would let me go. I observed him as he put the steel into the intense heat of the coals. If he left the iron in long enough, and if it got red enough, he could do something with it. I would see him take the iron or the steel from the forge, lay it over the anvil, then begin to pound it and shape it. Whatever shape was needed from that metal, round or square, he could form it on the anvil.

God is likewise wanting to fashion our lives into unique patterns of His loveliness, but first He must find us surrendered to the fire of His purpose. There is much refining to be done in us, and, as in my grandfather's forge, it requires the fire. Sometimes it is the fire of His love as we wait in secret. Often it is the fire of affliction. Occasionally it is the fire of persecution. But God places us in the fire that we might be made malleable to His higher purposes.

I heard a pastor once tell a story of a godly blacksmith who was afflicted much of the time. People would ask him, "Why are you so afflicted? Why are you so tried? If God loves you, and you love God so much, why are you so tested?"

And he replied, "When I reach in with my tongs and take out that red-hot steel, I can tell when I put it across the anvil and strike it the first time whether it is going to take temper and bend. If it won't take temper, I scrap it. God is trying to temper me so that I will bend easily to His purpose and won't end on the scrap heap."

Most people will not take the temper; they won't accept the bending; they refuse to be smitten. Few are willing to bend from self-desires to the purpose of God. Many persons who begin with Jesus at conversion are unwilling to press on into obedience that they might be shaped according to His will. They get out of the hand of God by going their own way, making their own plans, and arranging their own lives. Few throughout the centuries have learned the mystery

34

of God's divine hand molding and shaping the lives of His beloved ones.

Oh, how God wants to take out of us the many things which hinder Him. There is so much in a man when he thinks he can still do something in himself. God has revealed to me that we can do nothing but fail. Therefore, He must refine out of us many wrong attitudes and considerable self-reliance before we begin to discover that we are only full of failure. **Until we are willing to be nothing, God can shape us very little, if any.**

Grandfather Dickson died in 1941 when I was twenty-five. I cannot reminisce long about him without weeping, for he was a man tall in nobility. He was a man of great meekness. Most persons, unless they have been thoroughly cleansed by the Spirit, can sometimes become jealous or angry and rage when they don't get their way. But my grandfather underwent great suffering, and passed through situations which would break your heart if I would share them; yet, he did not complain or murmur. As a boy I can remember hauling gravel, shucking corn, and building fence with him while on the farm. Not once did he become angry with me or get after me.

He was one of those rare men who was willing to go the second mile. I can recall that after his hip had been crushed, the doctors didn't know until too late how seriously he had been hurt. The hip joint healed imperfectly and afterwards pained him severely at almost every step. Yet, when Joyce Lee, our first daughter, was born and my wife was recuperating in her parents' home, Grandfather Dickson came to Taylor University to stay with me and assist me. We lived in a little apartment upstairs, and he climbed those steps through much pain in that injured hip with very little said about it.

You see, my weeping is because of pleasant memories of a man very rare in the earth. I have seldom seen his like in all of my travels. My father said of Loran O. Dickson and his

35

brother, Tom—because of the gracious spirit in their lives—
that they stood head and shoulders above other men in the
community. He has told me many times, "I wish I had been
more understanding of my father-in-law. He was a bigger,
greater man than I was able to esteem at that time."

It was his sister, Aunt Libb, who was such a gracious,
gentle, compassionate woman. She and her husband, Uncle
Billy, loved me very much from the time I was first born. I
recall Uncle Billy putting on a record of an old hymn: "How
tedious and tasteless the hours." The memory of this song
lingers in my heart over the years—

> "How tedious and tasteless the hours
> When Jesus no longer I see:
> Sweet prospects, sweet birds, and sweet flowers
> Have all lost their sweetness to me.
> The mid-summer sun shines but dim,
> The fields strive in vain to look gay;
> But when I am happy in Him,
> December's as pleasant as May."
> —Words by John Newton, 1725-1807

He would sit in the old chair as this precious hymn would
play and tears would course from his kind eyes, over his
round cheeks, and drop into his lap.

As I mentioned earlier, my mother's mother, Elizabeth
Dickson, was an equally unique and gifted individual. Her
parents came from near Cincinnati, Ohio. Her father's parents, the Clarks, were religious people. My great-grandfather
Clark, a genuine and humble person, did daily work on the
farm. Great-grandmother Clark was an orphan girl. Her
mother died when she was a baby, so she was passed from
one home to another until my great-grandfather married her.
She was a step-mother to his six children. Elizabeth often
felt that Grandfather Clark's six children loved Grandmother
Clark as much as the children of their own marriage. Great
tenderness was in her life.

Elizabeth Clark Dickson was gifted in caring for the sick.
She not only cared for her own family, she was called into

different homes around the community to help in time of sickness. In fact, families would often ask for "Lizzie" before they would call a doctor, so confident were they of her skills. "She just seemed to know what to do," it was said of her. She was with many women when they gave birth to their children. "I used to wonder where she had gone when I got up in the morning," Mother tells me. "I would get up and find her gone, only to discover a little later that a tiny baby had come to live at 'so-and-so's house'."

Lizzie had the ability to go into a home and simply take over all the responsibilities. It didn't seem to upset her. Years later, when my father was her son-in-law, he often said, "If Grandma was there, everything was alright. I didn't have any worries when she was present. She was just like my own mother." Elizabeth was a woman of faith, of integrity, of service—a woman of sharing.

Her last activity before her mortal sickness was, appropriately, in service to others. While sweeping the church on a Wednesday evening in preparation for worship, she unexpectedly had a severe gall bladder attack. Thursday they took her to the hospital, but at first her fever was much too high for surgery. When they were finally able to operate, there was little that the physicians could do, for her gall bladder had burst.

The pain was intense, but she never complained. When the doctor would come to inquire of her condition, she would say, "You have other patients to see about. Don't worry about me." The doctors and nurses in that hospital concurred that she dwelt in the areas of outstanding faith and nobility. One of the leading surgeons of that time remarked that he had never seen anyone like my grandmother Dickson, for she was always wanting him to help somebody else rather than to attend to her.

When Elizabeth was dying, my mother was beside her, holding her hand. Grandmother had been so weak she could hardly move her arms, but suddenly she raised her arms and said, "Oh, child!—Child, there is Jesus!"

Amazed, my mother asked, "Mother, do you see Jesus?"

"Oh, yes," she answered, "just as plain as I see you. He is beautiful! Look right up there. Jesus is here! Oh— there is a light in The Valley of Death. I see Jesus, Child! He is wonderful. I can see now why all earthly things don't mean anything," she told my mother. "I see now why you didn't want to work in all those organizations," (for my mother had had an unusual experience with God some time before this and had felt led to withdraw from several organizations of men). "Oh, I can see Jesus! He is marvelous!"

While my grandmother was dying, she was privileged to see Jesus. When you can see Jesus, all these earthly things don't mean a snap of the fingers. The only thing that is going to matter is whether Jesus Christ has been first in your life; and He will mean so much more to you at death than I can tell you now.

And yet, as I say these words—even as I am speaking them—I know that very few will actually hear me. When I am in the pulpit and humbly striving to declare the whole counsel of God with all my might, somehow I have the realiz- ation that scarcely any of the people can hear what I am telling them. I will be preaching the best I know, as faith- fully as I can, and while I am preaching I can tell that the demon powers are stealing the Gospel truths right out of the people's minds.

When the sermon or exhortation is ended, instead of being contrite in their hearts, so often the congregation talks about farms, cars, and ball games. Instead of crying out in broken- ness, "Oh, Lord, I am so needy!"—they chatter about home, children, the job, and any other thing but the will of God and the love of Jesus.

You see, beloved, my heart is broken in church after church all across this country. The people are precious in every church. They are kind and generous; they would do anything

38

to help: but very few are hearing the true Christian message of self-denial, of the cross, of trust and obedience, down deep in their heart. There might be one, two, or three in an entire congregation who are getting the message of true Christianity inside the heart.

If dear ones were getting the message, they would be heart-broken. They would be weeping and crying. This is a fact. My heart weeps when I see how lost the world is and how far the church is from God's will. Jesus said, "Blessed are they that mourn, for they shall be comforted." But the professed church has this in reverse: after a man of God preaches, there is often laughter, light conversation, and joking among ourselves instead of repentant tears. It seems that some are saying, "Blessed is the man who has a hi-ho time and is able to get the boys to laugh."

Oh, my friends! Jesus cried out to His age and almost no one among the church leaders heard Him. Even the handful of His closest followers, who observed mighty miracles day after day, fell asleep when it came to the hour when Jesus most needed them.

And Jesus witnesses to me that the professed church today is spiritually three times more asleep than the apostles were in the Garden of Gethsemane. Think of that!—In about all churches today we are three times more asleep than the apostles were when Jesus needed them most.

I am so thankful that my grandmother had a heart awake to the life of Christ so that she could see Jesus as she was leaving this earth. Praise the Lord.

Eldon and Mary, about six months before Loran was born.

5 MY FATHER'S CONVERSION

Though reared in a religious home and delivered miraculously from death time after time, my father did not follow the path of Christ as a young man. Because of his wit and persuasive gifts, he had become popular with the men of the community. He had developed into a pretty rough-and-tumble fellow, even going so far as to smoke cigarettes and drink alcoholic beverages.

On the other hand, my mother was very quiet and retiring. Her grandfather, Andrew Dickson, had been such a quiet, gentle man. She never once heard him raise his voice. And her grandmother, although of a different disposition, was a righteous woman. If one would try to talk jokes or foolishness she would say, "Idle words. Idle talk." She would tell people whenever they were out of line in their conversation.

Mother's life had centered mostly around the church since her birth. She had learned to play the piano on a huge, ornate grand piano which her father purchased for a very modest amount. Then, to please his lovely daughter, he purchased a newer upright piano with money received from selling a fine horse. Mother soon became a gifted pianist and a talented singer.

She had not had an easy life, however. She was always a sickly child and suffered from rheumatism long before she ever went to school. It was called inflammatory rheumatism, and from time to time it created great swelling in her legs. At the age of fourteen Mother experienced such an encounter with this condition that she was not expected to live. It affected her eyes as well, and for two weeks she was blind. Soon the condition became even more serious, spreading into the entire nervous system. For days she lay helpless, unable to move her limbs or see the hand that fed her. The Lord, in His mercy, spared her, and she was free of serious attack from this particular illness until after I was born. Upon another occasion she contracted a serious case of measles. So my Mother had experienced a great amount of suffering before she met my father.

When God brought my parents together, He began to create a deepening love between them. Mother wasn't aware that Dad was drinking and smoking, but she did know that he was not born again. She insisted that he attend church with her.

Then came a Sunday night that was to be written down for eternity. Revival services were being held in the old brick church at the edge of Windsor, the one that sat on the banks of Stony Creek. Though the attendance had been fair, there had been no real stir in the meeting for two or three weeks. This particular evening Mother persuaded my father to attend the meeting, for Dad was not interested in religious things at all. In fact, the night before this memorable Sunday, Dad had been on the streets of Windsor entertaining the town people with a comical auction of any stray dogs that happened by. His plans were far from God's Kingdom.

But in service that Sunday night, at the time of invitation, Uncle Addison Fletcher came back and started talking to my dad. "Eldon," he declared, "you need to be converted." Uncle Addison was such a different man that few people could understand him. As he continued talking to my father, Dad suddenly stepped into the aisle and found himself kneeling at the front before he knew it. He had no intention of being saved, but Addison talked him into it.

At the altar he tried to pray, but was unable to find release from the burden upon his heart. People came to pray and counsel with him, but they could not lead him to

42

victory either. Then a woman who Dad didn't particularly like came over and began to pray. Soon the glory began to fall. She prayed Heaven down and my dad stepped into the Kingdom of God. He was transformed from head to foot, born a new creation, and his name was written down in the Lamb's Book of Life. Hallelujah! God had used a person Dad didn't especially appreciate to help him to salvation.

Dad had been such a man of the world that many who had known him as a sinner came to the revival services to see him on fire for God. He was so transformed, so miraculously changed, that his conversion seemed to stir the community and open the secret chambers of that revival. During the previous two or three weeks the preaching had produced no noticeable result. Now the obedience of one man began to spark revival flames, and others were soon responding to the call of Christ upon their hearts. "After that," Dad told me, "it seemed as if we had a countryside revival. Some twenty-seven young men were saved in that meeting."

For many weeks after his conversion my father had a most unusual anointing upon him. He has told me, "Though I was just a babe in Christ and knew very little scripture, almost everyone God sent me to would be saved. Of course, I wouldn't go talk to anybody unless I had a real strong 'impression' or 'impulse'." (He recognized the guidances of God as an impression on the soul.) Mother has said that she does not remember a single person who did not give his heart to Jesus once the Lord sent my father to speak to him. Somehow the Lord worked through him to melt the hardest hearts.

Here he was just converted, a youngster of eighteen, and God was working so marvelously through him. In testimony meetings, when one sat down, he was up and going again. Some of the folks thought him rather strange and unpredictable. I rather imagine that a number of the church people who had never really been born again felt

43

a little uncomfortable around him. They would have preferred that he not do such unplanned things as testify, exhort
people to obey God, and speak to individuals about their
souls. Dad might not have known the Bible declared it,
but he was a living example of the phrase, "For as many
as are led by the Spirit of God, they are the Sons of God."

Since Dad probably heard very little instruction concerning obedience to the Holy Spirit, God had to put this
awareness into his heart. In all my years in the ministry
I have seldom heard obedience preached from the pulpit.
In fact, after God has anointed me to share on the absolute
necessity of obeying God, dear ones have told me that they
have never heard a single sermon on obeying the Holy
Spirit in all the years they have faithfully worked in the
church.

A great portion of the people in our precious churches
don't even know about the life lived in obedience to the Holy
Spirit, yet obedience is the very heartbeat of Christianity.
If there isn't obedience, the spiritual blood stream stops.
If we are not following God's guidances daily, our spiritual
circulation is cut off. This organic spiritual relationship with
Christ is suggested in First John 1:7—"If we walk in the
light as He is in the light, we have fellowship one with another, and the blood of Jesus Christ His Son cleanseth us
from all sin." This implies a continual cleansing and purging
as we walk "in the light," or in other words—"in His guidance."

Ordinarily, many churches have not stressed a day-by-day
obedience to the Holy Spirit. They have primarily empha-
sized adherence to biblical commandments and to certain
earthly patterns. But the written Word and the Living Word
go together; they are inseparable. If we in the church are
not vitally connected to God by the Holy Spirit so that
obedience is in process constantly, we are like a body in
which the heart has stopped beating. We are either dead

or dying, for disobedience is sin; and sin is a dying process which takes us to death.

A few days after his conversion, Dad told his sweetheart goodnight at her door in Windsor and headed the buggy home. It was a good distance to his dad's farm some two-and-a-half miles northeast of Parker, and the hour was late. Looking up into the starry sky that night, he said, "Oh Jesus, you have done so much for me, and I have been such a terrible sinner. Is there any way that I can atone for my wickedness and evil life I have lived?"

And in the deep blackness of the night, as clearly as a picture painted before him, he saw an old abandoned church. It was called Plainview Church, located near Gaston, Indiana, where he had sowed his wild oats. The Holy Spirit spoke to him and said, "Go back to that old abandoned church and hold a meeting."

I can't tell you exactly how Dad felt when God revealed this to his heart, but I know that he was both surprised and thrilled. He probably didn't know the Bible as well as many children do now, because he had never read the Word much in eighteen years. It had been read to him a few times, but he scarcely knew Genesis from Revelation, so to speak. He was anxious, however, to do God's will.

The Helm family had been gone from Gaston only about three or four months and were well known by almost all in the community. Dad wrote to the minister at Gaston, Rev. Rector, telling him what the Lord had revealed. His letter probably wasn't much encouragement to the pastor, because my father's spelling was not very good. But Rev. Rector wrote back explaining that three retired ministers had been trying to hold services at Plainview Church for two to three weeks without any results. The services had been neither well attended nor had there been movement from the people. He wrote, "We have tried to have revival and haven't had any results. But, if God is sending you, we will try to get things ready. You come ahead." The announcement went out that

45

Eldon Helm, the young man who had been so wild and adventuresome, was coming to hold revival at Plainview. It took courage for this dear man of God to let a youngster of eighteen return, by his own announcement, to begin revival in his home community—especially when three experienced ministers had been unable to see any results after two to three weeks of preaching. But the key to what was about to happen was that God had truly ordained this revival effort. It was not a religious activity begun in the flesh, but a tiny branch in the Kingdom of God. The great God of Heaven had sent my father to that little church.

I would like for you to hear about this unique meeting in my father's own words, as he told me of this precious guidance of God several years ago:

"I was eighteen, going on nineteen, in a cold January, 1908," Dad told me. "The church was two-and-a-half miles southeast of Gaston. I got off the train on a Saturday and went to the home of my good friend, Willie Stotler. They took me out to Plainview the next evening. I had been saved just three weeks to the day.

"The first night of the meeting the church was so full that some people stood in the doorway. Even in the cold of January the windows were opened to permit the people outside to look in. Folk had come to see if it were true that I was holding a meeting, because I knew everyone there and everyone knew me. I had been quite a mischievous fellow.

"When it came time for the message, I don't know whether I even preached. I just read the scripture and talked, and the Spirit was upon me. The Holy Spirit hit the crowd and the meeting was on. Folks later made the remark to me, 'The first night that you stepped into the pulpit you said that we were going to have a great meeting, and you said it so emphatically we just knew that we were.' Of course, God had promised it and had sent me there: that is why people felt the power.

"There were no visible victories that first night, but after that I don't believe there was a meeting day or night when there weren't folks at the altar. Sometimes the altar would be full."
46

The power of God's Spirit upon that community was to be evidenced during the day as well. One young lady, who knew my father prior to his conversion, experienced this wonderfully. When she first heard that Dad would be returning for services she laughingly said, "I know why Eldon Helm is coming back here—he is coming just to see me." But when deep conviction seized her Sunday night, it became evident that such was not his motive. The next day, while she was washing dinner dishes, God fell upon her in such strong wooing that she couldn't resist His call upon her heart. She was converted at the dishpan, threw her dishcloth in the air and shouted through the house for joy.

"God was there in such strength," Dad told me. "The days of trances had been over (so we thought) long ago, but people felt the power of God so tremendously that they would fall in trances. God gave wonderful victories —eighty-four truly converted, several reclaimed, and many helped. Some of those who were saved became preachers. That revival, lasting two weeks and two nights, was one of the greatest meetings I have ever been in. But just as clearly as He told me to begin the meeting, God told me to close it. Some thought we shouldn't end the meeting at all, for on the final evening six or seven were at the altar. But God had revealed to me that we should close it, and that is what we did.

"Many who had gotten victory in this meeting were so hungry for the Word, however, that the next evening they streamed to the Methodist Church in Gaston, which had been endeavoring to conduct a revival even before our services began. And the Lord just bounced the meeting right over there! My, they had a revival! Many were redeemed in those old-fashioned, Holy Ghost services."

And God began to use my father in various revival meetings among the churches. Without question, the hand of the Lord was upon him.

Loran with his first brother, Richard, within a few months of the day God spoke to Loran's heart: "YOU BELONG TO ME. I WILL USE YOU IN MY KINGDOM SOME DAY."

6 GOD FIRST SPEAKS

Three years and three months later, on May 6, 1911, my parents were married. Dad was twenty-one, Mother going on twenty. They loved each other so much that there was no question in their minds that God had chosen them for one another.

So strong was their desire for a family that they hoped for a child within one year. But the first year passed into a second, and then into a third, and they were still without a little one. They began to pray earnestly for a child, and continued to pray into the fourth year of marriage. Most of their family gave up hoping, but Mother and Dad continued to trust and pray. In May, 1915, God was pleased to grant their heart's cry: their first child was conceived.

"From the time we began to look for Loran," Mother once told friends, "it seemed as if we just dreamed and thought of him all the time. When Dad left the factory he couldn't get home quickly enough to see if I was alright, for I suffered a great deal. He would say, 'Mary, as much as you are suffering, surely this will be a good child.'

"We began to anticipate his coming. I prayed for a man child, a man of God. I didn't pray for a preacher: I prayed for a man of God. I gave him back to God before he was born. I told God that I would raise my son for the Lord the best I knew."

I was born at home on February 3, 1916, with the doctor, Grandmother Dickson, and a friend, Aunt Mandy, assisting. Mother said, "We all sensed something unusual in the room.

Aunt Mandy said that she had never before been in a place like that, and my own mother sensed something out of the ordinary as well. I never told anyone about the Holy Spirit falling on me when Loran was born, until many years later."

Not long before his death, Dad told me, "Son, I don't know whether there was any child more welcome in this world than you. We so looked forward to your coming." How can I thank Jesus for the privilege of being placed into the care of parents who loved God and wanted to do His will? I am truly grateful to God and much indebted to Jesus.

In this Christian heritage I was taught to love God, to love Jesus, and to put the church first. As soon as they were able, my parents began to teach me to pray. My mother said that I could speak plainly at the age of nine months. While I was strapped in my little high chair, she began to teach me how to fold my hands and pray. I suppose I was praying at the age of one year, bowing my head and trying to say a few words to God. My mother and dad had me praying before I knew what prayer was. Prayer seemed so natural and normal.

There was such a deep love of the right, the pure, and the upright in our home. Because of this, I have been shocked whenever I have seen anyone drinking liquor or dressed immodestly. I cannot become accustomed to it. When someone curses, I am shocked; when somebody in a restaurant swears or takes the Lord's name in vain, I find myself turning around to look. I love everyone just alike, but when I see or hear things impure and unholy, I seem to suffer. It hurts my heart. I know that I have so little of Jesus, but when I observe certain iniquitous things, my heart is grieved.

I recall once stepping onto an elevator while with a fellow pastor. As the elevator started up, a man began to swear terribly, using vulgar oaths and taking the precious name of our Lord in vain. It had never happened before and probably will never happen again, but, all of a sudden, I began to praise God almost as loudly as this man was cursing. I began praising Jesus for His wonderful Self and magnifying the holy Name of God.

I tell you, things began to happen in that little elevator. My minister friend wasn't sure what that man was going to do. He looked at me with such animosity. But, you see, my heart had been taught to love and honor God. When such awful cursing began, God simply started praising Himself through me.

My mother carried me to church when I was very small. I was in service almost every time the church doors were open, whether Sunday morning or evening, prayer meeting, or revivals. I grew up not knowing you couldn't go to church. The only time I missed church was when I was quite sick. Even when I became an adult and was in the ministry I missed church only when I would be on special call, when I was waiting on God in prayer, or when waiting for Him to guide me. (And right now, as I tell you this, the Holy Spirit speaks within me, saying: "I will guide you; I will direct you; I will tell you what to do.")

My parents taught me that the Bible is the Word of God, the Supreme Voice, the revelation of God's love to us, the Volume of Life, and outside it was desolation. I believed it when they first taught me, and I believe it today. I knew nothing of modernism and liberalism, of doubting God or Jesus, until my second college experience. From my childhood until then, I had known nothing about these dark and sinister liberal views which questioned God's Word and hurled doubts into the minds of young Christians. When I first heard a professor bring his own thoughts, analyzations, and opinions to class, I was deeply hurt.

My Mother tells me (only because of Jesus and all to God's glory) that she recognized early that God's hand was upon me. As she was working one day, the lady who lived right across the street came to the door and said, "I wish you could see what I see. It is wonderful."

Mother said, "What is it?"

51

The woman replied, "You couldn't hear what I am hearing and not know they have been in church."

Mother still didn't quite understand: "What do you mean?" she asked.

"Why," she answered, "your oldest boy is out back on top of the rabbit pen preaching to the other children." She was quite a woman of the world but she said, "If I ever heard a preacher preach, he is a preaching one. No one could tell me he doesn't know how to go to church." And when Mother went to look, sure enough—there I was on top of the rabbit pen as the neighbor had described. I was trying to preach exactly like I had seen and heard Rev. Gilmore every Sunday.

I was but a small lad when God first spoke to me. It was a very serious and sacred event in my life. (And when I tell you that, God whispers within me in the operation of His gifts, "I am with thee.") I do not share this lightly, but with a profound sense of my unworthiness before almighty God, for I do not belong to myself: I am His and I am on this earth to do **only** His will.

It was while I was making a little journey for my mother that I suddenly had this marvelous experience at the fringe of the Kingdom of God. I wish that I were able to tell the wonder of it, but my words are too inadequate. Though men were to speak like angels, they cannot tell about the wonder of the Kingdom of God.

From time to time my mother would send me to the farmhouse of Ollie Gilbert to get a quart of milk. The Gilbert home was a little outside the limits of Windsor Village to the north. While on this errand for my mother that beautiful Saturday morning I had a quart Ball jar in the curl of my left arm. Since we were quite poor, I tried to be careful not to drop it.

As I was on my way, some 250 feet past the old church, I noticed that the wind was rushing through the leafy branches of the trees, and it looked like they were waving, giving greeting to each other, saying "How do you do?" at morning time.

I looked at the brilliance of the sun, the brightness of the blue sky, and it all blended into a symphony—all trying to talk, all endeavoring to say something of thanksgiving and gratitude to God. A song sparrow was singing this melody, also, when, to my sudden astonishment, God spoke in my heart and said, "YOU BELONG TO ME: I WILL USE YOU IN MY KINGDOM SOMEDAY."

Florence Spence while attending Ball State College.

7 TITHING OPENS THE WAY

In those days my parents were very poor. Dad had gone into the business of testing cream for farmers, and was also running a school hack. I think perhaps their income for the week ran somewhere between eight and twelve dollars. But my father came home one day with the announcement: "Mary, I just heard a sermon on tithing."

She said, "What?"

"I just heard a minister preach that we are supposed to tithe," Dad answered.

She asked, "What do you mean?", for her ministers had not preached the giving of the tithe. My parents had never heard it mentioned before. Up until that time, Dad and Mother were giving two dollars a year to the church and thought they were doing fairly well.

"Why," Dad said, "they tell me that the Word of God teaches to give one-tenth of what you have to Jesus, to bring your tithe into God's storehouse."

"Why—Eldon!"

"Yes," he said. "You know, I believe Jesus wants us to start tithing."

"Eldon," Mother said, "you know it's been taking every cent we have to live; every penny to pay our rent and buy groceries. We can barely manage to get the boys shoes when they need them. But, if God has revealed that we are to tithe, I am ready to begin."

The first week they took their one dollar or so out and gave it to the Lord, because it was already His. The next week they did the same thing. It would vary each week according to their income. And they began to marvel. "We can't understand how nine-tenths can go as far, or a little farther, than ten-tenths. We don't understand!" They exclaimed about the fact that God could extend less money (and it was truly a little amount) and make it go so far. Of course, they were trusting with the One who never loses a battle. They were trusting the One who could not fail. We fail, but Jesus never does.

They would kneel by their bed at night and pray, "Jesus, you know we have very little business. Lord, we are simply trusting you. We just want to do your will." They submitted everything into the hands of the Lord, and God began to bless them. He would send a little money in here, and then a little in there. My parents never ceased to be amazed how God honored them for faithful tithing according to His Word.

All was not obvious blessing, however. Mother's rheumatism began to return soon after I was born. They tell me that while she would be holding me on her lap, she would appear so ill that they thought surely she had suffered a heart attack. They didn't know whether she was going to live or not. But God was merciful and gracious to her. In a little over two years, in spite of her weak physical condition, she bore my brother, Richard. I was so proud of him. I can remember getting my Uncle Billy by the hand and taking him to the side of the bed where Richard lay beside my mother. I asked everyone to step aside, because I had to show Uncle Billy my new baby brother.

The doctor said that it would be impossible for Mother to ever be able to have another child; but two years later, Warren was born, weighing eleven pounds, three ounces: the largest of all her children at birth. Twenty months later, then, my third brother, Terrance, came into the family.

During one of my mother's very severe attacks, when I was yet a tiny fellow, my father earnestly promised the Lord, "If you spare the life of my companion, I will go back to preaching." Of course, my folks had attended church regularly, and Dad had filled in for several ministers from time to time. But, soon after his conversion, when God was using him so wonderfully in various revivals, certain religious people began to oppose my father's religious views. They said awful things to him, and it discouraged him so badly it appeared as if he weren't going to make it through. It was by the strength and assistance of the Holy Spirit that he was able to continue his ministry after such severe opposition. For nearly fourteen years my father had been striving to obey God and not become discouraged.

It was before my third brother, Terrance, was born that three men from the small congregation of Carlos City came to ask Dad to be their minister. "Well," he said, "I just go out and preach. I don't feel like I am capable of being a minister in a church."

But this committee requested him to pray about it. "We will come back to see you again," they said. Some time went by, and they came again to see how Dad felt about their request, but he still was undecided. He would go preach for one service, but he couldn't feel certain about assuming the responsibilities of their pastorate.

Mother was still bedfast following Terrance's birth when Dad came in by her side. He said, "Mary, these men have come back to see if I will come to Carlos City to preach, and I don't know what to tell them."

Mother answered, "Well, this makes three times they've come. I would think that if you want to preach, now is the time to go."

Dad was reluctant, however, and insisted that he didn't have clothes proper to go among strangers and preach. He had a fairly new suit, but it had been torn in the back of the coat. So my mother said to him, "Why Eldon, I know that I can fix that coat, and when it is pressed, no one will ever know it's been mended."

Dad's mother was there also, and he said to her, "How

57

will I get to church? I don't have a machine. All I have is this truck."

My grandmother replied, "Eldon, I believe if you just promise God you will go, when the time comes, you will have a way. I believe that."

After some conversation my father said, "Well, if that is the way you feel, I will tell them I will come to preach."

It was not long after my parents had begun to consistently tithe, and only a short while after my parents consented to assume preaching responsibilities at Carlos City, that a stranger walked in one day and said to my dad, "I want to sell you some motor oil." He, no doubt, mentioned a rather sizable quantity of oil. And, of course, my father didn't have enough money in his pocket to buy one gallon of oil, let alone twenty-five gallons, or fifty gallons, or a quarter of a drum. In all probability he just laughed and laughed, because he was quite a fellow to express himself in laughter, and he had a beautiful way of doing it.

After they had talked quite a while the man said, "Mr. Helm, I didn't really come here to sell you some oil. I came to hire you as my agent for the Standard Oil Refining Company at $180.00 a month plus commission."

My father replied, "You have just hired me, Sir." In a matter of moments my parents' income jumped from approximately fifty dollars a month to $180.00 plus! But, you see, their tithing made the way. Their obedience opened the door—giving to God, when they thought they didn't have enough to live on. They gave their tenth back to God, and, in return, God gave them dividends in abundance.

This new opportunity moved us to Parker City, Indiana, in September, 1922. It brought us to the village where I was to find Christ Jesus as my Saviour, and where I was to discover my wife. It blesses me as I think that the willingness of my parents to give to God that which was His, started us on the upward path of victory. Praise God.

8 CHILDLIKE FAITH

I would like to share with you a story of trust and faith. It is a simple story, but an important part of my early experience in believing God. It has since taught me several lessons. The Lord helping, it continues to do so.

While we still lived in Windsor, when I was four or five years old, my friend across the street received a beautiful, little Shetland pony from his uncle. From the front yard of our home I watched as the little crate, in which it was delivered, was opened. Having never journeyed far from our village, I had never seen a pony before. I didn't know what to think!

That animal was beautiful! It was brown and white, with a perfectly shaped face which told me that it was good-natured and well-behaved. I was anxious to get a closer look, but for some time my mother would not permit me to go over to the neighbor's home, fearing that I might be an imposition on them.

Since I couldn't see the pony very well from the ground, I would climb up on our fence as high as possible and look down across the road at it. Hanging there as long as I was able, I would watch it graze or move about. When it disappeared behind the shed or beyond the hill, I would have to get down and wait until I could catch a glimpse of it again. As soon as I would spot it, I would climb the fence, crane my neck, and look and look. I thought, "Oh, won't it be wonderful if Mother someday lets me go over to see that pony!"

On that memorable day when my mother said, "You may

go over to see Keith's pony now, Loran," I ran as fast as my little legs would carry me. Across the street I went, down the lane, into the neighbor's barn, and scrambled up over the manger. That beautiful pony was only about seven feet from me! I was thrilled. "This is great!" I said to myself. I thought that pony was one of the most wonderful things I had ever seen, and began to hope in my heart that someday I might have a pony like Keith Patty's.

(Over the years, as I have reviewed this experience of deep excitement which I had as a little boy, I have sometimes wondered how God finds us. Does He see us jubilant and impassioned over the marvelous truths of His Word? Is the Faith burning in our souls so that we care more for our relatives and friends finding Jesus than we do about the latest fashions or the newest baby in town?

(I have seen many people so excited at ball games that they would yell and jump up and down; at prayer meeting, however, most individuals are listless and greatly lacking in enthusiasm. It tells me that there is great need in most of our congregations, or we would be more inspired by the Kingdom of God than by these passing activities of earth. It appears, in many of our churches, that those professing to be Christians actually need to be truly converted and transformed, or they would possess an innate excitement over the things of God's Kingdom.)

A few years later, when we had moved to Parker and I was in the third grade, I remember returning home from school one day for lunch. Rounding the corner at the porch I looked east toward the little red barn, and what do you think I saw?—There stood a black Shetland pony! It was a beautiful, beautiful pony, with one white spot on the forehead and two above the shoulder!

As fast as I could, I ran down to where the pony was grazing. The owners, an elderly couple by the name of Henhizer, were sitting in the buggy nearby having their lunch. He saw that I was delighted over the pony and asked, "Would you like to ride Queen?"

"Oh, yes!" I told him. I had been waiting a long time to get this close to a pony, ever since I prayed in my heart, "I would like to have a pony like Keith Patty's."

Mr. Henhizer said, "Just a moment and I will get her ready." I learned that they had come that morning approximately eighteen miles in their little rig from the town of Ridgeville. They were enroute to Muncie, but instead of taking the more direct route west through Albany to State Road 67 they had come all the way south to Farmland, then west on Road 32 to Parker. "We needed to have a sandwich," the Henhizers informed me; "so we unhitched Queen here to let her rest awhile." They could have stopped many places up and down the highway, but they came to our house, a block off the main road. Of all the seven hundred people in the village, here they were at our place!

I'll tell you, if you walk with God and trust Him, He will have the very thing for which you are waiting come to your place sometime. One of these days, when you are not planning it and least expect it, He will send it by. You will probably not receive what you plan, but if you are really looking to Jesus and wanting Him more than anything else, He will give you the desires of your heart when you are not anticipating it.

Never try to get anything, only walk with Jesus and He will trust you with the best: what you need when you need it. He might send it soon, maybe later, perhaps after a long time; but God will provide. He's known to give surprises to all His faithful pilgrims.

And I was certainly surprised that day. I rode a pony for the first time in my life. Oh, the delight, the interest, the enthusiasm that was in my heart! If I could paint it in a picture, you would each chuckle, I am sure. In fact, it would do your heart good, because I was so wonderfully overjoyed. My child heart was thrilled to the limit.

When mother called me to come in for lunch that day, I wasn't much interested in food. Of course, when she said, "Come," I had to go; there wasn't any question about that. I tied the pony to the fence and went to the house. We had prayer and ate our soup beans, but I wanted to finish as quickly as I could to get back outside and ride Queen every possible minute before school took up. And that is what I did.

When I ran back to school that afternoon the bell was already ringing and I had to hurry. I said to myself, "For two to three years I have been waiting for a pony, and this is the one!" All afternoon the pony was running through my mind. "When school is over," I thought to myself, "I will get Howard, my friend. Both of us can hitch up the goat to the little wagon and haul the debris out of the barn to the garden. We will get the barn ready for my pony, because this is the one I have been waiting for." Somehow I knew in my heart that Queen belonged to me.

Howard and I worked diligently that night, and again the next evening, cleaning all the accumulation of rubbish from the barn. By the third night we had completed the task. Now wasn't that unusual for a nine-year-old boy to decide to clean up the barn so that his pony could come? I wanted to have everything ready. I simply had a child-like faith that this was the pony God had promised me.

I have since discovered that we cannot have faith unless we have love, for faith works and lives by love, as the Bible tells us in the fifth chapter of Galatians. If you wish for more faith, remember that your faith will be in proportion to your love. If you love, you will hear the Word of God: and faith comes by hearing, and hearing by the Word of God.

Faith will flourish in the heart filled with God's love, the precious love of Jesus Christ. Sensual, worldly love will fail you, but the love which Jesus gives never fails. A heart of love provides the right soil for faith to grow. If there are any rocks of doubt, darkness, sin, or lust in your heart, then faith is choked, twisted, and blotted out.

In order to maintain a holy faith, you will be making everything ready in your heart by clearing out the debris of pride and self-reliance. You will be confessing all of your bitterness and resentment, for faith recoils from such inward disorder. Nor can faith dwell in a heart cluttered with criticism and contention. You must clear out as well all questioning and analyzation (trying to find out all the answers, seeking to know "Why?" and "How?")—because faith only makes its abode in a heart free from the litter of carnal characteristics.

After three days I was saying, "Let's get the manger fixed up for my pony!"

Many years later my mother shared with me that, during those days, my father was somewhat alarmed. He would ask her, "Did you give that boy reason to believe that he was going to get that pony?"

And she would insist, "Eldon, I haven't told him a thing."

"Well, I can't understand it," Dad would say. "He has been cleaning that barn for three days and telling everyone that his pony is coming."

About ten days later, my father took my brothers, Richard and Warren, and myself into the Standard Oil bulk plant in Muncie to get some petroleum products. We were in one of those old Fords which had a middle door. The windows, you may remember, didn't crank up: there was a strap with which you pulled them up or down. In the front, a rather tiny seat folded forward to permit one to get into the back seat more easily.

The gravel on old Route 32 was worn into ridges, like a washboard, and it just bumped, bumped us much of the way. During the ride home I had become drowsy. I was somewhat peevish and wanting to lie down to really rest. Pulling up to the front of that little red barn, my father said, "Loran, how would you like to open the barn door?"

Now, if you ask a child if he would "like" to do something, he will probably respond as I did. You see, I was a peevish and sleepy nine-year-old boy. You know how they can be sometimes. Many older people occasionally get that way as well—cross and contrary, not wanting to be disturbed; wanting to keep comfortable in their own little corner. I said, "No."

Then my dad spoke again. This time it was not a request, it was a command. "Son, you get out now. Open the door." When I received the order, I moved right away. He only had to tell me once, for I was taught not to delay. If an earthly parent needs to tell a child more than one time, then there is something in that child which must be broken. God cannot do much with a man or a woman who has not obeyed when he or she was a child. There is so much to break up in persons who have not been taught obedience as children. They are unwilling most times to pay the price which God asks.

This is why we are hesitant to obey God. This is why we are so reluctant to obey God and do what He tells us. **The lack of obedience in the church goes all the way back to the heart of a child when he was very little, whether or not he was tender and willing to be obedient to his mother and father.** Much of our disobedience to God now goes back to our inner life when we were very young (and I can feel God operating within my heart as I tell you this).

When my father gave me the order, I was quickly out of the car and on my way to the barn door. Taking hold of it, I started to push it open. It was easy to move; I didn't have to push it much at all.

Just as soon as that door opened a little bit, I saw my pony! Queen was right there before me! I jumped up and down! I hollered! I ran and got my arms around her neck and cried over and over, "Oh, my pony has come! My pony has come!" I was so happy. You talk about a child being happy—I cried with laughter and with joy. I was so thrilled. I said, "Daddy, let's hitch up Queen, go to the elevator, and get a bale of hay and some corn right away!" My pony had come, and I wanted her to have something to eat.

I was elated! I'm even getting blessed now as I share it with you. Isn't it amazing that I am being blessed today about something which God did forty-eight years ago? When you are trusting Jesus, you still get blessed about the things God gave you twenty years ago, forty years ago, fifty years ago. You are delighted about it, because the more you appreciate it at the time, the longer it will last; that is, if you are broken enough, keep praying enough, and obey sufficiently to maintain it.

Of course, if you don't obey all the time, you will lose the appreciation, you will lose the praise and the joy out of your soul. The joy and the praise will stay in your heart as long as you obey God, and it will leave you when you disobey Him. Disobedience prevents joy from coming into your heart, leaving you desolate and lost. Obedience brings a true holy joy to blossom and bloom, and its fragrance grows sweeter as times goes on.

Over the years I have often thought about that evening when I was riding, peevish and sleepy, and my father asked me if I would "like" to get out and open the door. I was hesitant and not really wanting to respond, but back of that door was the very thing I desired. My father's kindly request for obedience was lovingly taking me toward that which I had long expected, for which I had prayed and trusted. Yet, because of my human weakness, I did not want to open it when the opportunity came.

In a similar way, many people miss the very thing for which they have prayed and trusted, because they hesitate to obey God's gentle command (for He only requests us, He does not coerce us). Instead of responding with joy when the Holy Spirit prompts them, they either ignore the leading or begrudge the effort to open the door.

If there is something you want very much, keep trusting for it. Be prepared when you come to the door of opportunity. Listen to your Father's voice when He speaks. Hop right down from your comfortable corner and push back the obstacles.

Don't let the bumps of misunderstanding and struggle in this life lull you to sleep. In this spiritual slumber you won't move for God and do what He says. But as you persevere upon the way of trust and praise, you'll be alert and able to know when you are near the goal.

Do you know that when the pony arrived that day, my father gave a check for the complete price of it? The very day my Queen came, she had been purchased in full for me by my father. Sometime there will come a day when that very thing for which you have been trusting so long is right here, and it is yours: all you have to do is continue trusting and believing. Your Father has provided all that you need. You will receive it after a while. Don't press to get it: it will come in time, as you let Him bring it to pass. A number of persons serve Jesus in order to receive certain things which they secretly desire. But the Lord will bring to the trusting heart everything that he needs, as he serves God only for Himself.

9 A CHILD'S PRAYER

In June of 1925 Standard Oil transferred my father to Yorktown, some fifteen miles west. Dad had been preaching in Carlos City those three years we were in Parker, and in Yorktown he was called to preach in a little church at Reed Station. It was there, at the age of nine years, that I took part in my first revival, helping my father by leading the singing.

While in prayer one day, the Lord spoke to my mother concerning my father's ministry. After she had put us boys to bed that night she came out and said, "Eldon, God has revealed to me that you will be called by the District Elder of the church to preach in his district."

"Oh, no!" he remarked. "That couldn't be! I have only a fifth grade education. I don't know much about speaking grammatically correct. I haven't had any training. I'm not qualified, Mary."

"Yes," she answered, "but Jesus has told me that you will be called soon into full-time ministry."

"I just hardly think so," Dad insisted.

Some four days later we were eating lunch when the phone rang. A voice requested, "Mr. A. E. Helm, please." When Dad took the phone, it was the District Elder. "Eldon," he said, "I want you to take Centenary Church (now Trinity) in New Castle. I can't guarantee you much—about sixteen hundred dollars a year at the most. I will need to know your answer by four o'clock today."

My mother said that my father's face turned as white as

death. "Mary!" he managed to say. He was shocked; but my mother was expecting the call. Glory to God! She knew it was coming. But my father felt so unworthy, so feeble, so limited in education. Surely he wouldn't be called. "Do you think I can do it, Mary?" he asked. "Of course you can," my Mother replied. She knew that God was in it. Here my father had a job with Standard Oil paying a few thousand dollars a year; and three or four thousand dollars a year income before the depression was times and times more than that amount now. He had a wonderful position.

He was a born salesman and doing well. What he was sold on, he could sell. He was so talented in selling that when he started in Kimmel Circuit in 1945, many years after that, he decided to sell a Christian publication to as many as he could. There had been seventeen subscriptions the year before he came but five had cancelled, leaving them with only twelve people subscribing. The first year, my father went from home to home selling this publication and signed seventy-seven subscribers, the highest increase in the entire conference.

Now he had but four hours to decide what he was going to do. He then had four little boys and was expecting another child, which turned out to be two more boys at one time. Would he remain with the business which was supplying him with an excellent income and promised him much more; or would he take this small church which could afford only a limited salary way below his present earnings?

With such a short time to decide, my father was praying with Mother, "What will we do, Lord? Will we give up this job and all its potential to go to a precious little church? What do you want us to do?" They earnestly prayed to know God's will. A few hours later my father called the District Elder and told him, "The Lord being my Helper, I will assume this pastorate."

I shall never forget going with my father the next Sunday

to that little church. Do you know how many persons were there that January morning?—I think there were four women, one man and a few children. Five adults! Did that look very promising to a man who had left a profitable and growing business?

But Dad bought himself a good pair of shoes and began to go from house to house working with the people, praying with them, talking with them, and loving them. It wasn't long before there were twenty in service. Soon there were forty. Not long after there were sixty, then eighty, and one hundred. God was bringing in the people.

After several months, father felt that the church needed revival; so he began leading the services himself. For about two or three weeks he preached his heart out, and although the Lord was helping him, the folk did not respond. They weren't really listening. Nobody would move. Even today, the heartbreaking fact is that a great number of people in the church really aren't obedient. There are very few people who actually obey God. We simply gather together, preach, testify and pray a little, and think that this is ninety percent of Christianity. But that is only about ten percent.

Ninety percent of Christianity is our walking with God: denying Self—what we want, what we desire and what we think is good or reasonable—to do what God wants; pressing to obey the Holy Spirit; assuming the cross joyfully; dying out to the carnal nature minute by minute and second by second. **Actually living for Christ** is true Christianity, and it has seldom been lived consistently in the ages.

Dad preached and preached, but the key individuals, like keys on an organ, wouldn't operate, and the divine melody was unable to play. If the key people would only get right with God, Jesus would be able to save communities by the thousands.

Once I shared from a pulpit God's revelation to me that if the key people of that congregation would humble themselves, confess their faults, and get everything right with God, then there would be hundreds of souls brought into the Kingdom within a short time. God revealed to me that there were eight thousand individuals ready to be saved within a radius of three miles of the church at that time, if we could only persuade everyone in the church to get right with God.

When God showed me this that night, I was so surprised. I shared it from the pulpit, and it witnessed to the pastor's heart strongly. He scarcely had ever had a burden hit his heart with such power. Several of the congregation also said that when this revelation was shared, it struck their hearts like an arrow.

You see, it is God who brings the sinners in. We can't do it. Preaching doesn't do it. Singing won't do it. People and personalities can't do it. It is the power of God that brings sinners in and changes them.

Many churches want you to have revival by "Caesarean birth." This is the method whereby the revival services are scheduled at the time the church wishes, with the assumption that the evangelist will bring the sinners in and get them saved. We might manage to get a few saved in this manner, but if the church is not cleansed of its criticism, disobedience, and hidden sins, before long the lambs die. They die on spoiled milk and clabbered fellowship. Lambs feed primarily from the flock. They can seldom feed from the shepherd. Many think that the pastor should take care of the new converts, but it is the sheep who feed and care for the newborn lambs.

The "milk" on which the lambs feed is the "joy of the Lord." The new converts feed on the joy which the congregation has in Jesus. They are fed on the praise flowing from obedient hearts. They are nourished by the thanksgiving of mature saints, the sharing of how Jesus has led and directed. When the church is not in glorious victory, however; when God is not able to be leading His people and accomplishing His will through them, many times the new converts are discouraged and soon gone. They are some-

70

times in a worse condition than they were prior to a knowledge of salvation.

The power of God will work through any church to draw
sinners to Jesus as soon as that body of believers pays the
price. Isaiah tells us: ". . . for as soon as Zion travailed,
she brought forth her children." (Isaiah 66:8) Very few
people have ever come to soul travail. I have preached forty
years throughout the United States, and I have seen only
two people in soul travail, let alone an entire church body
able to arrive at this holy place of agonizing intercessory
prayer.

Why, beloved, it requires a price; it takes yieldedness and
going with God completely before we know much about a
"soul burden." To come, then, to "intercessory prayer" is
some distance beyond this. But far, far, far beyond "soul
burden" is the "City of Soul Travail," and I know very few
people who have ever arrived there.

We make our way to soul travail by self-denial, under a
cross, yielded, obedient, and faithful to Christ: letting God
remove from us all carnal characteristics which hinder His
Spirit and wound others. Waiting on God is a necessary
requisite of this pruning process. But, once God can find
a body of believers willing to make the sacrifice—who will
come to brokenness together, confessing all hidden resentments and criticisms—He could prepare that body to come
to travail in the Spirit, and thousands would be brought into
the Kingdom, wonderfully transformed.

The grand impediment to such glorious victory through
Christ is simply this: the church acknowledges adultery, mur-
der, cursing, stealing, and drunkenness as sin; but very few
church people are aware that if Satan can manage to inject
the slightest tinge of malice or criticism into only one heart,
he has stopped the spiritual progress of that body just as
surely as if that person had committed a more obvious
wickedness.

The reason a number of our churches are bearing little

fruit for Jesus is because our roots are planted in the bitter springs of the carnal mind. Dear ones harbor a touch of malice, nurse a time-worn grudge, linger over resentments, or conceal a private criticism in their hearts. These carnal patterns are of Satan, not of Jesus.

The natural mind tends to minimize the intense serious-ness of these inner attitudes of the heart; but they are as devastating to the true spiritual effectiveness of the church body as those evils which we commonly recognize as sin. They are wicked, horrid, vile, abominable unrighteousness, and grievous to God. Like any other sin, they stop the entire spiritual life of the church.

When such carnal attitudes are not confessed and put under the blood of Jesus, that church body is rendered powerless in the Spirit. Powerless! Oh, the program and activities of the church may proceed apparently undisturbed, but the true fire of God will not be operating in its midst.

Paul tells us in Ephesians that Christ so loved the Church and gave Himself for it in order that ". . . He might present it to himself a glorious church, not having spot or wrinkle or any such thing; but that it should be holy, without spot or blemish." God wants His purpose to be fulfilled through holy people in His church.

My father had preached diligently to these precious people night after night with no results. One night, Dad asked the people to come up around the altar that they might pray. They were willing to come, but none would pray. I was only ten or eleven at the time, but felt so strongly my father's situation that I began to pray. "Jesus," I cried, "come down here and help my daddy! Come into this church, Lord. We've got to have help!"

I don't know what all I prayed, but it seemed to reach the hearts of these dear people. They began to weep, and before long the Lord had sent a little awakening. Jesus used a little boy to break the stony hearts of those good church people. But the Lord wants to work through adults as well as the

72

children. He wishes to operate in our lives. He longs to move in our souls.

My father had relinquished his job and a secure future to go with God, and Jesus honored his trust by saving souls in that community. Hearts were truly converted. Individuals were transformed by the power of His blood, and God began to raise up a faithful people.

Dad preached there from January, 1926, to April, 1928, although we moved back to Parker in September, 1927. Father didn't think he could live thirty miles away and still do justice to his charge, but the congregation said, "We want you to continue to pastor the church here." So he drove thirty miles each way from Parker to the south edge of New Castle to conduct services throughout the winter.

Mother and Dad owned a Chevrolet, at that time, which had no side windows; but only curtains, which flopped back and forth in the wind. Our folks would cover the six of us boys with blankets, and we would huddle as close together as possible. With the temperature sometimes down to zero and the wind pouring through those curtains all the way home—my, it was cold! Sometimes it was rather late when we started home. I recall one night when my father prayed till midnight with one man before he met Jesus.

On one journey I was with my father alone, and it was so very cold driving home. Dad said that I would have frozen to death if he hadn't sheltered me from the wind. But because he protected me with his own body, he was so frozen by the time we arrived home that Mother thought she would never get him warm. She had to heat comforts and blankets to put over him for several hours, and he was quite sick the following two or three days.

On another occasion, returning home late one particular Sunday, it was so cold that the radiator froze. Dad stopped by a stream and told Mother, "I'm going to see if I can find a can or a pail underneath the bridge here, then go down to that patch of swift water to fill the radiator." If you can,

73

picture my father out in the bitter cold of this dark night, groping through the snow beneath that bridge hoping to discover a can or pail. The chances of him finding even a tiny can in condition to hold water were mighty slim. In the meantime, his family of seven all sat shivering in blankets, trusting that he would get them home safely.

Suddenly his foot clanked on something! He reached down, and up from the snow rolled a five-gallon pail with a scoop on it, and the bottom was still in it! Praise the Lord. My father made his way to the rippling water where the stream hadn't frozen, and with that pail carried the water necessary to fill the radiator. He wrapped a blanket around it and it didn't freeze again all the way home.

My parents were striving to be faithful to the purpose God had for them, and He, in turn, provided for them time after time.

10 PARENTAL DISCIPLINE

"Mary," my father told my mother one day in New Castle, "we must go back to Parker City."

"But, Eldon," she replied. "Why?" She felt that they were working where God wanted them.

"I need to go back to get some finance so that I can give our eldest son an education," Dad replied. "God is calling Loran. (And when I share this with you, the power of God goes right through me.) He needs to have an education. We must return to Parker."

It broke my mother's heart, for she didn't want to leave the pastorate; but we returned to Parker in September, 1927. My father borrowed three hundred dollars from Mr. Mark Broadwater to buy a little old tank truck and start out to sell White Lightning gasoline.

Dad's finance was quite limited during the next two years, but he and Mother continued to pray and trust. He sold very little gasoline, because he had to start in at the very beginning again. But he and Mother held on in prayer day after day, and God began to bless. After a time he was hired as the agent of the Sinclair Refining Company, but his predecessor had been selling only two thousand gallons a month; scarcely enough to pay the light bill and the taxes.

One day my mother answered a knock on the door. A man said to her, "Tell your husband to come and see me." My father signed him as a customer, and earned four hundred dollars a month from him alone. In depression times, four hundred dollars would be equivalent now to about fifteen hundred dollars. Only one account! The Lord began to honor the trust of my parents by this great increase in their business. Praise the Lord for supplying.

Mother has shared that, because of God's watchful care of us, in the midst of the depression my father was able to buy boxes of groceries and have them sent to needy homes. He would buy baskets of supplies and tell the grocer, "Take these groceries to so-and-so, but don't tell them where they came from. I don't want anyone to know that they came from me." God was blessing him so wonderfully, and he had to share with others some of the increase.

Mother was suffering greatly from time to time during this period, troubled both with gall bladder and heart ailment. Raising six boys when their mother was ill was not an easy task for my father, but he handled the assignment well. He was a strong and powerful man. He seldom told us something more than once. What he said, he meant, and we learned that we had best do what he said, exactly as he said it.

I wanted to please my father in everything. If he told me to give so much corn to the hogs, I wanted to provide just that amount. If he ordered so much hay for the cows, that is exactly what I wanted to give them, no more and no less. When he showed me how to hoe beans, I tried to do it just as he showed me. I never enjoyed gardening. My second brother liked to work in the garden, but it was real work for me. I believe the Lord had work for me in another garden—the garden of the soul; plowing up hardened hearts, planting the seed of God's love, and hoeing out the weeds of doubt, fear, hatred, and animosity.

The six of us boys were taught to obey quickly and cheerfully. Whenever we were out of line, our father brought us back in line quickly. After we were older, Mother taught us to sing, and we would sing in various churches. Looking back on that early training period we have said, "Mother taught us to sing, and Dad kept us in tune."

He employed a special method in tuning us up. He had a buggy tug about eight to ten inches long. Right up where the buggy tug went over the singletree it was hard leather, and there were three holes in it. Do you remember that? In about every buggy tug there were three holes, and about an inch or two up from the last hole the leather was very limber. Dad cut it off about eight inches up beyond that third hole, split it down the middle, folded it up and carried it in his hip pocket. Whenever any of us six boys got out of line, he took that whip and laid it on us real well.

I remember that when my father whipped me, he whipped me hard. He would discipline me because he loved me. The more you love someone, the more you want them to go straight. I know this is true not only because of experience, but also because the Word says, "Whom the Lord loveth He chasteneth." When we get out of line, if we are really His children, God will apply the rod to us.

My father disciplined each of us boys differently, but when he punished me, I didn't want to do that which caused the whipping anymore. But, because I needed much help and instruction, I would receive another tanning in two or three weeks about something else. He disciplined all my brothers as well. If he had failed to do this, we could have missed what we are in the world for. If I had not had a father who disciplined me, and who was willing to be severe and consistent with me, I do not believe that I would have been called as God has called me (and when I tell you this, I receive the witness of the Holy Spirit that this is true).

Think of the seriousness of this! The Holy Spirit witnesses to the fact that, unless my father had lovingly disciplined me— whipped me severely upon each disobedience, and consistently put me in line—I would have missed the glorious Church and never known the purpose for which I was put on earth.

You see, the need of our flesh is greater than we know. It requires a heart firm in discipline to walk the path of self-denial under the cross. Without self-denial after conversion, we never reach the cross. And unless we take up a cross, we never truly become a disciple of Jesus, for He said in Luke 14:27: ". . . Whosoever doth not bear his cross, and come after me, **cannot** be my disciple."

The cross is not some trial, struggle, or tragic situation which may befall you. The cross is an instrument of death upon which Self is crucified. It is never forced upon me or you. Each person must personally resolve in his heart to unalterably pursue the way of the cross, even as Jesus steadfastly set his face towards Jerusalem where His ignominious death awaited Him. The cross is actually the life lived in accordance with God's perfect will, and we must **volunteer** to seek and do only God's will.

Once we choose God's way entirely, we are pointed in the direction of the cross, but we have not yet taken up the cross to follow Jesus. The only hands which grip the cross are "self-denial" and "obedience." **The spiritual hands which actually apprehend and maintain a life lived according to God's will are "self-denial" and "obedience."** Unless we deny Self and obey God moment by moment, we'll not even be able to take hold of the cross. **If we do not daily deny ourselves—what we want and desire—to wait upon God until He is able to teach us what the Holy Spirit wants us to do, we are missing what Christianity is all about.**

Do you begin to see how narrow this Way is? And, because it is more narrow than the fleshly mind is either willing to admit or even able to comprehend, we must be consistently disciplined in order to prepare our hearts to remain on the Narrow Way once we begin.

I recall a class discussion in college regarding how soon we should discipline our children. Some said at the age of three years, others said at two months, six months, a year. But a voice spoke up, saying: "We probably should begin with the grandparents fifty years before the child is born." He was suggesting that we need generation after generation of disciplined individuals. We need discipline in the home, in the church, in the school, and at work. We need to press to walk uprightly and circumspectly before God, with clean hands and a pure heart; not lifting up our heart to vanity nor swearing deceitfully.

If we are going to walk with clean hands, it will surely be because we have been disciplined and because we are continuing to be disciplined. We must go to the cross and remain humbly under the load of God's holy assignment. We must discipline ourselves to live lives of self-denial before the Throne in prayer, crying, "Oh, God, lead me, help me, direct me," otherwise we will bypass the cross and not know it. It is a great challenge to live a life of self-denial. It is a continual pressing, and we must discipline ourselves rigorously. Now this is simple, but it is worth the entire book if you are willing to hear and assimilate this in your heart.

We must also discipline our children or we will lose them. Sometimes we work so earnestly to save other children that we lose our own. Many people in the church are working unsparingly to win souls, but lose their own children by not chastening them, by not disciplining them. We lose our young people as well by praying inconsistently, by criticizing people before them, by failing to be a true witness of Jesus in our daily lives. It is not what we preach and teach that matters so much: it is how we treat our companion, how we really love our neighbors, and what we actually do or say that tells our children what we truly believe in our hearts. What we are in our hearts springs out of our everyday life, and we are not aware of it.

About twenty or thirty years ago, an idea began to receive popular acceptance which said, "Let the child express himself. Let him do as he pleases. If he wants to mark on the wall, let him mark on the wall. If he wants to sit on the floor, let him sit. Whatever he wants to do, permit him self-expression." We have been in a whirl ever since.

Susanna Wesley, mother of nineteen children and the woman who gave the world John and Charles Wesley, recorded, upon request, her principles of child-rearing which produced such monumental success in forming Christian character.   She is very brief and to the point:

"When turned a year (and some before), they were taught to fear the rod and cry softly; by which means they escaped the abundance of correction they might otherwise have had. . . .

"In order to form the minds of children, the first thing to be done is to conquer the will and bring them to an obedient temper." *

She tells, to some extent, how she did this.   Her children, once strong, were confined to three meals a day.   They were never permitted to eat between meals and made to eat whatever was set before them.   They were corrected early in order to avoid a stubborn nature, which, once ingrown, would have taken excessive punishment to remove.   She called those parents "cruel" who playfully develop patterns and habits in the children which later must be broken.

She insisted that once a child is corrected, he must be conquered.   He is to be brought early to revere and stand in awe of his parents.   No willful transgression was ever permitted to escape without chastisement.   She wrote:

"I insist upon conquering the will of children betimes, because this is the only strong and rational foundation of a religious education; without which both precept and example will be ineffectual. . . . I cannot dismiss this subject.   **As self-will is the root of all sin and misery,** so whatever cherishes this in children insures thereafter wretchedness and irreligion.   Whatever checks and mortifies it **(self-will)** promotes their future happiness and piety."

This woman of the eighteenth century put her finger on the very culprit which is now crowding our divorce courts, overflowing our prisons, discouraging our precious teachers, and causing many of our police officials to resign—SELF-WILL. **She cites Self-Will alone as the cause of all misery and all sin.**

*Quotation from: "Children Can Be Taught To Obey," William W. Orr, Scripture Press Publications, Inc., Wheaton, Illinois. (Emphasis inserted by the editor.)

Declaring herself absolutely an enemy of this innate perversion, she determines to drive it from the heart of her children before it crushes the principle and substance of goodness from them.

To many, this may sound severe and stern. This is because our minds have been instructed by the counselors of this world. We have been bent to the ideas of the earth, whereas God wants us lifted to the heavenly pattern of His Word.

She continues very soberly:

"This is still more evident if we further consider that religion is nothing else than doing the will of God, and not our own; **that the one grand impediment to our temporal and eternal happiness is this self-will.** No indulgence of it can be trivial, no denial unprofitable.

"**Heaven or hell depends upon this alone.** So that the parent who studies to subdue it in his child, works together with God in the renewing and saving of a soul. The parent who indulges it does the devil's work, makes religion impractical, salvation unattainable, and does all that in him lies to damn his child, soul and body, forever."

So this sacred assignment of raising children is much more serious than we can imagine. It isn't an easy task, although it is a wonderful privilege, filled with great joy and innumerable delights.

Mrs. Wesley also confessed:

"**No one can, without renouncing the world in the most literal sense, observe my method (of child-rearing);** and there are few, if any, that would entirely devote above twenty years of the prime of life in hopes to save the souls of their children, which they think may be saved without so much ado; for that was my principle intention, however unskillful and unsuccessfully managed."

And my father made "much ado" about our obeying. He didn't have many who sympathized with his efforts, even as Susanna Wesley predicted. He had to renounce the opinions of most of the world. His relatives and church people thought him much too strict. But I want to testify, and my five brothers would likewise declare, that it paid off marvelously to the credit side.

If I had had any trouble with the school teacher, I would have had trouble with my dad as well. Therefore, I saw to it that I didn't have any trouble at school. I didn't look for the faults of my teachers, I looked for the good qualities. If they had any faults, I didn't dare think much about them.

But if I hadn't been disciplined, I wouldn't have been that way. I would have brought back tales of how the teacher didn't like me and made things hard for me. I would have whined, found fault, and criticized her to my parents; that is, if they had listened or sympathized with me.

One of the biggest things we do to our children is pamper and pet them with sympathy toward the flesh, which passes for Christian compassion. What we are actually doing is training our child to feel sorry for himself in disappointment and find excuse for the satisfying of his own desires. When he is older, he will retreat from any situations demanding fortitude and courage; he will by-pass human activities requiring inner steadiness and maturity of mind.

I tell you, friends, there are things in us that need to be taken out, and if we don't take them out of our children—if we don't break our children when they are little—they will break us and grind us down when they are twelve or older. **Unless we severely discipline our children, they may not make it to Heaven.** In fact, the chances are slim that an undisciplined child will ever continue to walk with God even if Jesus can bring him to conversion, for the heart bent in childhood to self-satisfaction and self-desire will seldom bend to the will of God following conversion.

Now I know that many believe that once you have been converted, your reward in Heaven is secure. But God's Word tells us very plainly through the voice of Jesus in Matthew 7:21: "Not everyone that saith Lord, Lord shall enter into the Kingdom of Heaven; but he that doeth the will of my Father which is in Heaven." These precious ones feel that the will of God is just to be converted. But the Holy Spirit has revealed to me that God's will is to direct us and to lead us in our daily lives. This means that we are to obey God in every aspect of our lives. It declares plainly that we are to be holy, yielded, and submissive to God's will and to His plans. **This is the cross**—it is accepting gladly and doing willingly not what we wish or what we choose or what we select, but doing what God wishes for our day by day activities. **This is what the Christian life is about. It is obeying Jesus just as He obeyed God.**

But the undisciplined heart will by-pass the cross; it will resist self-denial, and will insist on having its own way. Once we choose our own way, we are headed the opposite way from God's Kingdom and from Heaven. You say to me, "Why, Brother Helm, this is serious!" Yes it is: more serious than I can ever say. Not many people want to hear it, but I must declare the truth to all persons faithfully, always.

I recall coming home one time and my wife informed me that one of my brothers was having difficulty with his son, two to three years of age. It seemed that every time they brought him into a church he would just scream and yell and carry on. So, they had to simply take him out of the sanctuary and go home. They couldn't bring him into the church or else he would make such a commotion. I asked my brother, "May I give you a little advice?" He said that I might and I suggested to him, "Next Sunday morning when your little one starts carrying on like that, you take him down in the basement and tune him up so well that he won't ever want to go back."

He said, "Oh, I hadn't thought of that." The next Sunday, the little son began the same thing—screaming, crying, yelling—and my brother took him out. The child stopped crying right away, of course, because he thought he was going home again. But he wasn't. His dad carried him to the basement and gave that little fellow a tanning. He punished him soundly.

(Many parents give their children two or three spanks and feel they have corrected them. However, this simply irri-tates the child. Children need to be switched until the rebellious spirit is broken and their crying is no longer angry, but repentant. We are not to carnally correct our children, but firmly administer the rod or some other proper chastening in a right manner. Many parents are undecided about how to correct their son or daughter; consequently, the little child has the father and mother under his control. He is saying to them essentially, "I am going to do what I want to do."

(I never once told my father that. If I had said anything back to him, I would have been on my back quickly, and that is where I should have been. It would have been good for me.

(If our children aren't corrected early, they are going to grind us to powder someday. People will tell me, "I just can't control my twelve-year-old son." If you can't control your twelve-year-old son, he will have you in the courts one of these days. He will go his own way and break you to pieces. Our children must be disciplined, but we must discipline ourselves first.)

When my brother brought his little son back upstairs to the sanctuary, he sat him beside him on the pew and that little fellow sat quietly. He started once to make a little move and my brother said, "You be quiet." Looking up at his father, that little guy knew that he would get another whipping if he didn't mind. He sat right back on the pew and behaved like a reasonable child from then on whenever he was in church.

When I look into the faces of little ones, I often see things in their lives which frighten me. It is difficult for parents to see these harmful attitudes lurking under the surface of their child's personality. But as we discipline ourselves to the walk with God, the Holy Spirit will begin to help us detect elements in our own natures which need the correction from our Heavenly Father. While we are being corrected, occasionally we are granted better understanding of how we need to discipline our own children.

Sometimes your child will display a spirit of disobedience, rebellion, stubbornness, harshness, impatience, or many other carnal attitudes for which you will need to discipline him. In the process of chastening your child, you will be chastened as well by your Heavenly Father for a similar spirit hidden in your own heart.

There is much for God to do within each of us, if we will only yield to His all-wise hand. He knows that, unless a parent is cleansed and filled with the Spirit, the discipline from that parent is liable to be angry and carnal, which can do as much damage to the child as no discipline at all. **Our chastening must be controlled by the Holy Spirit, not by anger or wrath, for carnal tactics never help, but hinder.** We must be disciplined ourselves, and our little ones must be given loving, consistent correction.

When our youngest daughter's child was only a few weeks old, she would take her bottle so rapidly. It concerned me some, so I told my daughter and son-in-law, "Why don't you simply take the bottle out of her mouth every thirty seconds or so and let her rest for a few moments. That way it will be better for her digestion, and she will be learning disappointment at the same time."

(I rarely tell anyone what to do, for a man of God is slow to give advice to anyone, except to encourage them to love Jesus with all their hearts and to obey His will. However, my youngest daughter and her husband are striving to follow Jesus the best they know how, and have asked me to tell them whenever God shows me something concerning them. A number of other dear ones have requested me to do this also. It has not always been easy for me, but it has been good.)

At first, each time the bottle was removed from her mouth,

that little child screamed and fussed. She didn't like it one bit. Of course, she was a darling child, but she simply wanted her food at her time and at her speed. We are all exactly like that. This is the Carnal Nature. This inborn self-will is what we acquired from the Fall in the Garden, and it is much worse than I could ever share with you. I know that I have only a very limited view of the desperate wickedness of the heart, but what I do see frightens me.

After ten days of having the bottle periodically withdrawn, that little child became accustomed to taking her milk slowly. Her parents could remove the bottle from her mouth and she would simply rest and wait. It required ten days for her nature to become accustomed to this denial. She knew by then that the bottle would return. While she waited, her tummy was resting and her nervous system was learning to be disappointed. If we do not early learn to take disappointments in stride, we will grow into adults who are immature in behavior. We will be at the mercy of any sudden difficulty or every change of circumstance.

Because of this method of early disappointment, accompanied with consistent chastening and correction, this child is able (by God's grace only) to take disappointment with a minimum of upheaval. She is pleasant to be around and a very happy two-year-old. And—may I share something for the encouragement of parents?—This little girl loves her mother about as much as I have ever seen a child love a parent: yet, her mother has spanked her severely ever since she knew that the infant could discern between "yes" and "no". She was five months old when her mother could recognize that she had a knowledge of obeying or disobeying.

I am certain that when a child is grown he will seldom return to his parents and say, "Mother and Dad, thank you for not spanking me when I was growing up." But, most children who have been lovingly and consistently disciplined will return to their parents many times with the words, "I am so thankful you chastened me hard, Dad, when I was a kid.

86

Mom, thanks for loving me enough to punish me. I needed more whippings than I received."

There is a mystery in correcting a child, and it defies analysis by the intellect. We know it is absolutely necessary, because the wisest man in history (except for Jesus) gave us several specific instructions regarding child-rearing. Most of these tell us to use the "rod of correction" when the child is disobedient. In fact, he said that if you "hate" your child you will spare the rod; if you "love" him, you will chasten him before it is too late. At another place he says, "Foolishness is bound in the heart of a child; but the rod of correction will drive it far from him."*

He counsels parents to chasten a child while there is yet hope, and "let not thy soul spare for his crying." These admonitions are recorded in the book of Proverbs, which also contains the promise, "Train up a child in the way he should go, and when he is old he will not depart from it." Many Christian parents cling to this latter promise, but have failed to comply with the many specific instructions to also chasten and correct the child sternly. Consistent chastening is much of what it means to "train up a child in the way he should go." Many think this scripture simply means to take their children to Sunday school and church, and to teach them the doctrines of salvation and repentance. But, to "train up a child in the way he should go" means that we are preparing him to walk with God. The "way he should go" is in lowly following of Jesus. We are to bring that child's rebellious inner nature to an obedient and submissive character.

If the child is not taught to obey his parents, he will have difficulty obeying God. It will not be easy for the undisciplined child to comprehend God's absolute authority over his life when he is converted. Jesus wants to lead all His people, but so few are prepared as children by their parents to obey without question or debate. This explains to a great measure

*See end of chapter for other scriptures related to correction.

why God has seldom been able to find a people who will really trust Him and obey Him. As children growing up, we have had our own way for so long that we can scarcely grasp the fact, after conversion, that God's desires supersede our own plans and wishes.

We tend to treat God in a similar manner as we did our own parents. We expect God to give in to our wants and permit us to run things along the lines of our own ideas. Because of early self-assertive patterns, few in all the ages have been willing to die out to Self sufficiently to really consistently do God's will and not their own.

To correct a child from his own ways into an obedient and submissive behavior is not easy. It cannot be done without God's help, without His constant wisdom and counsel. To the observer, correction appears cruel. But the mystery is that it is just the opposite—it is ultimate kindness. Correction grows out of a heart deeply rooted in divine love. To do less leads, sooner or later, to tragedy.

As we begin to walk with God, leaving behind the ideas and opinions of the earth, He will begin to teach us of the love hidden in His chastening arm. He will begin to reveal the future gifts that are ours because of His present denials. He will open to our limited vision the great principle of His Kingdom: "He that loses his life shall find it." He will make plain the understanding that in having our own way, we always lose; but in yielding to His inscrutable wishes, though it appears we are losing all we had desired or hoped for, we are actually brought to a land laden with more than we had ever dreamed possible, all for His glory and honor.

My parents instructed me in many areas. Mother told me how I should treat my wife if I were to be married: to be kind, gentle and thoughtful. I was never to say to her, "I wish you would have prepared this like my mother," or, "I wish you could do this like my mother." She taught me to consider ways of expressing kindness to others.

All six sons were instructed in washing floors, dusting, and keeping house. We were taught to cook simple meals and be independent. Mother constantly advised us to keep our clothing neat and to hang them carefully in the closet when we removed them. She instructed me in integrity, cooperation, and thoughtfulness.

My father taught me to be conscious of all my investments and purchases. "Never purchase anything when you can't see your way clear," he would say. I was shown never to be involved financially above that which I was able to bear. "If a man loses his credit, he has lost everything," Dad told me. "A man's credit is his word, and his word should be as good as his note, if not better."

I was taught to be truthful. My father said that he hated a a liar more than a thief. "You can watch a thief, but if a man tells you something that is untrue, you aren't sure whether he's telling you the truth or not." He drilled into me that telling untruths is a desperate, wicked thing.

Along this path of integrity and honesty, discipline and responsibility, my parents led me and compelled me, for which I am deeply in debt to Jesus.

The following are references from Proverbs, with which you are perhaps already familiar, but which I include for encouragement in what God's Word instructs us about child-rearing:

"A wise son heareth his father's instruction; but a scorner heareth not rebuke." (13:1)

"In the lips of him that hath understanding wisdom is found: but a rod is for the back of him that is void of understanding." (10:13)

"He that spareth his rod hateth his son: but he that loveth him chasteneth him betimes." (13:24)

"Chasten thy son while there is hope, and let not thy soul spare for his crying." (19:18)

"Even a child is known by his doings, whether his work be pure, and whether it be right . . . Train up a child in the way he should go: and when he is old, he will not depart from it." (20:11, 22:6)

"Foolishness is bound in the heart of a child; but the rod of correction shall drive it far from him." (22:15)

"Withhold not correction from the child: for if thou beatest him with the rod, he shall not die. Thou shalt beat him with the rod, and shalt deliver his soul from hell." (23:13,14)

"The rod and reproof give wisdom: but a child left to himself bringeth his mother to shame." (29:15)

"Correct thy son, and he shall give thee rest; yea, he shall give delight unto thy soul." (29:17)

11 CONVERSION

I was fifteen years of age, during a revival at the Parker church, when a saint of God slipped up beside me on one of the front seats and humbly asked, "Loran, are you saved?"

Self wanted to say, "Yes!" After all, I had been reared in a Christian home, prayed every day, went to church faithfully, tried to obey my parents as best I could, and didn't fight or fuss with my brothers. From the age of twelve on I seldom missed a prayer meeting, even though I was about the only boy there my age. I was janitor of the church at the age of thirteen or fourteen, but janitor or not, prayer meeting was on the program for me (and you can generally tell who are really serious about God's work by observing those who faithfully support this service dedicated to prayer).

But when I told this person that I was saved, I discovered for the first time in all my life that I had a living heart. My heart felt as if it literally flipped or turned over when I answered "Yes". I have to marvel how God convinced me in a second or two or three (and He tells me now that it was three seconds) that I was not born again. Now no person informed me about the marvelous operations of God within the heart and the body, but the Holy Spirit has instructed me little by little, over many years, how He reveals within the heart. At that moment, I was being instructed about the operation of Holy Spirit conviction within the human heart.

I was deceived about my true condition because I had been going by what "seemed" right, not by what God said through His Spirit. I wanted to think that I was a saved boy, but the Holy Spirit convinced me quickly that I wasn't what I thought myself to be. I don't think I had much conviction ever touch my heart until this saint obeyed God by asking me about my soul.

God's convincing men of sin will really come to a congregation when all the followers in that church are faithful and obedient. Great conviction will fall when the entire body has paid the price. Occasionally, however, God can bring revival in spite of opposition and disobedience. We experienced this when several of the board members at one of the churches we served rather felt that we couldn't afford to have revival. The Lord had revealed that we were to proceed, and He sent revival right over the top of every difficulty.

But usually conviction does not fall severely upon sinners in a community until those of the church humble themselves, confess their faults to one another, get everything right with God, and do exactly what He wants them to do. Conviction upon the lost will many times be in proportion to the burden which the church carries, and a burden for the lost cannot be achieved: it is a gift from God to the broken, obedient heart.

This is the reason we have so little true conviction in a great number of our churches today. So much secret sin, hidden iniquity, disobedience, and self-assertion in the lives of professing Christians grieves the Holy Spirit. Bible doctrines are still being preached in many congregations, but the power of God to convince men of sin has been greatly limited.

We cannot convict anyone of sin, for conviction comes not to the mind, but to the heart; and only the Holy Spirit can convince a man's heart of sin. We may have the proper theology and the correct ideas in our churches, but unless we as a people are one together in Christ Jesus through His love, the Holy Spirit is grieved; because of this, God seldom sends His convicting power. Without His divine power moving in their hearts, men will be totally unaware of the desperate lostness of their souls, just as I had been.

In December 1932 or January 1933, in a conversation unknown to me at that time, our pastor, Rev. N. E. Smith, came to my father and said, "Eldon, I have an opportunity to get an evangelist by the name of Rev. E. R. Lewis. I know that if I bring it before the board, it will probably not be approved, and I have only a few days in which to procure him. He has a cancellation and can come at this time."

My father told Rev. Smith, "Pastor, you invite him, and I will stand behind you."

So our pastor scheduled Rev. E. R. Lewis for revival in January. He was called "the word painter," for he could take the Bible stories and simply bring them alive. There was no one like him. Even today, though he is over eighty years old, Brother Lewis has not changed. He still has the fire, the keen mind, and the same goal he once had. I was amazed when I visited him a few months ago, for he was able to recall in detail many incidents of that revival in 1933. His wife is not well, but he never mentions it. He doesn't even act like she is sick. I would never have known it if his son had not informed me. Isn't it wonderful that a man could continue faithfully and not faint—simply be joyous and overcoming as if everything were normal? Why, most of us would be lamenting, "I tell you, we are having a hard time. Mother is not very well." But he didn't say one word about her sickness when I visited with him a few months ago. Praise the Lord.

In the first month of 1933 the meeting started, but I didn't come for a few nights because we had basketball practice. Of course, on Sunday night and prayer meeting I had to be there, but on other week nights my father would sometimes permit me to be at school functions. Not many nights went by until he said, "Now, Son, I think we will go to church tonight. We need to be at the revival." I wasn't too anxious to attend, for I was under dreadful, deep (the Holy Ghost says within me "deep") conviction. But, as soon as my

93

father said that I was to be in church, I was on my way.

A few months ago Rev. Lewis reviewed what actually took place, unknown to me at that time, during the revival:

"Before church started that night," he told me, "your daddy came up and sat down beside me. 'Brother Lewis,' he confided, 'don't look back, but my oldest son, Loran, needs to be saved. He needs to find Christ. God has called him and the devil is fighting terribly. Don't look around, but I just pray that some way God will help you in this revival to bring him in.'

"I said, 'Yes, Sir, we will do the best we can, Brother Helm.' And when I looked around, if I ever saw a picture of despair, I saw it painted on your face. You looked like you didn't have a friend in the world."

When a person is under conviction, he doesn't look too happy. Many people in the church do not appear too happy because they do not have the happiness on the inside. When you are saved and have the joy of Jesus on the inside, it shows on the outside, because your mind will tell your face.

True happiness, a genuine inner joy, is a result of obedience; and obedience is never experienced except by humility and self-denial. If we fail to deny Self, we disobey God. In order to obey the Lord regularly and consistently, one must continue to die out to himself and to things. Here is where **true** joy is to be found! **The secret of living is in dying: dying out to what we want and what we plan, in order to do what God wants and what God wills.**

As the revival services continued, conviction was apparent upon me. When we pulled up to the curb of the church Sunday morning, January 22, 1933, my brother Richard said, "They're going to get you today."

"What did you say?" I asked.

He replied, "I just have a feeling that they are going to get you today."

"Going to get me!" I remarked impatiently. Richard said that I didn't respond too cordially. I was under severe conviction. God was calling and the devil was fighting.

94

That evening after the Epworth League service, I came down the church steps onto the curb as my mother and father came up the walk to attend the evening service. I said to my father, "I am going with the young people to the Rivoli Theater tonight, Dad."

Without hesitation my father said, "Son, you will sing in the choir tonight."

Here I was almost seventeen years old, president of my Junior class in high school, and my friends were getting into their cars to go to the theater. But I simply turned around, walked back up all the steps, made my way down the aisle, and found a seat over on the left side of the choir loft.

I didn't question my father or whimper and whine until he let me have my way. My dad had never permitted us to have our own way. When he told me that I would sing in the choir, I obeyed his order immediately without question or contention. In a few minutes I looked up and here came my good chum, Thomas B. He said, "Well, if you're not going to the theater, I'm not going either." So my not going to the theater brought him back into the church also.

When the sermon ended, one of the saints came up into the choir loft to invite me to Jesus. I was hard; I was obstinate; I was stubborn. "No!" I insisted. But the evangelist, by the help of the Holy Spirit, led a young man to Jesus while he was praying with souls. All at once he said, "Now everyone who is a friend of Howard M., come down and shake his hand."

Why, Howard had been my friend since 1922. I had to go shake his hand. That brought me out of the choir right down to the old-fashioned "mourner's bench." It was composed of two benches, one on either side at the front of the sanctuary.

When I got there to shake his hand, the young people gathered around me and I couldn't get away. I tried to leave, but it seemed that I couldn't move at all. It was almost as if I were nailed to the floor. Folks were pleading with me to give my heart to Jesus. I looked to my left, and there, just a few feet from my side, was my mother at the altar praying.

After a few minutes in this struggle between dear ones who were pleading and Satan who was fighting within, I said to myself, "God, you have been on my trail ever since I was born." Now why did I say just those words—"God, you have been on my trail ever since I was born" when I did not even know that my mother felt the Holy Spirit falling upon us at my birth? It was the Lord speaking through me.

Still talking to myself I added, "I can see that if I don't go with You it is going to be dark. But, God, I don't want to be a fifty percent Christian or even a ninety-nine percent Christian. I want to be one hundred percent for you, Jesus." When I said that, I dropped to my knees right there and Tom B. fell to the altar beside me. He got victory in about nine to ten minutes; but I continued to pray and plead with God, my head in the curl of my arm.

I thought myself to be the worst of sinners, even though I had never had as much as a puff of tobacco in my mouth. Most boys, when they are little, will go behind the barn or into the field, get some corn silk, roll it, and smoke it. But I never did. My father and mother had said to me, "I trust you will never do that. If you will not smoke, we will make you a present the day you are twenty-one." Because of their admonition, each time I was tempted by the fellows, my mother's face would come up before me. I would resist the temptation and go home. Not a swallow of liquor had been down my throat either. But when I knelt at the altar that night, I was aware that I had come so far short in pleasing Jesus. I had grieved Him so much. I was such a terrible sinner.

Then Jesus began to speak to me. "I am calling you," He said. "You are Mine. You are going to be my servant."

"I can't do it," I told Him.

He said, "Yes, you can. I am calling you to preach the Gospel."

"No," I replied. "I am not able."

"You are Mine," God continued to deal with me. For the longest time I cried out. It was so black. "You are going to preach," He kept telling me gently.

"Lord, I can't preach," I insisted. (Now whenever a person wants to preach, I rather doubt if God has called him. Nearly every man of God I have known has tried to get out of preaching. He has told God that he is unable to do it. If a man feels himself totally incapable of this high assignment, I believe God will be able to work with him. I wanted to be a lawyer, but God was calling me to preach the Gospel.)

My mother tells me that the power of Satan was so very great around the altar that it seemed as if one could cut it with a knife. The enemy was there in terrible power trying to keep me back in the Kingdom of Darkness. I suppose that the devil fought me at my conversion as severely as any man I have seen or heard about in this age, because I believe Satan knew that if I started for Jesus, I didn't want to be half-way in this business. I wanted to be one hundred percent for God. Satan didn't want me to get started because he knew of all my appointments in the coming years with dear ones from coast to coast and in a few nations.

(When I would be with the clerk of the little village of Parker, Indiana, in 1951, I would share with him my walk with Jesus and answers to prayer in different parts of the nation. He would be blessed and thrilled over how God was directing me. One day as I shared with him, he lifted his hand across that big desk to make a statement, and I received the witness of the Holy Spirit to the truth of his words before he could even speak them: "What would have happened," he said, "if Loran Helm hadn't come down this lonely trail?")

That January night, Satan knew of the determination of my heart to do God's will. He knew why God had called me as a little boy, and he was fighting with ferocious power to keep me from getting started on this marvelous adventure with Jesus.

97

God continued lovingly to call me, but all I could repeat over and over was, "I can't preach—I can't preach."

Suddenly a beautiful light appeared right above me. I was amazed! I don't know how to describe it to you, for it was the light of the Kingdom of God. (Now don't you look for any light. What you anticipate and work out for your own conversion seldom happens. Simply take what God gives you and be glad for it. Every person's experience will be different, because God treats us as individuals.)

As soon as I saw this marvelous light, my sins fell away, all the darkness was gone, and a great load lifted out of me. God reached over His index finger, dipped it in the sacred blood of Jesus, and wrote my name down in the Lamb's Book of Life. Praise the Lord! On a page white and fair He wrote my unworthy name.

When He gave me a new heart and a new life I suddenly experienced a love and peace that I never knew existed. Jesus, through the power of God, by the work of the Holy Spirit, performed divine surgery on me: He grafted me into His side, and the Light and the Life and the Love of God began to flow through the veins and arteries of my soul. I wanted everyone saved right away.

I had heard my father and other pastors preach on the joy of the Lord, the peace of Jesus, since I was a little boy three years of age; but I didn't know a bit more of what they were talking about than if they had read a paragraph in the Hebrew language. I had studied the Bible, prayed daily, and attended church faithfully, but I didn't know about the divine joy that flows through the great heart of Jesus until I was brought from sin's terrible darkness into Christ's glorious light.

Oh, I know that I was only beginning, that I was just on the fringe of His great love; but God made a new person of me that January night. I was unworthy of this new life. I was so undeserving. It was a gift from God through Jesus Christ. I wasn't expecting the miraculous, but when you walk with God, it will be a supernatural walk. The holy

Word of God verifies the fact that the way of Christianity is supernatural.

To try to have Christianity without the supernatural is like trying to have apples without orchards, homes without dwellings, factories without machinery. To try to have Christianity without the miraculous is like trying to have human life without breathing, water without wells or springs, and light without electricity. Christianity began in simplicity with a supernatural birth, and continues to live in the miraculous through childlike faith.

But don't seek the supernatural; don't seek for experiences: seek first the Kingdom of God. (Matthew 6:33) One doesn't seek gifts or things, one seeks the person of Jesus alone. When you seek Jesus alone, He never fails to give you what you need and what other persons need through you. He cannot fail.

Jesus saved me right there at that altar. (And do you know what God is telling me right now as I share this with you? He is saying, "I will guide you and direct you." Isn't that wonderful? Just as I shared that Jesus saved me, He spoke within me and said, "I will guide you and direct you." To walk with God and have Him reveal Himself to you is one of the most wonderful things in the world! I sense His presence in my heart right now. Thank you, Jesus.

(I get excited and I can't help it. I am wonderfully glad about Jesus living in my heart. If you have Jesus in your heart, and if you are walking with God, you are really going to be excited about the Kingdom of God. You are going to be enthusiastic about everything that Jesus is in. You don't have to work up excitement; it is simply within you, and it gets better as you go along.

(I am convinced that very few people are following Jesus with all their hearts. Some people claim to be Christian, but there is scant evidence of joy in them. Precious persons stand in services to testify that they love Jesus, but there is so little of the love of Jesus in them. Their faces are full of shadows, and through their eyes one can see hidden darkness. There is a great possibility that at home they find fault, complain, murmur, or criticize. Some individuals claiming to be Christian say beautiful words at church, but at home they can be harsh and cruel, complaining and hard to get along with.

(Listen, dear ones—if a man is a Christian, he has the joy of Jesus and the fruits of the Spirit in his life. The time is short, and we need to be examining our lives for solid evidence of Christ's indwelling. We must go with Jesus wholeheartedly and rid our lives of all these unclean things. If you are in this with all your heart, God will begin to work through you to help someone: to encourage, to lift, or to heal.)

When I rose from the altar to a standing position, I felt like I was going to lift right up off the floor. Really! I actually thought that I was going right up. I didn't say a word to anyone, but Jesus had so lifted the load of my heart that I thought surely my feet would come off the floor. Others could sense this divine presence too, for John Wesley Lewis, the son of the evangelist and the song evangelist for the meetings (who has been in the church for over fifty years) told me recently: "I have been in many revivals and in many church services; but the night you were converted, I felt the most power of God that I ever felt before or since."

Only a few had remained to pray with me during this deep struggle of the soul. Satan had been there determined to own me forever; but Jesus delivered me by the power of His blood and started me on a heavenly path.

The beginning of my salvation was so wonderful that, by God's grace, I have never wanted to give up and turn back. Even though Satan has fought me severly, I have had to say, "Get behind me, Satan, I am going with Jesus of Nazareth. I belong to God." The Lord being my Helper, I want to be faithful. I don't want to be up and down, in and out. I want to be true to Jesus.

Observing this tremendous day in my life from the distance

of these intervening years, one brief moment stands out in bold relief: it is the moment when my father said to me, "Son, you will sing in the choir tonight." If my dad had not been firm in his decision and given that command, I would never have met Jesus as my Saviour that night. It might have been months or years before I yielded to God, or perhaps never.

But that was the night God wanted to graft me into the True Vine. That was the hour He had appointed to start getting me in readiness for the calling of God which had been upon me since birth or before. I would have missed that appointment had it not been for a father who expected obedience and demanded it.

You see, that fleeting moment on Sunday evening, January 22, 1933—when I faced my parents on the walk of the church and informed them of my own plans: "I am going to the Rivoli Theater with the young people"—had been emerging for nearly seventeen years. Every time Dad had corrected me in the preceeding months and years; each time he had needed to whip me and disappoint me: these moments were preparing me for that particular evening and this apparently insignificant encounter of wills.

I did not want to go to church. My will was to go with the young people to the theater. But, because my dad had unswervingly demanded my obedience in the past; because he had not yielded to the pathetic persuasion of a cute and adorable youngster in the preceeding years; he carried with him absolute authority that night which spoke volumes in a few simple words: "You will sing in the choir tonight."

Without the years of consistent adherence to continued discipline and obedience within my life, I would have resisted my parents that evening. Either I would have argued and whined, trying to get my own way, or else I would have done what they wanted me to do, but with resentment and grumbling in my heart.

But because my parents had broken me as a child to obey

101

their every command, and obey willingly and joyfully, I didn't argue or fuss. I didn't murmur or complain. I didn't carry resentment or a grudge into the church with me. As best as I can remember, by God's grace, I didn't greatly mind not going to the theater, and this was only because I had been accustomed to disappointment time after time in the preceding sixteen years.

Because of my father's command, not only was I brought into the necessary place to be drawn to Jesus, but my friend, Thomas B., was affected as well. His salvation, as well as my own, hinged on my father's life of discipline.

As I observe across the years how hundreds and thousands of divine guidances have been intricately intertwined with the preceding leadings of Jesus, the significance to my salvation of my father's life of discipline and obedience increases profoundly. If it had not been for God working through him in this way, a great host of appointments in the Holy Ghost would have been missed. I would have been out of step all along the way.

We have discovered through experience that when God orders things, a matter of a few seconds can mean the difference of someone being saved or lost, a loved one being healed or left in affliction, a family avoiding tragedy or going to accident. It is all because of the guidance of God, the direction of the Holy Spirit; but if I had not started at God's time on this precious path of trusting and obeying, I might have missed hundreds or thousands or many more who were waiting on a lowly servant of Jesus to come their way.

My words aren't adequate to relate what I am seeing, for in this walk with God, one revelation leads to another. There are no short cuts in God's ways or in God's timing. If we fail at one point to obey His word or follow His guidance, then we set out of joint all that He had planned for us in the seconds, the minutes, the days and the years ahead.

Of course, He is so gracious to forgive us and help us when we have failed. But, if we only hold steady, continue right on trusting and following the best we know without looking back, He will bring us, by His grace, to those precious and sacred appointments with people or situations where He will work His Kingdom through us entirely for His glory. Almost every leading which the Holy Spirit has given me over thirty-some years has been like this: the preceding guidance leads to the next. **What God is able to do through me today pivots on what He has helped me to obey of His guidance months and years before.**

Therefore, I am striving to appreciate the great debt I owe to my parents for training me in the way that I should go —in absolute obedience to their wishes—for when the eternal fate of my soul, and that of many others, hinged upon a single response to my father's command, I was able to obey immediately and without contention. I owe all to our loving Jesus; to the work and leading of the precious Holy Spirit of God.

Graduation from Parker High School, April 26, 1934, fifteen months after his conversion.

12 FIRST OBEDIENCE

I thought I was going to be translated. I hadn't any word from God yet. All He had sent into me was His peace and joy. I had no order but to rejoice and look to Him.

Taking the keys, I drove the family home, stopped at the door, let them out, and drove the car out through the old barn-yard to the garage. When I walked back through the lot toward the house I looked up at the sky filled with stars and said, "Lord, I am a new man. I am different. Everything is different!"

I was very happy in Jesus and not expecting anything unusual to take place. But the moment my left hand touched the yard gate, the Voice that had been silent for almost twelve years suddenly revealed within me, "Go to Austin Holloway's for prayer."

I came through the kitchen door greatly excited: "Daddy! The Lord has just spoken to me and told me to go to Austin Holloway's for prayer!" (Mr. Holloway was my basketball coach, and I had never been in his home before.)

Dad said, "Wonderful! The car is nearly empty of gas, Son. You take the car to the bulk plant, put gas in, and Mother and I will be ready to go with you as soon as you return."

I didn't realize it at the time, but when my hand touched the old iron gate and God spoke to me, "Self" was meeting head-on with "denial." I could not continue with my plans to relax, rest, and go to sleep—I was supposed to go on a journey of obedience. In less than ten minutes after con-version, "Self" was meeting right up with "denial." Now most Christians don't get to go that long without denying Self. God tells me in my heart that **two seconds** after most conversions, self-denial will begin.

When one is converted, when his sins are covered with the precious blood of Jesus and the joy of the Lord fills his heart, the Holy Spirit will nearly always impress the new convert to stand and witness for Jesus. God wants him to say, "Praise the Lord for saving me! I want you to pray for my mother and dad to be saved." He will ask newborn lambs to testify: "Oh, the Lord's joy is so wonderful!" He seldom asks us to say much, but He wants us to witness for Christ.

As soon as the prompting of the Holy Spirit begins in the soul, Satan and the flesh are right there to tell you, "Don't do it! People will think you are crazy. Your friends will think you are aiming to put on a show. They'll think you are trying to be somebody." The devil will attempt to throw fear into your heart and body by causing your legs to tremble and your voice to shake. He will try to tell you that you won't have any friends left and that you are foolish and should just be quiet. "Nobody cares what you have to say anyway," he will insinuate. In this battle of self-denial he will try to tell you many things to prevent you from being partaker in the experience of obedience.

In most cases, Self succumbs to the pressures of Satan, and the flesh wins the battle. Not many people are successful in their first opportunity of self-denial. The flesh wants to be respected by everyone and applauded by all; it wishes to be seen as discreet, orderly, and above ridicule. But as soon as you are willing to resist this pull of the earth, immediately you will have a little blessing. A little lift always follows self-denial. There is always a little vineyard or a small oasis after Self is denied to do what God has wished.

However, this victory in Jesus is only occasionally known. The devil doesn't want it to be known, for the life which begins at conversion to deny Self has a great advantage over the life which fails in this first assignment. Overcoming grace is supplied to a self-denied heart, as well as strength to resist temptation. Until a new convert learns the absolute necessity of obedience through denying the desires of the flesh and the mind, it is likely that he will suffer numerous setbacks and backslidings. On the other hand, the life which learns the secret of self-denial soon after conversion experiences the divine joy of Jesus within, which enables it for the coming attacks of Satan and the trials of earth.

Self-denial is more urgent to Christianity than I can tell you. It is like breathing to the body: If I do not breath, I die.

My first breath had come after ten o'clock that evening, and my second breath came when God revealed what I should do and I started getting ready to do it. All the breaths of obedience which I have taken since that first night have been dependent upon those first two. Thus, my entire walk with God these many years pivots upon my willingness to deny what Self wanted ten minutes after Jesus had saved me.

We must not delay when God leads. There is injury in delay when the Holy Spirit prompts us to obey. When God does not speak, waiting is golden as well as silence, because there are gold mines of His love in waiting. I probably never would have had the victory if I would have failed to tell my father what God had revealed to my heart. It was late at night and Self could have reasoned: "Now they'll think this is foolish. It will be nearly eleven-thirty by the time you can get to your coach's home." But I had to deny what Self thought in order to tell my parents what God had commanded me to do.

Most parents would have said, "Now wait a minute, Son; wait just a minute. Look at that clock. That clock says that it is late and people ought to be in bed at this hour." They could have told me, "We are tired, Son. We have been through two church services today, and tonight's meeting was a long one. We must get to bed. You wait until it is more convenient." Instead, they said, "We are glad. We will go with you." Their hearts were saying, "Our son has heard from God! He is going on his first mission. We want to go with him!" (Glory to God! I feel the power of God going through my arms and my body as I share this with you.)

I headed for the bulk plant, still dressed in my Sunday clothes. We had two trucks at the bulk plant for delivering gasoline, and you know how greasy and dirty they can be. I had to walk between both of them to get the gas for the car. How I ever squeezed between two dusty, oily trucks and never got a smudge on me is a mystery. I am still marvelling at this, for I know that the Lord had to help me. When you can't do something in yourself, God can do it for you. I didn't have time to change, I just had time to obey; so the Lord helped me not to get my clothes soiled.

When I returned to the farm, not only were my mother and father ready, they had called three of my best friends and the evangelistic singer to go along. All seven of us started in that old 1931 Chevrolet sedan for Austin Holloway's. We were going fine until we got about to the iron bridge east of Parker, a little distance from the home which God has now provided us. Until then I was still enjoying the happiness and deep peace I received at conversion. Never before had I known anything like this sweet wonder of Jesus; but I was totally unprepared for what was about to take place within my soul.

At that point along our journey, the joy of obedience suddenly flooded my soul! The joy I had at the altar when Jesus saved me was instantly multiplied! Jesus has revealed to my heart since then that He tripled the joy which I had at conversion. It became three times greater because I obeyed the Holy Spirit. The glory of Heaven was so within me that I couldn't contain it. I began to praise the Lord and shout.

I had always been calm, reserved, and very quiet. I didn't want to shout. I never wanted to say "amen" or get happy. I wanted to be a quiet, dignified Christian. In fact, I had always been opposed to excitement in the church. After the age of fifteen or sixteen, if anyone became happy or said "glory!", I was rather offended.

When I said "yes" to my first obedience, nonetheless, God tumbled a boundless joy into my soul. It simply fell into my heart without warning. Oh! It was great joy! The first joy when Jesus redeemed me was so marvelous. But what was I to do with a joy three times greater? All I could do was shout, "Glory! Hallelujah! Praise God!" Everyone in that car looked at me surprised. Howard M. said, "I have never seen you like this."

To them I seemed like a different fellow than they had ever known. To be truthful, I wasn't the same fellow, because at that iron gate some minutes before, God had told me, "This is what I want you to do." I couldn't go to bed, lie down, or sleep. I had to deny what Self wanted and get started on God's assignment immediately.

And the joy which God poured through my soul was so tremendous that I never wanted to miss another leading of the Holy Spirit. The inner delight of His presence was so sweet that I wanted more of this heavenly blessing. I discovered the path of obedience to be the King's Highway. I never wanted to get off on a side road or take a detour. I wanted to stay right in the middle of God's will. (I know it is only by God's grace and help that I can do this. I need your prayers always.)

The lights of the little farm home near Stony Creek were still shining as we pulled into the yard. I got out of the car, went to the door, and knocked. Before long the door opened and I was looking into the face of my teacher and coach.

It had been only two hours since I had last seen Mr. Holloway at church that night. He had come down the crowded aisle of the church, while Tom B. and I were standing un-decided at the altar, put his arms around both of us, and said, "Boys, don't let the school stand in the way. This is the right step to take and I am for you."

No doubt his heart was throbbing when he came down to

us, for the church was full—more than two hundred persons were there that night—and he was a backward, quiet man. He did not live near town and I had never seen him in that church before, nor have I seen him there since. I seldom heard of him testifying or never knew much about his Christianity; but he surely obeyed God that night.

A few hours later he faced a boy nearly seventeen years of age on his first mission for God, and told him, "I am not surprised to see you." That was the first thing he said! —"I am not surprised to see you. When the headlights turned in, I thought it might be you." Think of that! I had never been there before, yet he wasn't surprised to see me.

"Brother Austin," I spoke up; "Jesus told me to come out and have a little prayer."

"Fine," he said. "Come on in."

We went into the living room and I prayed. I had just met Jesus, but I tried to pray. One might have asked, "Well, what are you going to pray?" Simply pray—praise God, start talking to God. I imagine the prayer wasn't much to remember, but I wasn't to worry about the quality according to men's standards. All God told me to do was to go and have prayer, so that is what I did.

Then I became happier. Yes. My joy didn't go down, it went up and kept on going up! I shouted all the way home from there. I couldn't stop it. Somehow it just came out of me. Oh, if only we could persuade people to deny Self right away and do God's will, the world would be turned right side up shortly. If we could only encourage dear ones to yield themselves entirely unto God.

I tried to tell each one in the car how wonderful God's blessing was to my soul. I was rejoicing over how God had guided, how He had led, how He had blessed. Believe me, when you have the joy of salvation and obedience in your soul, you are telling it. In fact, you will have to pray for grace to be quiet. If it is joy unspeakable and full of glory, you will have to labor to be still. When we arrived home after midnight, the joy still did not stop. (Oh, it is marvelous just to deny Self and walk with Jesus!) It didn't fade away like a dream: it brightened.

Four of us boys slept in one room, and Richard, my oldest brother, was my bed companion. When I lay down to rest that night, the joy of the fellowship of the Holy Ghost was moving within me. Do you think I could be quiet in that bed? The power of the Spirit would lift me right out of there! Down the steps I would go to my parents' room. I would stand by the bed and tell them how Jesus had saved me. I would try to tell them how wonderful He was, what wonder was taking place within my heart. And they would simply listen. Dad was an early riser: he liked to get up about five in the morning. Yet, here I was still preaching to them near one o'clock in the morning.

Coming back upstairs, I would try to lie down and sleep, but the joy would well up so great I would leap out of bed, run down the stairs, and tell them more about Jesus, until I didn't know what else to say. I had a lot of the Holy Spirit moving within me, but I didn't have much knowledge to go with it. I would preach all I could remember about the scrip- tures, would run out in five or ten minutes, then go back up and try to sleep. It took much patience for them to bear with me, I know.

After this was repeated many times, my brother, Richard said, "If you don't be quiet, I won't get any rest tonight."

"You are right about that," I told him. "But, I can't help it. I just can't help it!"

My folks thought I preached to them until about two or three in the morning, when I was finally able to get to sleep. Years later, when conversing with my brother, I asked him, "Do you recall, Richard, that seventeen years ago tonight I started with Jesus?"

He looked at me from his chair and nodded. "Say," he said, "I want to make a confession to you."

"Confession?" I asked.

111

"Yes," he replied. "When you went to the altar that night, I thought to myself, 'Loran is going to the altar to be saved; but like most saved people, he will soon become lukewarm and lose out.' But I want to tell you, before morning came the next day, I changed my mind about you."

He decided that we had the little end of the biggest thing in the world—sweet as honey, rich as cream, good as gold, fine as silver, refreshing as a stream; never tiring, never disappointing, always better than anyone had ever dreamed; it was beyond the orators of men to describe, colors to paint, and the languages of earth to express; it was Jesus, the Pearl of Great Price.

13 JESUS REVEALS MY COMPANION

At school the next morning, one of my friends cursed when he learned that I had accepted Jesus. He had ridden many, many miles with me in my father's car, and since I worked for my father, Dad had provided the gasoline for our pleasure rides. I also had often supplied this young man with refreshments. But in spite of these past kindnesses, he gave me a real talking to that morning and used some strong language in my direction: "You won't last two weeks," he chided. "That is all—two weeks!"

But Jesus helped me to deny myself again. By God's grace, I didn't retaliate or feel sorry for myself when my friend cursed and reprimanded me. The Holy Spirit kept me from becoming upset and saying, "Now look here, you can't say that about me!' I simply spoke to Jesus in my heart, "By your grace, Lord, you can take me on," and He delivered me. (And God tells me, "I will direct thee and tell thee what to do," as I share this with you. Praise the Lord!)

After three weeks I talked to him about Jesus for one to two hours on the sidewalk across from the church where I had been converted. Seven years later, when I told him how wonderful these many months and years had been and how Jesus had helped me last past the two weeks which he predicted I could last, he said, "You have will-power, that is all."

"Will-power?" I exclaimed. "Brother, it takes more than 'will-power' to live this life. It takes the divine power of Jesus."

Seventeen years later, then, at the death of his father, I had opportunity to again talk to him about Jesus. I was trying to share with him how marvelous it had been to try to walk with God these seventeen years, what wonderful adventures He had given me. He said to me as we sat together that day: "Who knows but what someday you may lead me to Jesus." Isn't it precious that after seventeen years this man who first ridiculed me could begin to see that there was something more to this transformation than the eye could see; that God had done a true miracle within this unworthy servant?

This would never have come about if I had failed that first test at school the day after my conversion. If I had begun to argue or strike back when he was upset with me, I would have lost his confidence forever. There never would have been occasion for the exchange of thoughts in three weeks, the discussion after seven years, or the sweet conversation in the seventeenth year. These all hinged upon my response to the first test just hours after my conversion.

Now the secret of Jesus helping me through that vindictive attack Monday morning following my conversion was in my hearing the voice of the Holy Spirit the night before, just minutes after getting up from the altar. If the Lord had not helped me to obey that first guidance of Jesus, I would not have had the joy, the glory of God within me, to withstand the fury from my friend a few hours later. My strength to stand was dependent upon my obedience the night before, when God tripled the joy I had at salvation and brought me into a land of such inner delight that I never wanted to miss another leading of the Lord.

I have found that very few persons actually obey what the Lord wants them to do. And when we fail to obey the leading of the Holy Spirit, then we lose the precious abiding with God which we so very much cherish. For many, the joy they once knew at conversion seems to vanish for no specific reason. However, all too often this joy is lost through disobedience,

114

for joy continues to flow into every heart which obeys the Holy Spirit consistently. The Word tells us that "the joy of the Lord is our strength." This indicates that we are only as strong as the joy we have in our daily walk with Jesus.

Now joy does not come from within us. Joy is a gift from God as we obey the Holy Spirit. Joy is not on our part: obedience to the leading of the Lord is on our part, and joy is the remuneration. Always the joy of the Lord is as we humble ourselves in obedience through self-denial.

God is seeking simply an obedient people. He is trying to find men and women who will do what He wants them to do; but He has had a difficult time finding them down through the ages. There are many who are willing to try to obey the written commandments as found in the scriptures; but this so subtly leads to a legalistic Christianity—a fulfilling of a minimum degree of service or adhering to a certain set of beliefs. God is seeking a people who will not only obey His written Word, but who will also actually walk with Him day by day, moment by moment, listening to and doing what the voice of the Holy Spirit says.

The person who hears and heeds this still, small voice will many times experience a river of joy pouring into the interior life, because joy flows from God freely into the obedient heart.

As I review this sentence, the Holy Spirit operates more in my heart on "heeding" than on "hearing." This tells me that God has already commanded us many things which we could have heard, but we have not done what He required us to do. We have not "heeded;" thus, our subsequent "hearing" is dull and insensitive.

Our "heeding" today assists or sharpens our "hearing" tomorrow. We "hear" as we have "heeded." And "heeding" intimates a following. "Heeding" is applying or carrying out what we have heard, and we never "heed" God's wish without first relinquishing what we are doing or have planned to do. Self-denial precedes "heeding."

It is difficult for the natural man to receive spiritual things. It is only as we permit the Holy Spirit to have His way with us—as we deny Self, die out to Self, and are inwardly crucified—that we are made sensitive to spiritual things. As Self is slain, we are then more able, through the Holy Spirit's guidance, to receive revelation that God has for us: revelation to the mind, as well as to the inner heart.

Now Self will oppose this spiritual death; the mortal will oppose it. In order that the Holy Spirit can so crucify us, we must resist the devil and deny Self. It will be only by the blood of Jesus purging us and cleansing us that we will be able, through the Holy Spirit, to discern what God is revealing to us.

He wants to first slay the inner man so that he can teach us how to discern His will. This comes slowly. It comes by prayer and it comes by waiting and then still more waiting. It comes always by doing all that God wants us to do while we are waiting. The great difficulty is that Self wants to get busy doing something; Self wants to go; Self wants to be planning something. All this is an enemy to hearing God and heeding what the Holy Spirit wants to relate to us.

The very core of our nature will resist and rebel against God having His way with us. The earth within us will oppose and resist God who made us and Jesus who died to purchase us. The main parts of our inner make-up war against it. They neither want to comply with the divine will nor come down in humility and brokenness, where this is found.

This spirit that is within us, this great power of the earth which is so contrary to what God wants, we acquired in the Fall. It is this power in the earth, in the fabric of the mortal and the flesh, which battles to pull us upward from the lowlands of brokenness and surrender (where the mysteries of God's revelations are learned) to set us in the high places of man's knowledge. For this reason, most people have been striving to acquire insights of divine truth by means of knowledge, books, and the intellect.

Through the ages, however, God has been seeking a people who would simply wait upon Him until He could slay them, refine them, indwell them, and instruct them how His Holy Spirit operates; how He guides and checks. Very few people have been willing to pay the price and wait upon God long enough for Him to reveal Himself. This comes in time: God's time, not our time.

Man has always wanted things his way, at his time, and by his methods. It doesn't work this way. It must be the reverse. It must be that we die and are slain so that it will be God's will, God's way, God's time, whether that is a short time or a long time (and I have the revelation that it is "a long time"). Man is impatient. We are all impatient unless we are slain and die out daily. It is our nature to want spiritual growth to be rapid; we covet divine revelations right away. Therefore, we must die out to these impatient tendencies and simply trust for God to help us know how to proceed.

Jesus said, "I thank thee, oh Father, Lord of Heaven and earth, that thou hast hid these things from the wise and prudent, and hast revealed them unto babes . . . " Now the wise and prudent have been trying to theorize and speculate about spiritual secrets. But Jesus has plainly said that the Father **reveals** unto babes. They are the lowly ones, the ones way down in the low-lands of humility and brokenness, obedience, and yieldedness.

Divine guidances do not come for any advantage of our own; they come only for the praise and glory of Jesus. These mysteries of God are not found in books or in reading material. They are revealed little by little to those who are walking with God and waiting upon Him, who are trying in their hearts to be faithful and pressing to obey the Holy Spirit. I want to greatly emphasize that **the things of God are not given to those seeking to know how to be led of the Holy Spirit**—they are given at God's pleasure to those who are losing their lives for Jesus, who are loving God for Himself alone.

Here is one of the secrets of the universe. **God is trying to find people who will give all to Him and just let Him be all to them.** If we are willing to lose all because He gave all, lose that He might **be** all, then He will reveal Himself to us in time. (And God is telling me now, "I guide thee and direct thee and tell thee what to do." Right now!)

These spiritual guidances—these wonderful, most delightful things of God—are not given because we are worthy, because we know so much, or because we are seeking. They are given to those who are willing to lose all for Jesus' sake and lose it for life. They are given to those who are not trying to get anything. Most people are trying to get somewhere, to something, for self-advantage. And this, you see, is not the right spirit. We are to come to the end of Self, losing all for Jesus so that He can have full, complete guidance of our lives. We, then, become mere servants: not trying to become somebody, but remaining like children.

Unless we become like a little child, Jesus tells us that we are going to miss the Kingdom. (Matthew 18:3) Perhaps this is the reason many have missed the Kingdom of God: we have tried to become adults, grown-ups, somebody who knows something. But God's Kingdom is in the lowly. That is where He lives; that is where He walks; that is where He reveals Himself.

To some extent, organizations, groups, and personalities have been seeking to advance God's Kingdom. But often, in the back of their minds lurk the questions: "How can we get what we are wanting? How can we obtain this victory? How can we see all these souls saved? How can we see our group benefited? How can we see our church enlarged?" God knows all these hidden motivations and deceptions of the heart, and He is unable to trust His Kingdom work to such self-seeking souls.

For this reason, His revelation to my heart in 1942 was,

"I am in search of a people who will trust me with all their hearts—trust me with **all** their hearts—totally and wholly depend upon me and obey me in everything; a people I can trust to come into their lives with the Kingdom of God." So you see, God reveals Himself to the trusting heart. (And now God says within me, "I will guide thee and direct thee and tell thee what to do.")

God has been seeking a people who will simply trust Him since the Garden of Eden experience. He was anticipating that Adam and Eve would trust Him and obey Him; but they chose to procure knowledge and insights of Good and Evil rather than simply rest and rely wholly on God. In gaining knowledge that they desired, they lost and we lost with them: we lost about all; we lost unto death. The only path back to God is Jesus; and **the steps back to life in Him are taken through obedience to the Holy Spirit.**

We have been living too much on the fringes of the land that He has promised us rather than on the center. We have been living on the marginal rather than on the central. Only a few ever really press into the center of God's Kingdom, on into becoming like a child and losing all just for God Himself. The persons are rare who are not seeking something in return for loving and serving God.

But God would save millions of people right now if He could find a church that would really trust Him—**really trust Him.** I am sure that very few people know what real trust, continued trust, is. We often try to work out God's Kingdom a little bit ourselves. This is not trusting: it is our own manipulation, our own programming, our own desires in process. It is our own ideas in progress and we want them to live. But our ideas don't mean a snap of the fingers unless God is in them and leading them.

We are trying to have church with our own insights, our own descriptions, our own programs, our own methods. But God wants the leadership. He wants to guide us in every detail of our endeavors. We must wait before Him that He

119

might teach us how to be led. We must first learn to trust and die out to our own desires so that He can bring us to the place where we can discern His will in the Word and in the Spirit. He has given us the outlines and descriptions of the true Christian walk in the Gospel, but we are not following all the tiny, intricate lines. They are so simple, but we pass over them.

Church work too often can be a performance rather than actual heeding and following. We try to lead persons to Jesus, and this is good: but unless we have been heeding and following ourselves, people are saved and become copies of us. If we are not dying out, rejoicing, holy and pure in heart, our influence causes new converts to become performers. It is wonderful to lead persons to a knowledge of salvation, but too often they are converted to the church, to the denomination, or to the local fellowship and its particular religious styles rather than to the Lord Jesus Christ. What we need to be saved TO is Jesus so that people will wait on God until He can actually guide them and direct them.

This has been one of the missing links in Christianity. **Men have tried to implement the plans of God by means of their own programs and ideas.** All meant well; all wanted to do well; but few in all the ages have waited and died out sufficiently for God to really teach them His will.

He teaches best those who are lowest in brokenness and humility. Until we come to the absolute admission that we are nothing and capable only of failure, we will seek to achieve, to become knowledgeable, to become recognized. We think learning, training, philosophies, and theologies are going to help us. Too easily, instead of bringing us closer to Jesus, these interefere with divine communication. They become the static of Self, the earth, and man's knowledge. Unless the Holy Ghost leads you to these areas, they only deflect God's revelations; they only obstruct your view of His plans; they only dull your sensitivity to His operations.

I cannot adequately express how lowly we must become

120

before spiritual revelation can enter the inner life. This is a mystery. It is supernatural. The simple, lowly life in Christ is opposed by people who don't understand. This is not to be understood. It is to be practiced, followed, and experienced.

This is faith—a living faith. We cannot have faith other than in the areas of the interior life. The more faith a person has, the more willing he is to lose all. He has confidence that in losing all, he will gain Jesus. **God is seeking a people who will trust Him; who are willing, through self-denial deep in the interior life, to come by faith to the loss of all things.** Too often we want to instigate a little, suggest a little, insert a portion of what we want. This is self-assertiveness, and because of it, we as individuals and as a people have rarely come to the place where God can guide us.

Here is one reason we have come so far short of the will of God. We have missed so much of the marvelous privilege and potential God would work through us because we have been unwilling to yield all, to lose all, absolutely: not only in word or thought, but in actuality through continued trust and obedience.

These precious mysteries of God's Kingdom which I have just shared with you are only a little of what God wants us to experience of the word "heed." As I inquire of the Holy Spirit, He tells me in my heart that this is merely a little of our heeding His word.

During this revival, a number of young people were converted and formed a very active Gospel Band. This group of young people went to various churches to lead in special services. Either a young lady or I would bring the message. I believe, to Jesus' glory, I saw a number of souls find Jesus my first year as a Christian.

Only a few weeks after I had been saved, I was preaching in my home church when I felt impressed to turn around and also direct my comments to those young people who were seated in the choir loft behind me. I was looking into the face of each one as I preached. When I came down the second section of seats to my left, I found myself looking into the eyes of Florence Spence, the daughter of Ora and Grace Spence. Her blue eyes were looking straight into mine.

The instant our eyes met, an operation of the Holy Spirit moved in my heart like a light. (And this light is in my heart now. It is right inside of me! Praise the Lord!) In much less time than it takes to tell it, Jesus revealed within me, "HERE IS YOUR COMPANION."

By some marvel of God's help, the sermon was never interrupted. Even though the Holy Spirit had never dealt with me as He did at that point, Jesus helped me to continue preaching as if nothing had happened. I was so greatly amazed because I had never said so much as "How do you do, how are you?" to Florence Spence in over ten years. She was already a graduate of Ball State, with an equivalent of a Master's degree in Music and Art. I was a young man still in high school. I felt so unworthy of her. But when God revealed to my heart by the Holy Ghost that she was to be my companion, I simply believed Him.

I marvel that a young man of seventeen, who had never been taught about the operations of the Holy Spirit in the body, could somehow know that God was speaking, and understand what He was saying. No one taught me how God speaks to the heart. I never heard anyone mention much about the workings of the Holy Spirit within the heart and throughout the body. I believe that the secret of my being able to understand was that the Holy Ghost had fallen on me at birth. God had a plan for my life, and Florence Spence was a part of that sacred plan.

At each interval along the way, at each crisis of my life, He has revealed what I need to know by the Holy Ghost. One incident which demonstrates this abiding care occurred when we were with Homer and Rebecca Pumphrey. Homer and I were planning to go for prayer, but decided to have supper first. We started for the kitchen to prepare the evening meal, but as I came through the kitchen door a burden came over me. I said to him, "God is burdening me. I will not be able to eat."

For many years God would occasionally burden me as I sat down to a meal. I thought He was telling me not to eat. It took some years of instruction before I recognized that He was often trying to reveal to me about some person or situation related to the food on my plate. He might be speaking to me about the man who owned the beef, the one who grew the carrots, an individual who helped process the catsup, the person who delivered the bread to the store. Our Heavenly Father knows all things about each person in every place on the earth. If it is His will, He can reveal any particular need to those servants attuned to His voice.

I fasted many times when God was trying to send me little S.O.S. messages about the needs of those in some way connected to my food. He was telling me of needs in their bodies, struggles in their lives. Sometimes persons had been called to the ministry or the mission field, and God wanted me to pray for them to hear the sacred call upon their lives. It took me years to discern what all God was telling me, and I am still learning.

We have been privileged now to teach some of our brothers and sisters in Jesus a few of the very sacred and precious workings of the Holy Spirit. These are holy secrets and mysteries of the Kingdom which we have learned after years of waiting upon God; years of crying out in prayer, of doing God's will and pressing to be true in order that the Lord could teach me how the Holy Spirit operates within the temple of our bodies. I am only in the kindergarten learning my ABC's.

After about an hour the food was prepared and on the table. We had grace, and Rev. Pumphrey picked up the salmon platter to take off two small patties. Just as he slid them off the platter onto his plate, the Holy Ghost started right in my heart, came up my throat, and spoke through me, "Poison!—That is poison! Don't eat it!" I warned. I got up from the table, rushed to the cabinet, and picked up the can which had contained the salmon. "Look at this can!" I said. They examined it, and discovered it to be partly corroded inside.

That is what God was revealing to me when I came through the kitchen door, but I didn't know what He was telling me until He spoke through me the revelation. This knowledge came to me by the Holy Spirit in a similar manner as on that day years before when He revealed to my heart, "Here is your companion."

I will never know another thing, unless the Holy Spirit is so precious to reveal it to me. I won't be able to perceive it, except God see fit through Jesus to reveal it. Now if I am faithful, by God's grace, and give Him all the glory and all the praise; if I keep broken like a child, do everything He reveals for me to do, and keep happy about it—am appreciative and don't run out of thanksgiving—then He can give something else, if it is His will. But it all must come from Jesus for God's praise and honor.

And that night, while turning to preach to the young people, I knew that I had found my companion for life. I felt very unworthy that He would choose my companion for me. Only He would know the mate which the years ahead would demand. We have been together over thirty-nine years now, but it seems like only a little while, because of Jesus. No one will ever know how precious my wife has been to me.

Our first time together was on April 14, 1933. That prayer meeting night we had a heavy April shower. Since ours was the only car at church that evening, all the young people piled into it. I still wonder how so many got into the car, but young people can really stack into a place if they want to.

I decided that this would be a good night to be alone with Florence Spence. Although God had shown me the last of February that she was to be my companion, I hadn't had the courage to ask her for a date. That night I said to myself, "I will arrange it so that she will be the last one taken home." After delivering all the young people to their homes, including my own brother, Richard, I was finally left alone for the first time with the girl who was to become my wife. She was the last girl I ever dated.

After Florence and I had gone together about six weeks, we were returning one night from church, driving very slowly down the street about six to seven hundred feet north of her parents' home. Suddenly a ray of light from Heaven fell into my heart. I saw another ray of light fall into her heart, and these two lights leaped together like static electricity. Through a miracle of God, we were joined together by the Holy Spirit.

Young people, it is so urgent that you find, through waiting on God and prayer, the companion which God has selected for you. Recently the Holy Spirit has revealed to my heart that eighty-seven percent of all marriages in the United States are out of divine order. They have not been led and arranged by the Holy Spirit. The couples have married because of a physical attraction, personality similarities, or particular interests. Sometimes a boy has pressured a girl to marry, or vice versa. Anyone who pressures another into marriage is bringing that person to a life of darkness near the edge of despair.

Every major life choice—such as a companion or a vocation—which is not made by the Spirit, will continue to produce consequences for the remainder of that person's life. (Often these choices are made between the ages of twelve and twenty.) Even if one is converted after these major decisions have been made, though Jesus will freely forgive all past sin and error, one will still grapple with the results and suffer within the confines of these choices which God was not permitted to make for him. There is no way to adequately convey the seriousness of waiting on God's **specific** guidance concerning our vocation, our companion, our place of dwelling, and our choice of a school or a college.

This is why so many homes are unhappy, without romance, in constant upheaval. Most of us are so in the flesh when it comes to the opposite sex. We have certain ideas about the companion we wish, and we set out to get what we want. But God knows exactly who we are, what we will be in ten or twenty years, and precisely where He wants us in His Kingdom. We are absolutely incapable of making an intelligent choice of our companion by ourselves because we cannot see where God is going to want us in the years ahead. The choice we would make of a companion, no matter how ideal and perfect it might appear at the moment, will not stand the tests of time and circumstances. Only God can have the knowledge and wisdom for such a choice.

Now Satan will tell you all kinds of things to make you anxious and fearful. He will likewise try to get you attracted to many persons along the way to keep you from meeting the one God has chosen for you. That is why it is so important that the Holy Spirit be given the freedom to choose your vocation and where you are to attend college (if you go). It could be that unless you follow God's leading from the very beginning, you will be late in finding your chosen mate, or you may never get there.

But if we start at the moment of conversion and simply seek to deny what we want and follow every leading of the Holy Spirit, He will lead us in time to everything that we need in order to be used as He sees fit in the Kingdom. Sometimes we must wait a long time; sometimes a very short time. It was a surprise and a delight when Jesus revealed to my heart that our youngest daughter and son-in-law were to be married in less than a month. We didn't work this out in our own understanding. The Holy Ghost revealed it.

I urge every unmarried person reading this book: **be absolutely certain of God's guidance before you marry.** It would be much better to never marry than to go into a union which isn't led of God. One could never tell you the sorrow and anguish you will have if you marry out of divine order. Neither are there words to tell the wonder of a marriage led of God.

God was also letting Florence know a little that He had brought us together someway in His Spirit. I learned later that even before I knew she was to be my companion, if she were in the church facing the pulpit and I would come through the vestibule doors at the back, she sensed my presence when I entered the sanctuary. This is a miracle of Jesus. This doesn't always happen.

I believe this occured because God had called me for a specific purpose into this world. I needed a wife who could wait for hours in a car without being upset, while God had me sharing with dear ones about the Kingdom. One who would bear with me when I failed to get home on time for dinner and her meals became cold, because my schedule was at God's bidding. I needed a wife who would understand that the things of earth were secondary always. When meals, family, and home are upset, most wives rather want to talk about it and let it be known that they don't particularly appreciate it. I had to have a companion who would say "yes" to the will of God; a wife willing to die out to her hopes and her wishes.

It took this supernatural union because of the seriousness of God's call upon our lives and also because of the difference in our background and education. God had been working to keep her in the Parker area, even though it was not easy on her at the time. Her excellent achievements musically had made her a favorite of Mr. Palmer, the professor of music where Florence had earned her degree. He often took her to play for the Lions Club, the Rotary Club, and other organizations. She didn't ask to do it, but of all the pianists at Ball State, she was chosen.

She had excellent recommendations for a good teaching position that previous fall, and a few people were wanting

127

to help her; but God closed the doors. As a result of her not finding a teaching position, Florence was very, very restless. No doubt, she was also disappointed, for she wanted to teach. She was excellently qualified to instruct, but God had another appointment for her instead. I would have missed her if God had not closed the doors on her teaching opportunities.

If you remain true and faithful to God, He will be working out the important concerns in your life. He will arrange them in His own way, if you will wait upon Him, praise Him, and honor Him from your heart as well as from your lips. It might not be the easiest on you, but it will be the best for you.

Once I became acquainted with the one God had chosen for me, I didn't want to go home at night. I didn't want to leave her, because I had a treasure there. When you have a treasure, you will want to be near it. When God joins you with a companion, you are simply not happy without her, for He brings you especially close together. The more you obey, the closer you become, because you understand one another better. You learn when to keep quiet and when to speak. Sometimes we don't learn for a long while, but God helps by teaching us what to say and what not to say so that we won't make our companion appear small in the eyes of others. He teaches us to be careful of what we do and how we live, so that we won't hurt or hinder the ones we love, but rather help and encourage them along the journey.

Florence and I began to anticipate marriage. One night we were in the car outside her parents' home, right in front of the old maple tree. She was talking to me about one of her married girlfriends who already had a little home with furnishings. While she was talking I was praying in my heart. I was crying out to Jesus, for I had only a very few dollars in my pocket, and there was my education yet to pursue.

Suddenly, as I was silently crying out to Jesus, He revealed to me a home which He would someday build for us. I saw our home as a light in my heart, far off in the future. I could never begin to tell you exactly how it was, but it was vivid within my heart.

"Oh, Honey!" I said. "I can see our home as a light. I can see that if we go where God sends me, take His message, embrace the cross, be obedient and win men and women, boys and girls to Jesus, He is going to provide a home which will be a testimony that God provides for His servants of today as He did for the prophets of old. I see that you have lovely furniture, too."

One can never capture the splendor, the wonder, the excitement of a revelation which comes from God. It is usually so very simple and direct in content; yet it is always such a surprise. To hear directly from Heaven is a privilege beyond the words of earth to describe. Because of my limitations, I am not able to convey the specific excellence of this moment in our lives together. It was a very precious revelation to me.

We held to that promise through many dark and difficult years, the promise which came unexpectedly and quietly in my heart as my wife spoke about her friend's home. Approximately nineteen years and eight months later, that home became a reality.

Loran William Helm and Florence Martha Spence joined in marriage, May 27, 1934.

14 SANCTIFICATION

On May 27, 1934, Florence Spence became my wife in a small private ceremony in her parents' home. We had only a few belongings, and lived for the remainder of that summer with my folks, one block west of Grace and Ora Spence. My five brothers loved Florence as well as if she were their very own sister. After all, she was the first girl in the family. They still love her in a very special way.

God had called me into His ministry. I didn't know much about our future, but I did know that God had laid His hand upon me. I recall my father, on January 24, 1933, lifting his old Bible high overhead and saying, "Son, if you're going to preach the Gospel, get this Book in your heart; because through this Book operates the power of God." Since that day I had been endeavoring to obey his admonition, and still am striving to do so.

Knowing the Bible alone, however, is not sufficient: we must first know Jesus. I was sent once to a church for revival services south of Knoxville, Tennessee, and there I met a young man who had gone through four years of intensive Bible training. He sat through seven to nine services before that eventful night when he made his way swiftly to the altar to find Jesus Christ as his Saviour. He knew the Bible, had taught the Bible, had preached the Bible, but he didn't know Jesus in his heart. When he did meet the Master, he said it was the happiest day of his life. He had spent years learning about God's word, but he had never let the Word become flesh within him.

131

The Fall of 1934, I entered Taylor University. I was not much interested in academic study, but the Lord helped. I discovered that they taught sanctification there as well. I knew very little about holiness subsequent to regeneration. My father had never heard it preached either, and understood little about it. He had preached for years and knew people claiming a high state of holiness who wouldn't pay their bills. "Well," Dad would say, "I don't think there is much to it, because there isn't anybody much living it." He rejected sanctification because of the neglect of a few. And I was of the same mind. My professor taught me that after a person is justified, he should be sanctified. "I just don't believe it," I still said.

That next Fall we returned for our second year at Taylor. The college had scheduled Dr. Paul Rees as speaker for a week's series of meetings. Dr. Rees is probably one of the great preachers in the earth. He is called the Prince of Preachers, and is a very gracious, kind, gentle man. On the last night of services, September 22, 1935, he preached on sanctification. He had completed the message and the congregation was singing the altar call hymn, when all of a sudden, during the second or third stanza, I heard a voice say, "LORAN HELM—WHAT ARE YOU GOING TO DO ABOUT YOUR SANCTIFICATION?"

It frightened me. I said within myself, "I am not going to do anything."

A second time the voice asked: "WHAT ARE YOU GOING TO DO ABOUT YOUR SANCTIFICATION?"

I didn't know what to do. Again I answered, "No." The third time God spoke to me, and once more I said, "No!" When He spoke the fourth time, His power struck me on top of my head and operated all through my body until I thought I was turning to stone. When the power reached my heart, it began to bring the life right up out of my body. I tell you, when your life starts leaving you, you are going to do something about it.

You see, I was a stubborn person. If I believed something, I stayed with it regardless of what the crowd thought. And I was convinced that there was nothing to sanctification. But God was the One persuading me now, and He was desiring to move me to sanctification. His power was taking the life out of me.

I came out into the aisle and I thought I was crying at the top of my voice. My wife told me later that she could not hear me, but I felt I was yelling as loud as I could, because I was desperate. If God ever comes on you as He has come on me, it will move you around some. It won't make any difference who you are. God will move you.

The devil said, "Don't say 'sanctify me!' "

But I cried out, "Oh, God! Oh, God—sanctify me!"

When I cried out for God to sanctify me, the Holy Spirit operated in my heart. I knelt at the altar and continued to pray, but the work had already begun. My sanctification started not at the altar, but in the aisle as I went forward for prayer. I was so certain that I didn't believe in sanctifcation after conversion, but I knew it began right then in my heart by faith. I know that I am spiritually bankrupt and have so little of God's love, but He started a work in my heart that September night which has never stopped. It has continued on and on, by His Spirit.

Before this work of God in my heart, I would get angry. I would become hostile. I was a fast mover and my wife was slow. I would say, "Hurry up, Honey, let's get started; we are going to be late!" The more I talked the more frustrated she became. After I was sanctified, I could help her instead of making her feel badly. I found I could help bathe the children. I discovered that the Lord was making me longsuffering and granting me patience. He began to take out of me the harshness that was under the surface of my personality. He began to eradicate the anger. He started slaying those things out of me which grieved Him,

133

and still continues to refine the inward man. Praise the Lord.

Now when you are saved, you are saved from the sins you committed since you reached the age of accountability, when you first knew right from wrong. When you are sanctified, you are cleansed from the Sin Principle with which you were born, something you have inherited by nature of the flesh. The work of the Holy Spirit is to come into your life, cleanse out all this uncleanness by slaying you, and then to fill you as much as He can as quickly as He can with the fullness of His Spirit.

This doctrine has divided many churches, and we must not dwell on definitions, theological discussions, or anything that would divide us. The Holy Spirit works with every man and woman a little differently. Don't try to obtain an experience like someone else or follow another person's pattern. Only seek Jesus and His love. Set your heart and mind like a flint on Jesus, and resist all confusion, frustration, or up-heaval, permitting the Holy Spirit to lead you.

God wants the whole church to be sanctified, to be set apart for Him; and we must persevere all the while to maintain it. It has been my observation over the years that a good number of people who think they have persevered to be sanctified have really only been soundly converted. I think many persons have never actually gotten through to true holiness of heart. We stop short of it and are in a form. We are more conformed to this world than we are surrendered to God. If God could find a few who were all for Him—oh, what He couldn't do for Jesus' glory.

Now, beloved, I preached a good while before I knew this, and I am still learning. Many suppose that they can be sanctified when they are living rather casual, wishy-washy spiritual lives. But the candidate for sanctification is the person who is seeking first the Kingdom of God, who has the love and joy of Jesus in his heart, and is striving with all his might to obey God.

For many years my burden has been that God wants the entire church body—all of us, every part—to be sanctified. Jesus said, "Sanctify them through thy truth; thy word is truth. . . and for their sakes I sanctify Myself, that they also might be sanctified, through the truth. . . that they all might be one; as thou, Father, art in Me, and I in thee, that they also might be one in us: that the world may believe that thou hast sent me."

Twenty years ago that struck me so deeply: ". . . that the world may believe that thou has sent me." The world will never truly know that Jesus, the Son of God, is a real Person, the only Saviour, until the entire church is sanctified. I am more and more convinced that every man, woman, boy, and girl needs to be sanctified. If we don't persevere to it, we are going to come short of God's will, and untold millions of souls could be lost in an endless eternity.

Many who do not yet know Jesus could possibly be lost because we in the church did not press on in the Kingdom to heart cleansing, to the oneness for which Jesus prayed nearly two thousand years ago. And because we failed to arrive in the Kingdom where we were needed, the power of God was not able to flow through the Body and draw sinners to Jesus. **The power of God is able to work through any Body of believers in proportion to their whole-hearted obedience, their complete surrender, and their entire sanctification.**

When a person is sanctified by the Holy Spirit, he is wonderful to get along with. He is kind, gentle, longsuffering, and, by God's grace, does not find fault. He is a peacemaker, helping, lifting, and encouraging everyone. He is full of joy that is actually unspeakable and full of glory.

Of course, sanctification is merely the beginning of the walk with God. One can't sit down and think it is going to automatically last forever. Years ago people had the idea that all they had to do was go forward once to be sanctified. They would fold their hands and rest on that experience. But we are only in the beginning. Now we start the daily life of dying out to Self—that inner slaying which only the Holy Spirit can bring about. It is a waiting on God, looking to Him daily for our life and strength. It is pressing into continuous self-denial to take up the cross and follow Jesus. When we are sanctified, it shows all over. We become a light wherever we are. We no longer complain about the church, murmur over activities, or find fault with individuals. We are filled with praise and thanksgiving. When the pastor is preaching, we are there praying for him, crying out to Jesus for help, and laboring together with him. We won't be sitting on the back pew with a glum, disinterested face.

Once God begins the work of sanctification within us, we want nothing more than to hear the Word which will expose the yet-darkened rooms of our heart to the glorious light of the Gospel. We will delight in hearing the Word preached under the anointing more than we want to attend football games, basketball games, or carnivals.

Once we really start seeking heart purity and holiness of heart, we will start making things right with our fellow man. Pencils that we've "borrowed" from the office will be replaced. Tools that we have taken from the shop will be returned and apologies made. Old unpaid bills will be made right. Unkind remarks and criticisms about the pastor, our neighbor, relatives, boss, or employees will grieve us deeply, and we will need to ask forgiveness. Many little things will need to be put in order.

One day when in the seventh grade, I met my high school coach in the hall. The boys had tried him severely that day. and when I asked him when we were going to have gym, he turned and kicked me in the side. Though he didn't kick me hard enough to hurt me, I rather resented it.

There came a time when I had to be cleansed from that resentment in my heart and ask his forgiveness. I told him, "I am sorry. I am ashamed that I allowed any little thought to come between us like that." But when Satan put this resentment in my mind, I entertained it long enough for it to fall into my heart and lodge there. I had to ask the Lord to slay that out of me and make it right.

If we are going to seek perfection of heart, we are going to be making restitutions. We cannot detour making things right with our fellow man. Christ really wants purity of heart, a holiness of the interior life, in His Church. He says in His Word: "Follow peace with all men, and holiness, without which no man shall see the Lord." We are to seek to be a pure people. We are to persevere to perfection.

"Now Brother Helm," I can hear someone say. "Surely you know that one cannot be perfect in this life, and there is no use trying."

I want to tell you, if engineers and machinists had not tried to make those cylinders in my car perfect, I would be in trouble. If the interior of my automobile engine is not tooled properly, if the valves aren't seated just as they should be, it will lose compression and run short of power, and the engine may even be damaged. Likewise, the person who is bogged down spiritually and who is not climbing well has something wrong with the workings of his soul. Either the heart is not seated quite properly in love, or the soul is not quite in line with the perfect will of God.

Most people do not want to hear about Christian perfection. The carnal mind resents and resists any mention of heart purity or of absolute surrender. But the apostle Paul held it high. John Wesley taught it. Charles G. Finney, D. S. Warner, E. E. Byrum, A. B. Simpson, Bud Robinson, and many other humble servants of God preached it and sought to live it. I need to seek a heart of purity and determine at the very center of my heart to be perfect in Christ. If such a devout determination is not there, God is disappointed with me. I have been born in sin and am chief of sinners, yet Jesus died to save me not only "out of" my sins, but "from" all Sin. It is His desire to get me completely out of the sin business. He suffered on the cross that I could be sanctified, cleansed, and made partaker in His divine nature.

137

Jesus Himself encouraged us: "Be ye therefore perfect even as your Father which is in heaven is perfect." (Matthew 5:48) Many individuals are striving to attain perfection in worldly things. Every athlete, for example, is striving for perfection. Wouldn't it be wonderful if Christian people exerted every effort to be perfect in heart as these athletes daily run several miles to improve their skills and their capacity? The athlete is pleased at the fatigue his exercise produces. It gives him satisfaction. When it comes to striving for the perfection of the soul, however, the carnal mind will contend, "That is foolish. Don't do it. Let us alone. Don't try to tell us that we are supposed to be perfect."

But we are to strive for perfection. God is pleased when we endeavor to go on to perfection. He is deeply grieved when we settle for less than His best. Perfection is only known and arrived at through the grace of God; through the Spirit of Christ; by self-denial, under the cross, dying daily, as we are yielded and rejoicing.

I am convinced that there are very, very few persons truly sanctified. Some have started, but few have continued to press in obedience and persevere in self-denial until God could truly cleanse their hearts and come into their lives with His Holy Spirit. **It cannot take place without a crucifixion.** It is an inner dying out to the ways of the flesh, so Christ can really live in us.

John T. Hatfield, that marvelous man of God, had such a nature before he was sanctified that once, when his wife was not punctual as he was ready to go to church, he took the horse and buggy on and let her walk. She was a precious saint and never said a word. She walked to church, presently making her way into the service and sitting beside him with a sweet smile on her face. "She was as calm as a May morning and as patient as a jug of molasses under a kitchen table," John mentioned in his autobiography.*

*Thirty-Three Years a Live Wire, John T. Hatfield, Revivalist Press, Cincinnati, Ohio.

John had been saved eight years before he first heard of inward holiness of heart. But once his pastor obtained the blessing during a holiness camp meeting and began to teach sanctification, John T. was convicted for it. He prayed and cried out for this experience so fervently that he was soon blessed mightily and thought he had been sanctified.

One evening he and his wife began the task of moving a setting hen to a more desirable place. After transferring the eggs, John T. gently put the hen back on the nest. Instead of settling down quietly, the hen stood back up. John T. placed her back on the nest. Again the hen came right back up. Every time she jumped up, he set her back down, each time a little more forcibly. "Sit down on those eggs now!" he commanded.

Since she couldn't understand that kind of language, back up she came. He didn't know how to talk hen-talk and he tried to convince her to set on those eggs in his own way. By the time he was through, several eggs were broken, the hen had lost a few feathers, and John had found out that he wasn't sanctified. He had only been blessed.

On another occasion he thought he would wean the new calf from its mother to a bucket. It had nursed long enough, he decided. Placing some milk in a bucket, he very gently tried to coax the calf to sample it. Each time he got near the calf with the bucket, however, the little animal would stick its nose in the air. Sometimes a calf will drink the milk right away, but often it takes awhile. "Here," he said, "put your head down." Of course, the calf couldn't understand what John was telling him and every time its head would rear up.

After much effort, John got the calf's nose down into the milk. At this, it became wild with fright, prancing around and standing on its hind legs. Mrs. Hatfield had been trying to hold the bucket for her husband. Soon John was telling her how to hold the container, and in a very loud voice.

His store of patience exhausted, John leaped on top of

that little calf, grabbed it by both its ears, and shoved its head down into the milk up to its eyes. The calf gave one big heave, sending John T., his wife, and the milk sailing. If I recall correctly, he confessed to such anger that he kicked the calf out of the stall and threatened to kill it. He, like many of us before God cleanses us, had a powerful temper. Once again he realized that he wasn't sanctified. He really thought he had obtained it, but he hadn't. He had only prayed until he had been blessed.

However, there was a memorable night when John was asked by his pastor to pray for the seekers who were at the altar. God had blessed his soul wonderfully that night, but as the service continued he felt the need for a clean heart more than ever. He had never longed to be delivered of his evil temper more than at that moment.

He began to pray for the weeping seekers at the altar, but before long was praying for himself. For six months he had been seeking the work of entire sanctification in his heart. He had prayed through blessing after blessing, but still the "old man" held control of his life. On this night the Holy Spirit helped him to see that he had been praying himself up to the blessings, but he had not actually exercised his faith to take hold of God's promise. He reached the point where he said in his heart, "Lord, I do believe!" and instantly the fire fell. He knew the work was done! God had sanctified John T. Hatfield. (And as I tell you this, the power of God is flowing through my body witnessing to the fact that he was truly sanctified.)

The morning after this blessed experience he was out milking his cow, an animal which had given him considerable trouble. She often waited until the bucket was nearly full, then she would let go with a powerful kick that sent milk flying. In previous days John had kicked her, cuffed her, and called her all kinds of names.

This morning he was so lost in the joy of Jesus within his heart that he hardly noticed the cow. But just as he had finished and started to stand up with a full bucket of warm milk, the cow gave a sudden kick which sent milk flying. That warm, sticky liquid splashed all over John's head, his face, his clothing, and trickled down his neck.

Instead of cuffing and cursing her as he had in days before, John calmly stepped to the front of the stall, put his hand on the cow's back, and gently confessed that he had been the cause of her kicking. "You're a good old cow," he told that lowly farm animal, "and I love you. My kicking days are over. If you want to kick, you go right ahead. But I want you to know that I am sanctified—the kick is out of me."

The story tells that John's wife saw him coming up the path that morning from the barn, milk dripping from his hands, his face, his clothing, and a smile all across his face! She was satisfied at last that he had struck the Rock. The "old man" had been slain. John had been sanctified at last!

Loran and Florence with their three daughters—Joyce Lee,
Nancy Marie, and Martha Louise. Taken December 12, 1939,
while pastoring at Whitewater.

15 OUR FIRST PASTORATE

When I was twenty-one, my wife and I went with our pastor to speak with the District Elder about taking a pastorate while attending Taylor University. He had informed me prior to this time that there were three pastorates available. I was to make my choice at this time.

As I listened to my Elder describe the opportunities, I was trusting Jesus to help me know which one to choose. "You may have this one particular pastorate," he explained, "which is close to Taylor University and pays eight hundred dollars a year. This other one is farther away and has two parsonages. You may rent one and have a little more income. It also pays eight hundred dollars."

He paused, as if waiting for my answer, and I said, "Sir, you told me that there would be a choice of three pastorates."

A bit reluctantly he replied, "The third one is Redkey Circuit. It pays only seven hundred dollars a year."

The moment he said "Redkey Circuit," I knew that was where God wanted us. I could tell in my heart. "Redkey Circuit is where we are to be," I informed him.

This man was many years my senior and had preached for a long while; but when I told him my decision, he asked, "Why didn't you choose this pastorate near Taylor University? It is much more convenient and pays a hundred dollars more a year?" (Of course, one hundred dollars was a sizable sum at that time.) "You have answered too quickly," he suggested. "Give it some thought for twenty-four hours."

"It will never change," I assured him. "What God tells me never changes."

He replied, "You call back in twenty-four hours to give me your final decision."

The following day I phoned the District Elder to tell him, "We will go to Redkey Circuit." This charge consisted of two congregations, and the parsonage had neither a bathroom nor a furnace. In terms of human comfort and strength of membership, it could have been considered one of the least desirable pastorates of the district, if not the least. But this is where God witnessed that we were to be. We began our work there in April of 1937.

After we had been there six weeks, one of the dear praying women told my wife, "I have prayed for your husband's ministry in this church for thirty years." That meant that eight-and-a-half years before I was born, she had been praying for the work which God was doing through me. What if I had failed to seek God's will, had not gone where He had directed, and had missed this sacred appointment for which this dear one had prayed these many years?

When Florence and I started, we had little with which to furnish a parsonage. My father had bought us a small green couch which pulled out at the bottom and made into twin beds. Florence slept on the soft side and I slept on the hard side. That was our bed from 1934 to 1936. In 1937 we purchased our first regular bed with the $17.50 I had saved since childhood. Unfortunately, it was not a very good one, and before too long neither of us was sleeping well: the mattress gave way and both of us ended up in the middle. But we were thankful for it.

While praying beside this old couch in December of that year, God revealed to me: "I want you to have a meeting with your Board of Evangelism. Tell them that you are going to have a revival." When I spoke to the board, however, the two leading men told me, "We can't have revival. We don't have the money. We couldn't raise ten dollars from the entire congregation.''

I hadn't thought of that. ''Well,'' I informed them, ''God tells me to have revival.''

The precious mother who had prayed for my ministry, the only woman on the board, spoke up: ''Rev. Helm is right. God wants revival.'' The other two men expressed themselves by saying, ''We are on the fence,'' meaning—I could have revival if I wanted, and if I didn't, that was alright, too.

Returning home, I went to prayer. I was only twenty-one in my first assignment as pastor. I didn't want to do anything that I shouldn't. My Board of Evangelism was not in agreement: one thought we should have revival, two were definitely opposed, and two were undecided. ''Jesus,'' I prayed, ''what will I do?''

As I sought the Lord's guidance, He clearly directed me to call an evangelist in Richmond, Indiana. I was to ask him to arrive early Sunday morning for prayer, after which he could preach for me as guest speaker. Jesus said, ''You leave it all to Me,''—which I did.

Early Sunday morning the evangelist and I had a little prayer meeting before he preached. When the altar call was given, down the aisle came Arthur and Mrs. Brown. They prayed through, were converted, and the entire congregation agreed, ''This is revival!'' (Less than one year later, Mrs. Brown lay in her casket. How important God's guidance for revival was to this precious soul!)

Those special services lasted three weeks, the Lord guiding and helping. Forty-five were saved or sanctified, and bodies were healed. God did miracles among us. My wife still recalls that as one of the most wonderful revivals she has ever been in. We had twenty-five to twenty-eight in Sunday School at that time. When the power fell on that small congregation, the attendance soon doubled and continued to increase. Jesus had told me, ''You leave it all to me.'' He was the One who performed it.

145

At this young beginning, I did not believe in divine healing. The evangelist, on the other hand, declared, "God
heals today just like He always did."

"Is that right?" I remarked. I had heard about my father
being healed when he was a boy, but I was still a young man
and had no experience with healing.

"God is still the same!" the evangelist assured me.

"That's wonderful," I told him. When he shared that God
still healed as He did in Bible times, I began to believe him.

As it happened, one of the women in our congregation,
Edna C., had been in a very serious accident and suffered
severe pain almost constantly. Because of a fractured pelvis
and some fractured vertebrae, she had to be turned in a sheet
for three weeks. The evangelist learned of it and said to me
one day, "Let's go out to the home of these folks and have a
little meeting. We'll anoint this woman with oil and ask God
to heal her. It will stir the countryside for Jesus." When I
asked Edna for her permission to come, she gladly consented.

About a dozen of my laymen accompanied us there that day.
After singing "Amazing Grace" and a few other hymns, the
evangelist and I moved to the side of the bed, anointed the
suffering woman with oil, and began to call to our Heavenly
Father to come down and heal her.

In the midst of prayer, I saw a ray of light descend from
Heaven and the glory of God fell all over the room in great
sweetness. I looked over at Edna's husband, a man weighing
two hundred pounds or more, and God was moving so upon
him that he was literally shaking. The power of God hit my
wife, and she shouted. I never saw her rejoice like that
before or since. She had no idea she was going to do it, but
when the power of God came, it simply brought the shout
right out of her.

(We are so unaccustomed to God's Spirit being in evidence
today that few of us know how great His power actually is.
When He comes in a mighty Awakening one of these days,

everyone will know it. He will move everybody, whether they want to be moved or not.)

Oh, the glory of God that filled that room! Jesus went into Edna's body, immediately healing the fractured pelvis and the injured vertebrae. In an instant, God performed a miracle!

When we all left, her elderly aunt came into the room. "Will you please get my clothes?" Edna asked her.

"Oh, Edna," she cautioned, "you are a sick woman. You wouldn't want to try getting up."

"You mean I was sick," Edna told her. "Please go get my clothes, because I am going to get dressed and come help you prepare the evening meal."

"Oh, child! You aren't well! You are sick!"

"You mean I was. I want to get up out of this bed. I want to go to church tomorrow night."

"But Edna," the aunt insisted, "you are in bad shape!"

"I WAS in bad shape, Auntie," she explained again. "I am not now. I am well," and she got up out of bed! The dear relative was so startled. After Edna dressed, she helped her aunt prepare the evening meal, and the next night came to church. When this woman, who had been painfully confined to a turning sheet for three weeks, stood up and witnessed to the miracle of Jesus healing her—people were moved for God in that community.

This was my first experience in divine healing, and God made it unmistakably clear to me that He is just the same today as He was when Jesus walked this earth. By God's grace I shall never forget it.

God also performed a miracle for Mabel P., who had been unable to lie down because of a certain infection in her respiratory system. Upon occasions, a bloody mucous would start up out of her lungs and choke her; so she was forced to try to rest sitting up. We took a few of our laymen to pray for her.

As we started to pray, somehow God helped me to know

that everything was not quite right. "Something is hindering prayer," I said. "There is something in the way. People are not right with God." I then asked the people to pray for themselves. "Get right with God!" I would plead. Still, I could not pray for Sister P.'s healing. I cried out some more, "There is something in somebody's heart that is holding back the power."

Isn't it amazing that God could show a young and inexperienced pastor the need of the moment? I continued to plead with the people to get right in their hearts. It was not an easy place. Finally, after about three or four exhortations, two women came across that living room and asked one another's forgiveness. The channels of love were unblocked and the glory fell. We began to pray, and Mabel said that she saw Jesus standing in the gate of Heaven. As we were interceding for her, she saw Jesus reach His hand down from Heaven, put it on her head, and heal her.

But as soon as she was healed, this thick, bloody mucous began to flow out of her mouth. Quickly we had to get a container. All my people were alarmed. I could see by their faces that they doubted.

"Have faith!" I encouraged them. "This is the unclean coming out!" It was a terrible sight. I have never seen such a substance pouring out of a person's mouth and throat. "Don't disbelieve," I kept telling them. "Just have faith and say, 'Thank you Jesus!'" (Why, who told me that? What made me so certain that this was of God when the older people were fearful that she wasn't healed? It had to be Jesus helping me, I know.)

When she visited the doctor for x-rays, he said, "This is wonderful. All that infection is gone from your lungs." Jesus had healed her for His glory.

These are but a few of the marvelous things we would have missed in our first pastorate if we had made our own choice rather than God's choice. My District Elder had been thinking of my finances when he recommended the better-paying positions. But look at the power of God which was able to operate once we arrived where God ordained us to be (and the Holy Ghost is moving through my body now as I share this with you!). This was only the beginning of what God was going to accomplish for His glory, because it was His beginning, not mine.

Loran and Florence, 1973.

16 "COME WITH ME, SON . . ."

In April, 1938, we were transferred from Redkey to White-water. After one year had elapsed, out of Asbury College came Rev. Homer Pumphrey, who had been in school with the son of my District Elder, Phillip Brooks Smith. Rev. Smith was one of the great preachers in the state of Indiana, and gifted of God. He preached Jesus and Him crucified. Rev. Pumphrey requested a pastorate; so Rev. Smith sent him to Redkey Circuit.

When Rev. Pumphrey arrived, he heard of our walk with God and remarked, "I want to know that pilgrim of Jesus." In 1939, at New Castle, Indiana, I was privileged to meet Homer for the first time. He said, "I want you to pray that I will be a sanctified man and everything that God wants me to be."

When I returned to Whitewater parsonage I told my wife, "Never in my life has a preacher told me this!" How delighted and surprised I was to hear of someone who desired to be all that God wanted him to be. I have met few who really wanted to go all out for Jesus.

At that time I had begun the completion of my undergraduate studies in Earlham College, and God was continuing to work with me. I was trusting Him the best I knew how and was trying to do all that He wanted me to do. In the little churches we were serving, people were being saved, bodies were being healed, and faithful hearts were coming forward to be inwardly cleansed; but within me I knew that God was not calling me to the pastorate.

After a day of classroom study, I would say to my wife, "Honey, I am not in the right stall. When I was a boy on the farm, all of my cows had their own stalls. God is calling me to something. I am not in the right place yet." I was very thankful for what Jesus was accomplishing, but this strong impression never left me: "God is calling me to something—it is out there ahead of me somewhere."

By this time we had three little girls. Joyce Lee was born in January of 1936, our second year at Taylor University. The twin girls arrived May 24, 1939. Eight-and-a-half months before they were born, Jesus revealed to me that He was giving us twins. Coming home I told Florence, "Oh, Honey, Jesus just revealed to me that He is giving us twins!"

I shall never forget my wife's reaction when I informed her. Both of her hands came up to her bosom in a way she had never done before, nor has she done since, and she said, "Oh, no! Surely not me!"

When I told people what Jesus had revealed, I can't recall that even one person believed me. However, they believed when Florence gave birth to identical twins eight-and-a-half months after the revelation. Nancy weighed five-and-a-half pounds at birth and Martha weighed five pounds. Each had lost a pound when we brought them home from the hospital. They were so very tiny and most precious.

At the annual conference meeting in 1941, my District Elder told me where he thought I was to be assigned. This charge included two churches, with a parsonage which had a new furnace and new floors. He also asked me to be praying about Shideler Circuit, a charge with three congregations. The parsonage there had neither a furnace nor a bathroom, and one had to go outside to pump the water.

I said nothing; but while he was discussing with others at the conference where I should be sent, I returned to the home of the Swansons where my wife and I were being entertained during our stay. Florence was not well in those days. If you knew all that she has passed through in these thirty-some years, you would agree that it has been only by God's grace that we have made it this far. It will be only by His mercy that we can make it tomorrow.

Coming into our room I said, "Honey, I am going to pray about these pastorates." On my knees I asked, "Jesus, do you want us to go to the pastorate where there is this wonderful opportunity?" —And it was as black as midnight. I then asked, "Lord Jesus, do you want us to go to Shideler Circuit?" When I prayed about this pastorate, I saw a ball of fire a few hundred feet above me to the right. With great delight I announced, "Oh, Honey! God is sending us to Shideler!"

Three days later the District Elder sent us to Shideler Circuit, the place God had already shown me. In earthly estimation it was the least desirable pastorate among many scores of churches, but when we arrived there in May of 1941, I was so happy. Unless God would reveal it, no one could ever know how thrilled I was to be there, because this was the place Jesus had chosen for us.

Though the parsonage had no indoor bathroom facilities and we had to pump our own water, at times I would stand on the parsonage lawn with such happiness in my soul that I could never express it adequately to anyone. I would tell people, "I am as happy here as if I were in the White House in Washington." I was thrilled because God had brought us here! We were at the bottom but I felt like we were at the top. We scarcely had anything, yet I felt as if we had much. Now that requires Jesus, doesn't it? If He can trust us to be delighted with nothing, then perhaps He can trust us someday with something.

God told me how to make the three churches like one congregation. During our period of service, there were some ninety victories, and the three churches began to be joined together in an unusual love. God worked through them to put storm windows on the parsonage, drill a new well, install a pump, and provide running water. He gave me a group of men who could sing for the glory of God. When we first

153

began they said, "Why, we are just farmers, meat cutters, factory workers. We can't sing." But when we would get together, with my wife at the piano, the Lord would help us.

Having completed my undergraduate degree, my District Elder thought that I should pursue advanced training in theological studies. I was sent to a school near Chicago. On Monday I would leave my wife and family, journey to the seminary for four days of classes, then return home to conduct Sunday services.

As I walked among these beautiful academic buildings, often God would deal with me, and I would ask, "God of Abraham—God of Elijah—did you call me to this place? Is this Thy will for me?" And I received little consolation. I wasn't at home there. I had been going along with man a long while, doing what my dear ones wanted me to do: my father, mother, District Elder, pastor, ministerial brothers, Christian friends. I had been trying to serve God the best I knew and still please the ones I loved.

When I returned the second week to this place of higher education, God continued to deal with me. I was so moved upon by the Spirit that all I could do was talk to Jesus about it. I was uncertain what all God was trying to tell me, but He was working and moving within my soul.

On arrival the third week, I paid my week's portion of the board for the little suite of rooms where I lived with two other young ministers, and sat down to write a theme on "Ten things I believe about the Bible" for my Bible class. I was in a quandary, for I knew that my Bible professor and a few others there did not believe the Bible to be the inspired Word of God. When someone asked the professor how she could give the Apostle's Creed believing as she did, she replied, "I give the Apostle's Creed through respect for our forefathers."

I believe the Bible as it is. If I did not, the Holy Ghost couldn't work through me. The Bible is an account of God dealing with men, walking with men, working with men. It

154

has been given by the Holy Spirit. Many scholars seek to find discrepancies in it. I try only to look for God's will in it, for the Bible is God's Book.

As I was seated there trying to write, I lifted my head and silently cried out, "Oh, God!" The moment my heart cried out, God began to show me things I had never seen before.

I saw the earth. It appeared as if an awful storm were about it, the kind of storm I once viewed as a young boy, when the clouds would sweep in from the west during March and April. I saw the earth covered with thick darkness and engrossed in deep sin. Oh, it was so dark! Sin is far worse than we think. It is much, much worse than you and I can comprehend. I saw that the ugliness of sin had covered the earth; it had invaded men and women, boys and girls. This wicked Sin Principle was terrible. It was monstrous.

I cried out "Oh, Jesus! Where is the light? Oh, God— where art thou?"

I looked up, and there was a light. God was in the light and He said, "COME WITH ME, SON. . ."

When God called me to go with Him, and with Him alone, I said good-bye to my father, my mother, my elders, my friends—everyone! In my heart I said, "Good-bye, things of this world. I am going with God!"

My friend, the instant I forsook everything of earth to walk alone with Jesus, I entered into a land that was darker than midnight, even the blackest of midnight. It was a spiritual experience which words could never convey, yet as real as this book in your hand. God has revealed to me in these intervening years that seldom have men ever gone this lonely path to walk in absolute dependence upon Jesus.

Most mortals will never have this experience, because God called me into this world for a specific purpose. No one needs to pattern his life after this experience, for I was called by God and ordained by the Holy Ghost for a specific work in the Kingdom of God. I do not belong to myself, or to any certain group: I belong wholly to God. By His grace and protection, I must do what He wills, nothing more and nothing less.

God was calling me to this land seldom trod by men. Suddenly a demon voice above me clamored, "Your life is ruined! There is no hope for you! Take one step along this path and you will fall a thousand feet to the rocks beneath you!"

I said, "I am trusting Jesus."

I heard another evil voice above me, "What are you going to do? You have blighted the hopes and anticipations of your mother and father. They have spent thousands of dollars on your education. They have sacrificed and worked to help you all these years. Now you have destroyed their hopes. What are you going to do with them? How will you explain this to them?"

I answered again, "I am trusting Jesus."

A third evil voice demanded, "What will you do with your lovely wife and three children? How will you support them? You have no place to go. There is no way to go."

My reply was, "I am trusting Jesus." That is all I said: "I am trusting Jesus."

To me it is a marvelous thing that a twenty-five-year-old boy who had walked with God only a little while would reply "I am trusting Jesus" in the face of such great accusation. It had to be God helping, I know. Of course, that was His call upon my life—to trust Him.

I wasn't aware then that very few people in the professed church knew much about trust. I have since discovered that only a handful are really trusting God in their everyday lives. Most people in the church are arranging their own lives to some extent. I wouldn't be surprised that well over ninety percent of all professed church people are working out their lives by their own reasoning and according to that which appears expedient.

But trust only begins when we look, not to our own

understanding, but first to God for His leading through the witness of the Holy Spirit. It continues as we simply follow His guidance no matter what obstacles or trials seem to block the way. Trusting God is so simple a child can do it; but very few in all the ages have been willing to consistently apply it.

I wasn't aware then that most of us mortals were so far from God's will. I only knew that my call was to trust God and obey Him. I was just to walk with Jesus, follow His direction without question, and let Him work out all the situations.

As the Lord was calling me to trust Him, the powers of earth and hell were raging against me. It was a ferocious battle of the soul, though I was still seated at the desk in the little apartment. My minister friends were unaware of the struggle taking place within me.

When I entered this land of Absolute Trust, I found it densely choked and snarled with battles and trials. I saw that I couldn't take a step without wielding a sharp blade of determination to mind God and rely on Jesus. I had to hew a path through huge oaks of difficulty that no one would dream about. All these obstacles had to be cleared out of the way, and only God could do it.

There is no way of communicating what this land is like. Until one has walked in absolute faith—trusting and obeying only God and letting God have His way entirely—it is impossible to understand this experience. But those who have been trusting only Jesus through the years have learned that it is a pressing, that it is a rejoicing. It is not looking to the church, to religious leaders, or to anyone else, but it is looking to Jesus.

Through the ages, all men who have obeyed God's call to do only His will and have not tried to work out ideas and answers with their own skills, have found themselves in this lonely and wonderful land. True life is found here, for it is the Kingdom of God on earth, where God's will alone is not only sought, but, by God's grace, fulfilled. Since all of hell is against anyone reaching God's perfect will, the path to it is strewn with enormous difficulties and obstacles.

For this reason, whenever God sends a true servant to any congregation, that people will begin to experience unusual struggles and upheavals. Whenever God is truly endeavoring to accomplish His will, Satan will be there trying to stir up strife, create misunderstandings, and cause jealousies among the people. Few laymen are prepared for the battles which they will encounter once God sends a true servant their way. The average church person believes that the program of the church is to be handled like any other business, and should proceed along the path of least conflicts and most beneficial results.

Quite to the contrary, any time a church works out a program or a religious plan in themselves, it is not pleasing to God. This is not a popular statement to declare, but I must give the truth in love or be held responsible at Judgment. I know that we dare not devise our own church systems and programs because our ideas, at their very best, can only come from our human minds and insights. They originate from the wisdom of the earth and cannot satisfy heavenly requirements, for God's Word plainly states: ". . . they that are in the flesh cannot please God." (Romans 8:8)

I am not seeking to find fault with any church, but Jesus has revealed to me that unless our singing, our preaching, our Sunday schools, Bible schools, and revivals are led by the Holy Spirit, the fruit of these activities will not survive. Jesus tells us that "Every plant, which my heavenly Father hath not planted, shall be rooted up." (Matthew 15:13) This strongly indicates to me that the Holy Spirit must not only lead, but must be the Author of all that I do. He must be the One to plan my life; He must originate my programs or I will be living a life which is powerless and ineffectual. It is as I am submissive, broken, waiting on God, and loving everybody, that Jesus is able to lead me into a life of divine vigor and eternal glory.

Following this tremendous spiritual struggle, I finally related back to the physical world around me. My decision was clear. "I am going home," I told the ministerial student opposite me.

He looked at me surprised. "What's the matter?" he asked. "Can't you stick it out for at least one semester?" He thought I was simply giving up. He had no idea what God had been telling me for weeks and weeks, or what all I had been through in the past few minutes.

I answered, "I am going home." My friend didn't know whether I meant "go home" for a day, two weeks, or to stay. He continued to persuade me to stick it out, but I had to tell him, "I must purchase a train ticket and return home tonight." I had been away from home only since morning. It was then around eight or nine o'clock in the evening.

After packing my bags I was taken to the train station in downtown Chicago by two of my roommates. I paid them fifty cents for gas and had enough money to purchase a one-way ticket to Hartford City. At eleven-ten I boarded the train.

Satan was fighting furiously. "It is all over now," he raged. "You have ruined everything."

I replied, "I am trusting Jesus." Satan continued to hurl accusing thoughts at me to make me feel dishonest, guilty, and in error. I repeatedly answered, "I am trusting Jesus." Until you determine with all your heart to leave everything of earth to go with God, there is no way to describe to you the depth of my soul's struggle during this time. Yet, I was happy. I had no idea what the future held, but in my heart I was at peace.

The train moved very slowly, stopping at nearly every little village. A few seats behind me sat a drunk man. For four hours that train stopped and started, stopped and started. I simply looked to Jesus for strength and courage.

The devil repeatedly brought to my mind, "There will be no way for you to get home from Hartford City. You don't known anyone there. Your wife and children live ten miles away. They have no phone. The bus doesn't leave Hartford City for Shideler until five or five-thirty. It is raining. You will get wet, catch pneumonia, and die. You almost did," he whispered to me. "Don't you remember?"

"Yes," I thought to myself, "I almost did." Dr. Kramer told me that when I was a very little boy I contracted a swift pneumonia so severe that my parents could hear me gasping for my breath from the living room all the way to the pump-house outside the kitchen. He informed the men at the store, "The Helm baby will be gone by morning."

I am told that I had to fight for every breath. It was New Year's Eve, and Mother and Grandmother sat beside my crib, not daring to say a word to one another, both fearing the worst. Mother related much later, "I didn't think you were going to make it through the night." It was only by the mercies of Jesus that I was raised up. Satan was attacking my mind severely with the fear: "You will get wet, catch pneumonia, and die."

The Hartford City depot was dark that October morning when the train pulled in at three-thirty. My situation did not appear good, for I was ten miles from home and no one knew that I was returning. The main highway was closed as well, for they had been re-working the entire road.

When the train jerked to a stop, I picked up my bags and walked to the coach steps. It was very dark, but I noticed a tiny light ninety feet or so to my left. As I looked down, this light reflected from some object at the bottom of the steps. Out of the darkness, a man's voice unexpectedly asked, "Did you want to go some place, Sir?"

"Yes, Sir!" I exclaimed. "I want to go home!"

"My car is at the curb," he said. "Sometimes I meet this early morning train."

Praise God! As I looked closely, I could see an old gentle-

160

man standing at the bottom of the train steps, the light reflecting from the shiny black bill of his cap.   Oh! Was I ever glad to see him!   My heart was filled with such praise to Jesus that I didn't know how to express it!

What if this elderly gentleman had not been there?   Dwell on that for a moment.   He did not always meet this early morning train.   Since no one was there to help me, I would have been obliged to walk uptown carrying two heavy suitcases.   With the sensitivity in my body to sickness in damp weather, unless God protected me, I would easily have become seriously ill.   But, praise God, this gentleman was there to meet me!

God has had somebody to meet me every morning since, spiritually speaking.   When I have needed help, He has sent someone to assist.   When I have been in need, without fail He has always provided.   Bless the Lord!

For two dollars this kind gentleman drove me the ten miles south to the village of Shideler.   Thanking him, I lifted my two suitcases to the porch and gave my special knock on the front door.   My wife and I had arranged this secret code so we wouldn't frighten or alarm one another.

Never scare anyone.   Never try to frighten your wife, your mother or father, a sister or brother.   Never try to play a trick on people, because this grieves the Holy Spirit.   Often our little pranks backfire, causing hurt and damage.

Many folks, in the carnal, play tricks and pranks, thinking they are going to have a good time.   In contrast, Spirit-filled men are taught to be very cautious and careful, because the sweetness of Jesus doesn't work in the mold of cleverness and the way of the smart-aleck.   The sweetness of Jesus works in gentleness, humbleness, tenderness, and thoughtfulness for others.

My precious wife was sound asleep.   I can still see her coming through the house.   The porch light was always left on when I was away from home, and I could see her wiping the sleep from her eyes as she tried to bring her thoughts awake. She unlatched the old-fashioned lock, opened the door and looked up at me, her face all one big question. "What is the matter?" she asked.

I replied: "Honey—I have come home to go with God!"

17 "... AND PERFECT WILL OF GOD."

That is all I said: "I have come home to go with God." But that is saying a great deal.

You see, I am not sharing this pilgrimage simply to compile a book. I'm declaring what God has done. He is the One who has accomplished it. I am striving only to exalt Jesus, to make known what He has done for His Kingdom's work. The Holy Spirit is the One who has led this trusting life and directed its activities. So I honor Him for all these things.

I attempted to sleep the remainder of the night; but instead, I rolled and tossed on the banks of accusation. The devil was still flooding my thoughts with questions: "Now what are you going to do? What will the elders say? What will your father and mother say? You have broken their hearts. You have shattered their lifelong dreams."

This was indeed true. I had disappointed my parents more than anyone could know. They had hoped that I would someday become the well known and highly respected pastor of a large urban church. I had been told by dear ones that I was one of the young ministers who showed promise of a good future. Now it appeared as if I was turning my back on everything. Many probably wondered how I could ever expect to advance in the church unless I was well educated; and by leaving seminary, I was throwing away the key to a successful ministry in the church. I had broken the hearts of many of my loved ones and close friends, who had been expecting great things of me. Very few understood.

But my wife was not surprised. She had known that God

163

was going to do something. Isn't it wonderful that the same Light which told me that she was mine, also let her know about me and some areas I was passing through? It seems that God sometimes informs her about situations before I am able to tell her or need to tell her. Praise the Lord.

I am so glad she didn't say, "Now look here—you get back to school. You straighten up and get hold of yourself! We have to have a pastorate! Don't go off on some tangent now!" Often people will try to straighten you out. If I had not had the companion God knew that I needed, she might have been tempted to "bring me back to my senses," set me back in the order of earth, and put me on the next train back to Chicago. Most women, I believe, would have wanted to have a few explanations, at least.

But my precious wife realized that there was a Higher Power than man doing this. A Higher Authority than earth was involved in this. (Hallelujah! I feel the power of God when I tell you "a Higher Authority than earth was in this." Glory to God! The Holy Spirit tells me now that this was true! It is wonderful to have God tell you with power that He was the One directing you when everything seemed dark. It is something to get happy about, believe me!)

When I awoke the next day, I went to see my District Elder. I told him that I had stopped my seminary training. Thinking I had either become discouraged with school or planned to drop the ministry, he said, "Son, you have a promising ministry in our church. Just go over to this other seminary and finish your education."

Of course, I had no desire to leave the church or to stop working in the church. I loved every church then, and I love them more now. I love every church of Jesus everywhere. And yet, some people say that I am out to divide churches. They tell that I am out to take over churches. It is difficult for me to believe anyone would ever think such a thing, for all I want to do is walk with God, to seek and do His will. I am simply striving with all my might to help all people love

Jesus and their fellow man. I have so little of Jesus, I know. I need so much more of His love. I cry out daily to be filled more with the sacred Holy Spirit.

The elder inquired, "What are you going to do?"

I answered, "My Brother, God is calling me. He is calling me to trust Him."

"What?" he replied.

"God is calling me to trust Him," I repeated.

"I don't know what you mean," he said.

"Well, He has called me to trust Him," I told him again.

His demeanor at once became deeply serious. Solemnly he cautioned me, "Now I will tell you, Son—you may get along alright someway if you go into this kind of life. You may make it fairly well until you are forty-five. But if you don't obtain more advanced training, achieve more knowledge and wisdom—by the time you are forty-five your ministry will start down."

"Well," I answered him, "God is calling me to trust Him. That is all I know: only trust Him and do His will." I knew that unless God were leading, I would never make it to the age of forty-five.

I am unable to explain what it was like within my soul during this time. Nothing but naked faith supported my decision to live my life in absolute trust in Jesus. There was no flow of emotion to sustain me or carry me through. Within and around my spirit there was a darkness that I am unable to describe; but, oh—what peace was in my soul. I was happy in Jesus, although I was alone in the earth as I had never experienced aloneness. I was in a midnight walk of the soul all that week, from Monday night through to the following Sunday night.

That evening the church was nearly filled, for God had been doing miracles in this pastorate. Twelve to fifteen men from these churches truly loved us. That evening, this chorus of men was to sing, after which I was to preach. Since 1933 I had preached by outline, and as I went into the pulpit that

165

night, I sensed so deeply my inability to present a sermon. I felt that I knew no more how to declare God's Word than a four or five-year-old boy.

All too soon the men finished singing. I rose and started for the pulpit, not knowing what to do or what words to speak. I started to say, "Oh, Father in Heaven. . . ," when, suddenly I was on the hand of God going up like an elevator! The darkness of that preceding week blew away like a cloud and I was in sunrise! God was taking me far up somewhere in His love and revelation.

He said, "My Son, you will preach tonight on: 'I beseech you therefore, brethren, by the mercies of God, that ye present your bodies a living sacrifice, holy, acceptable unto God, which is your reasonable service. And be not conformed to this world: but be ye transformed by the renewing of your mind, that ye may prove what is that good, and acceptable, and perfect will of God.' "

It seemed that my life was a funnel: my mouth was the tiny spout of this funnel and God was pouring His revelation through me in such a quantity that I couldn't talk fast enough to get it all out. He was pouring so much of Himself into my life that I couldn't contain it, and it was flowing over the sides. I was so thrilled with Jesus that I was all over the platform. The glory of God was evident everywhere in that sanctuary as I was preaching about going with God, doing God's will. I was trying to tell them how God is so sweetly beseeching us by His mercies every day to do only His will.

I was striving to share with them the imperative of presenting ourselves holy unto God. Jesus was preaching through me that we must be totally His, a complete sacrifice; that we must be pure and undefiled; that this is our only reasonable service. As He had never done before, God was moving me from one side of the pulpit to the other, trying to get across His message that we must prove what is His good and acceptable and perfect will.

That's where God was taking me in His call to trust Him

absolutely. **That night I started toward God's perfect will.**
My people had never before seen the anointing of God upon
me like that. Jesus was preaching through me that we in
the church are living a thousand miles below where God wants
us to live. "There are too many missing links!" I cried.
"We are coming far short of the will of God! God wants to
work in us. He wants to have His way with us!"

People were at the altar. They were weeping and Heaven
was all around. I had never preached like that in my life.
I had never been in such a light like that. It was the first
time I had forsaken all the peoples of the age to go with God,
and He was working through me. Glory! Oh, the light
was wonderful! The darkness was gone and I wasn't alone.
For days I had simply believed and gone by faith. God somehow helped me not to look at the darkness or the hardships,
but to look only to Him.

(Now this is what you want to do all the time. **Don't place
your attention on any difficulties at any time.** Look only to
Jesus through every circumstance. Keep your eyes fixed upon
Him constantly. Maintain praise and adoration in your heart
even when you don't feel like it, when it is not easy to praise.
We will never be able to work out a single situation ourselves
anyway. Leave the working-out to God and simply keep your
eyes on Jesus, who is the Answer to every need and every
problem.)

My people were weeping, and I was trying to tell them
that God wants us to be faithful and true. He doesn't want
us hot and then cold, up and then down. He wants us to be
consistent, alive, radiant, rejoicing—through every situation
which we experience. He wants us to be overcomers.

I had discovered few Christians who had this victorious
overcoming experience. I didn't know the missing links in
Christianity then; but God has let me discover one or two of
them over the years. I learned that **the missing link which
connects us to a continuous life as an overcoming Christian
is self-denial.** We must learn to deny Self in a heart of trust;

for then we move, through the leadership of the Holy Spirit, to obedience and the cross.

We in the church can sing, preach, pray, read scripture, go along with the religious program, and never once deny Self. Often, instead of depending on God to guide us, we plan a little of what we want to do, sing the songs we like to hear, and preach when we want the preaching to take place. We pretty much arrange activities which suit our taste and conform to our schedule. But, you see, God wants **all** of the church's activities at **His** direction. He wants to be **all** of the content of our program. Christ must have everything.

We must wait on Him until He sends, until He guides, until He reveals. **We must wait on Him so that He can lead the church, lead the body, and become the true Head of His believing followers.**

According to the scriptures, Jesus must be the Head of the Church. If He isn't the Head of the body, it will be because He is not leading. And when He is not leading, the body becomes a headless body—a social organism incapable of sustaining life. Like a chicken with its head cut off, it thrashes around meaninglessly in all directions and is unattractive to the world.

God has shown me that any congregation severs itself from Jesus, the true Head, simply by working out a religious program which is not led by the witness of the Holy Spirit—even when that program appears feasible, beneficial, and helpful to both that church and the community. This congregation may consist of apparently beautiful, religious people. They may have excellent orthodoxy; they may preach conversion by the blood of Jesus; they might have the finest Christian ethics; they may be well-informed and well-trained; but, as yet, they simply have not waited on God to be inwardly crucified and learn the leading of the Holy Spirit.

Many in the constituency of the churches today have a fair knowledge of fundamental Christianity, and feel comfortable within the order of Sunday morning worship. But I fear that there are not many who have pressed from conversion on into a consistent experience of self-denial, willing to rely on God with all their hearts, and striving to follow each leading of the Holy Spirit. In fact, in all of my travels, I have met very few who have waited on God sufficiently that they are able to discern the Holy Spirit's guidance.

In the last few years, Jesus has begun to teach me that He has a plan for every occasion in which His children meet to have fellowship and worship. **It is absolutely essential that we get quiet long enough to discern that plan.** Once we are able to understand what He wishes and obey Him, then Jesus truly becomes the Guide, or the Head, of that group of believers. The Body of Christ begins to take on divine life when He is actually directing the movements of His followers. When He leads, it is like Heaven. When **He guides,** God's Kingdom comes to earth.

But if we as a congregation are not receiving His directions and doing what He says, then it is not God's Kingdom operating within the church structure—it is our own kingdom. The little kingdoms of religious activities, which we often construct because we don't know what else to do, have no divine power. As sincere as our efforts may be, our instigations are born of the earth, not of Heaven.

A multitude of sincere seekers will involve themselves in these church activities thinking they are serving God, when actually they are serving a man-made institution. A few dear ones may even be genuinely converted through our program; but, unfortunately, most grow lukewarm and cold within a short time, because they had no example of waiting on God, of denying self, of obeying Jesus. If they remain, they often become followers of the mores and styles of the human-dictated kingdom, and are detoured from the true walk with God.

Do you see how tragic it is going to be for us in the church if we have not permitted Jesus to be the actual Head of our congregation? If we in the church have been working out programs and services as we want them and think they should be, instead of as Jesus desires, do you see what terrible judgment will fall upon us?

It is not an easy assignment for me to cry out like this to the professed Church. But unless I make known what the Holy Spirit has revealed to me, I will be held accountable. It is very serious to call ourselves "the Church" if we are not striving with all our energies to deny Self and obey the leadings of the Holy Spirit. Unless Jesus is **literally** directing the activities of any congregation just like the brain in our head controls our own human body, then that group of persons—as precious as they are—becomes a headless body.

Are you gaining a little glimpse of how serious it is to be in the church?

Dear ones, we must be for Jesus with all our hearts. If He hasn't been absolutely first in everything we have sought or done, we will come short of His will.

Jesus said, "Not everyone that saith Lord, Lord, shall enter the Kingdom of heaven: **but He that doeth the will of my Father** which is in heaven." **It is doing God's will absolutely in Christ that matters!** And we are to wait on Him until He makes His will clear to us. We are not to work out anything or work up anything, but let Him work through us as He chooses.

The secret of God being able to work through His people in power is simply this: CEASE TO WORK IT OUT OURSELVES, AND LET HIM WORK THROUGH US. (Beloved, if you can digest this and get it into the muscle and bone of your inner man, it will be worth more than the cost of all books ever sold; because it will introduce you to the mystery of God's will being done in earth as it is in Heaven.)

Now the Powers of the Air will not want you to get hold of this in your heart. They will minimize the depth of holy truth in this little phrase. Many will say to themselves, "My, isn't that interesting?" and then read on, looking for something a bit more exciting.

But God wants this feeble servant's life shared just for this purpose: that God's people might begin to learn this divine secret. **We are to cease trying to do God's work, and let Him simply work through us His Kingdom.**

Several of you may already be asking, "But how do I let God work through me?"

First, we must truly repent of all of our sins. We must ask Jesus to forgive us and save us. We must be converted and become like a child.

We then begin to let God work through us by waiting upon Him. Set aside a time each day, preferably before you begin your day's activities, to be alone with God. It may be fifteen minutes in duration; it could be one hour or more. Simply talk to God from your heart. Tell Him how you love Him. Read some scripture and meditate on it. **Especially be attentive to the promptings of the Holy Spirit while you are waiting and listening.**

As we begin to learn to wait upon Him, He will start to slay us, refine us, and bring us into His likeness. He will begin to remove the short circuits, the briars, and the stickers which are hidden in our natures and our personalities: these harmful things which ruin more seed than we could ever plant.

As we trust Him, He will teach us to rest in Him, to rely upon Him, to really believe His Word. We will learn to love Him more deeply and praise Him more frequently.

Occasionally He will send us on an errand: perhaps we are to speak to a neighbor about how wonderful Jesus is. We aren't to argue or tell him that he is going to hell. We are simply to tell him how precious Jesus has been to us. Sometimes Jesus will ask us to stand in church and witness for Him. He may show us that we need to ask forgiveness of some person for our wrong attitudes. As we are waiting, He will be showing us the simple steps of obedience and how to walk with Him.

You see, one doesn't learn to walk with God overnight. I wouldn't dream of learning the Hebrew language in one day, in two weeks, or even in three months. This is a walk with God, and it is the highest privilege in the world. There is much to know, and there are many lessons to learn.

One of the first lessons God will teach us as we wait before Him is that we can do absolutely nothing good in ourselves. **He will begin to show us that, until He leads, we can only do damage by our own attempts.** It may look as if much is being lost and that something must be done, but simply continue trusting until He gives you guidance. **He can do more in seconds than men can do in centuries; and when He does it, it is done fully, beautifully, and lastingly.**

Before we wait too many hours in the secret of our own prayer closet, He will teach us that His ways are not our ways. While we are anxious to get things going, we will discover that God moves very slowly; yet, He moves swiftly when the time is right.

We will begin to observe that God has no set patterns, but that He works in infinite variety. We would like to set a scheme to things. But He will go to great lengths to demonstrate to us that He is above our plans and our arrangements. He will work out the situations which face us in ways that will constantly amaze and delight us.

These are only a few of the lessons we may learn as we press daily to seek God's face. He will not come short of His promises toward us if we truly are striving to love Him more than we desire to do anything else on this earth.

God revealed to me some years ago that He will send a mighty World Wide Revival that is truly of the Holy Ghost, once He can find a body of believers who will truly begin to wait upon Him and put Him absolutely first above everything of earth. This Revival, which I have been anticipating now for over thirty years, will not come by fanaticism, by seeking gifts and manifestations, or by striving to gain power with God. It will be given by the Holy Spirit in God's time as we seek only His will and His love in Jesus Christ. This mighty

172

work of righteousness to come is His, not ours. We are only the sheep of His pasture.

God wants to give us His Kingdom. The secret is: Cease from arranging our lives and permit Him to operate through us as He wishes: in a simple life of trust and obedience; in a consistent, continual denial of self-desires without variation or vacation.

Helm Brothers Sextet, May, 1950 — nine years after God called Loran to leave all to trust Him entirely. (Left to right: Warren, Loran, Richard, Terrance, Edward, and Edwin.)

18 ORDINATION

Near the end of the message I declared, "I am going out into the world to find the people of God! I am leaving all to go wherever the Lord leads me. I am going to find those hearts who are willing to trust and walk with God!"

During the last two-thirds of the message I noticed that the pianist, a woman seldom given to emotional expression, was weeping. When the benediction was given she came to the pulpit to deposit her offering which she had been unable to give from her position at the piano. Stopping where I was seated, she stated very simply, "Well—this is it."

And a shout came right out of my heart!

The previous September she had told me, "Rev. Helm, you are not a pastor."

"Why, Gladys!" I responded, a little amazed.

"Oh," she went on, "I know that you are pastor of the Pleasant Grove Church, but that is not who you are. You have a different calling."

And on this evening when God spoke through me the words, "I am leaving all to find the people of God!"—Jesus stood right behind her and spoke into her right ear, "Gladys, this is what I have been telling you about this servant." She related that this revelation continued throughout the latter two-thirds of the message. I don't believe she ever had such an experience before this nor has she had one since then.

A few minutes after she had told me this, I noticed Charles I. hugging the shadows of the north wall of the church. He was standing with his shoulder against the wall, weeping with his hand on his chin. When I went over to love him he said, "Well—I guess we will be coming along."

We prayed with people for some time that evening at Pleasant Grove Church. The meeting wasn't over until twelve-thirty the next morning, but still the people didn't want to go home. They loved me and I loved them. Oh, how I loved them! God had always given me an unusual love for my flock. While we had pastored in Whitewater, a minister friend from a distance away had said to me, "I never would want my congregation to know what thoughts were in my mind."

I was shocked. I replied, "Oh, my Brother, I wish my people could see into my heart. If they could see how I loved them in Jesus, I think they would be moved to weeping. If they could know how I really want to do God's will with all that there is within me, I believe my sanctuary would be full and the church basement crowded as well."

The dear ones at Pleasant Grove Church never did draw back from my ministry or question me. Even later, when God was working with me so mightily, not a member or church leader opposed me carnally. Of the seven churches I served, this congregation simply believed the report. They didn't get after me or line me up. If they had questions about how God was leading me, they just prayed about them.

And that night, even at twelve-thirty in the morning, they didn't want to leave us. I carried our three daughters out to the car, one at a time, and started for home. We had not travelled far when suddenly, from within the car, I heard music that was not of this earth! "Oh, Honey!" I exclaimed. "I hear heavenly music! It's right here by the rear view mirror! Put your ear over here and see if you can hear it."

But though she listened, she was unable to hear it. "Oh, it is wonderful! It's coming from right there!" I told her. I wanted so badly for her to hear it, for she is a musician and her soul responds to music in the Spirit. She would have been deeply moved, I know. It was the first time I had

176

ever heard such a heavenly melody, because it was the first time I had left everything to go with God.

When we arrived home a little before one in the morning, I carried the children inside, helped put them to bed, and began to get ready for sleep. For many years now my wife and I have endeavored to have family worship before retiring. Many things—in fact, nearly everything—will try to stop family worship, but you will need to do it regularly, either at morning or at night.

You will need to worship together for your own strength, because, if you haven't read the Word consistently and prayed regularly, you won't have the strength to resist temptation and the Tempter. The essentials of living an overcoming life in the face of trials and situations are: consistent reading of the Word, prayer, humble witnessing, and obedience to the Holy Spirit through self-denial. Jesus will grant you strength for every encounter as you obey Him in prayer, in the Word, in your testimony, and in yieldedness.

I was very much in the Spirit of God as I came from the bedroom into the front room to get my Thompson Chain Reference Bible, which I had laid on the old table my mother had loaned us. Generally I picked it up with both hands, but on this occasion I reached for that Bible with only my left hand. I never dreamed that God was about to give me one of the most wonderful and significant experiences of my entire life.

As I reached for that precious Book, the Holy Ghost suddenly took complete charge of my left hand and arm. Moving within that arm in a way He had never done before or since, God opened that large Thompson Chain Bible like it was a little New Testament. More perfectly than I could ever describe, the pages of the Word opened to the Gospel of John.

When my eyes fell upon the page, the sixteenth verse of the fifteenth chapter leaped right out, hit me on top of the head, and ran down to my feet. It said: "YE HAVE NOT CHOSEN ME, BUT I HAVE CHOSEN YOU, AND ORDAINED

YOU, THAT YE SHOULD GO AND BRING FORTH FRUIT, AND THAT YOUR FRUIT SHOULD REMAIN: THAT WHATSOEVER YE SHALL ASK OF THE FATHER IN MY NAME, HE MAY GIVE IT YOU."

My soul began to laugh, to cry, to rejoice. I am unable to tell you what all was happening in my heart, for the glory of God was burning in my soul. The experience which I had enjoyed in the service earlier that evening while under the anointing of Jesus had truly been marvelous; but this sacred event in the seclusion of the parsonage was somewhere higher in another area of hallowed bliss. I was unspeakably, gloriously happy! As I rejoiced I started to travel up and up toward the skyline drive of God's precious Perfect Will.

I had right to rejoice, for this was my Service of Ordination. During that previous week I had relinquished the honors of men and the approval of most religious leaders. In order to serve Jesus alone and do only His will, I had forsaken all that the earth had to offer, and this was the night of my ordination from God.

You see, my ordination is not of man. My Calling is right from the Throne. I am ordained from Jesus the Christ in Heaven, for He witnessed this to me in power and in the Holy Ghost through the Word: "YE HAVE NOT CHOSEN ME, BUT I HAVE CHOSEN YOU AND ORDAINED YOU. . ."

The moment was so sacred and so holy, I scarcely wanted to move. I knew myself to be utterly unworthy of this experience with God. I sensed that I would never be able to adequately convey what Jesus had done for His glory in those brief seconds.

Walking from the front room through the dining room into the bedroom, I sat down on the bed. About the time I reached the bedside, Jesus walked through the door behind me. I was not seeing Him with earthly eyes; it was a spiritual vision. I had never before seen Jesus in a vision, but I knew when He came through the door. "Oh, Jesus!" I said. "You are here!" As He came right up to me, I was privileged to see

178

His nail-scarred foot. His presence was to be sensed all about. The only words I could say were, "Jesus, You are here—Jesus, You are here," and began to praise and honor Him.

While I was adoring Him, that nail-scarred foot began to turn away. I thought He was going to leave me. "Oh, Jesus!" I cried. "Don't leave me! I am left alone now and forsaken by nearly all men. I don't have many friends in this world. Lord, don't leave me! Please don't forsake me, Jesus!"

And in the twinkling of an eye I was on my right knee in a land that I had never been in before. As I faced the southwest I saw a building of unusual design set in a landscape which I cannot describe. Everything was of the Kingdom of God. The hands of Jesus were close to me, and I was just ready to place my uplifted hands upon the Master's shoulders, when I heard His voice.

I heard the audible voice of Jesus!—The most beautiful, resonant, glorious voice of the ages! It was such wonderful, wonderful sound, that if you ever hear it, you will want nothing more than to hear it over and over. I heard His spoken voice twenty-two to twenty-four inches from my right ear say, beautifully clear: "I WILL NEVER LEAVE THEE NOR FORSAKE THEE."

(And as I share this with you, God operates within me by His gifts and says: "I will lead you and guide you and tell you what to do." I am thrilled that in the midst of sharing with you how Jesus spoke to me years ago in an audible voice, His Holy Spirit speaks within me in an operation of His love and tells me that He will guide, direct, and help me know what to do and say. What could be more marvelous in the earth than this!

(A few of you may receive a little thrill or an operation in your heart when you read certain passages of this humble pilgrimage. This is the Holy Spirit witnessing to you that something is of God. This is His way of helping you to know that these aren't simply words, but that whatever is being shared is truly of Jesus. John Wesley preached more on the witness of the Spirit than he did on many doctrines of the Church.

(God witnesses to the body because the body is the temple of the Holy Ghost. As long as our body is yielded to God, the Holy Spirit lives in us from the top of our head to the soles of our feet. When He has full control of the heart, He is able to teach and refine us. But there is much more to be done within us than we can know. Therefore, God continues to refine and purify our hearts; He repeatedly leads and instructs us in humble ways until we are more sensitive to His gentle promptings and holy guidances.

(We have only begun! So, be encouraged. Never ask, "Why does this have to be like that?" Or say, "I don't see why God has to work like this." No, no, no. Don't question, analyze, or attempt to fix everything to suit the intellect. Simply look to God, believe Jesus like a small child, and trust the Word.

(Above all, don't let anything discourage you. Keep pressing on in faith, in spite of all obstacles, always seeking to express and embrace the love of God. Be content with very little. The less you have, the happier you should try to be, because Jesus promised that the last shall be first in His Kingdom. Never permit yourself to be ruled by feeling or by emotion: go by faith in Jesus. Doing these things, you will begin to experience a day by day walk with Jesus which the choicest vocabulary will be unable to express.)

After this heavenly experience in the Kindom of God, as I was lying on my back in bed with my feet together, the loving hand of Jesus suddenly came to rest against the bottoms of my feet. I said, "Honey, Jesus' hand is on the bottom of my feet!"

"It is?" she replied. The moment was so hallowed that I scarcely dared to speak, yet I wanted my companion to know a little of the wonder of God's presence with us.

"I feel God here," she whispered.

How could you praise God sufficiently for the holy privilege of having the Master place His hand upon your feet? Praise God! He was getting me ready to walk with Him. Glory be to Jesus! I had been striving to follow Him for about nine years, but now He was preparing me to walk on the heavenly trail of God's Perfect Will. Hallelujah! He was getting me ready to go with God and not with man!

The hand of the blessed Son of God, the Stranger of Galilee, rested on the bottom of this unworthy servant's feet for about forty to sixty seconds, then moved. "Now Jesus' hand is on the top of my feet!" I told my wife. It remained there for a time and then passed up to a position slightly above the ankles. Slowly—very slowly—the hand of Jesus moved up my body, lingering for some seconds, then progressing slowly to another area. Each time I could tell where His hand was placed. When His hand reached the area of my heart, I fell asleep.

This was my first experience in walking with God after I had forsaken all of the earth to do only Jesus' will.

Ora and Grace Spence with their daughter, Florence.

19 BAPTIZED WITH THE HOLY SPIRIT

When I awakened the next day, I was starting a life altogether different than that which had gone before. I was no longer following the patterns of men or of the earth, I was simply trusting Jesus. God began to work, and before long the community was stirred up. I didn't know it was going to happen, for I wasn't aware that when you walk with God you stir people; but I began to learn it.

As you read about how God worked through each of His servants, you begin to discover that God's men create upheaval in the carnal heart. However, unless you get in the battle yourself, you'll only know this theoretically in your mind. To experience it is a different matter. But I was happy in Jesus. I knew little about the future, but I was looking to God who holds the future in His hand.

During November I would return to the parsonage and try to tell Florence what all God was doing with me. "Honey, God is slaying me," I would say. "I am dying—I am dying."

She would look at me, trying to understand what I really meant. "Is that right?" she would reply.

"Yes," I would tell her, laying my hand over my heart "God is slaying this self-life. I am dying right here inside." Day after day, for weeks and months, He persisted in slaying out of me little hidden things: little ways which weren't pleasing to Him; little ideas that were of the earth and not of Heaven. It was marvelous, but it was a death, believe me. This continued through December of 1941 into the following year, through January, February, and March.

The last day of March, 1942, I began a series of evangelistic services. When I entered the pulpit that night I felt normal in my body and soul. As soon as I opened the service, however, God began to take me into an area of the Spirit which I never knew existed. There is no way to describe how God was working within me and around me. I have seldom heard of anyone being in such a place. It was a realm of suffering, revelation, and crucifixion which words could never embrace. God was helping me to know: "Son, you have gone about as far as you can go on your own."

When I arrived home that night, I knew that I must get to my bed; and that is where God kept me for about two-and-a-half to three weeks. I was unable to get up; and if I tried, He put me back in bed.

God talked to me day and night. He talked to me more from midnight to four in the morning—when my wife, my children, and the village were asleep—than any other time. I was unable to sleep because God was revealing to me about Eternity. He was speaking to me about my mission on earth, about the great need of the Church. Because of the light I kept on, Florence couldn't rest and had to sleep in another room.

During the day I would call her to me. "God is calling me!" I would try to tell her. "He is talking to me. He is telling me some things!"

She would answer, "Yes, I know that God is doing it." Night after night, day after day, God marvelously worked with me. He would open the scriptures to my understanding and shine the light of His truth on various areas of my soul, revealing hidden needs and carnal ways in my heart, and in the hearts of men, which grieved Him.

Each evening, Rev. Homer Pumphrey and his wife, Rebecca, would come over to the house. The devil would try to tell them, "Don't go back tonight. You are wearing out your welcome. Just stay at home." But each night, here they would come from their parsonage home twelve miles away.

You talk about being happy to see somebody! I was so delighted each time they would come, for hardly anyone understood what I was passing through. I tried to tell a few what God was doing with me, but I don't know whether anyone comprehended it much. Even I couldn't grasp all of what God was doing. I was simply trusting Jesus.

I would tell the Pumphreys, "God is talking to me! God is doing wonderful things with me!" They would listen and try to grasp what I was striving in my feeble way to share. They were a great encouragement to my wife and me at this time.

One night I began to tell them the message God had given me out of the third chapter of Colossians: "If ye then be risen with Christ, seek those things which are above, where Christ sitteth on the right hand of God. Set your affections on things above; not on things on the earth."

When I first started to share with them, it seemed as if Homer was three city blocks from me in spiritual distance; yet, he had visited us night after night and was trying his best to understand me. Soon, however, the Holy Ghost got hold of his heart, picked him up in his soul, and set him down real close to me. I was sharing all that I could tell him as fast as I could get it out, and he was listening with all the energy that was in him. "This is wonderful!" he would say. "This is such a precious message!" The Holy Spirit was giving it and Homer was feasting. So was I.

It was while I was still on my bed that a precious handmaid of Jesus felt led of the Lord to pray and fast at the altar of Shideler Church. She went to the altar at ten-thirty Sunday morning while my father conducted the service for me. She prayed all day and on into the night.

She had prayed at that altar twenty-two hours when at eight-thirty in the morning, while I was still asleep, the power of God began flowing through me in waves of glory. Before I was fully awake, wave after wave of the Holy Spirit was moving through my body! I was being baptized with the

185

Holy Ghost under the glory, the power, and the presence of Jesus! This continued for nearly four hours.

It was the most wonderful experience of His love—for when the power would come through me at intervals, it came in wave after wave of love. There is no way of telling the love which flowed from my heart to my enemies, to those who hated me, to all men, following my baptism by the Holy Ghost.

Of course, the love of Jesus flowing from your heart to all people is the true manifestation of the Holy Spirit's indwelling. The initial evidence of the baptism with the Holy Spirit is not talking in a language unfamiliar to us. The true evidence is the flow of divine love to every person in the earth. Jesus did not say, "A new commandment I give unto you, that ye speak in an unknown language." He said: ". . . That ye love one another as I have loved you."

There is a gift of speaking in tongues, as Paul instructed us in First Corinthians twelve; but it is not wise to press for this particular gift. God administers this sacred gift to those whom He wills. Spiritual immaturity will pursue the gifts of God, but spiritual maturity will seek first the Kingdom of God and His righteousness.

The glory of God was so within me and about the parsonage that I couldn't begin to tell people about it. I sent Florence to bring my Sunday School superintendent and his wife, Addie. When they came into my room, I tried to tell them of the great riches God had for all who would follow Him. "It is for you," I would tell them. "God wants to do wonderful things!"

They didn't quite know what to do, but they knew God was there and it was precious. Addie knelt, praying earnestly until she was numb into the knuckles and into the toes. As she prayed she began to reach a little of the wonder I was trying to describe. "Oh, my dear ones!" she declared. "The presence of God is so great just above us! I can't tell you what I sense. If God would see fit to descend upon us, it would be marvelous what He would do in this age!" She caught a glimpse of the Spiritual Awakening God wanted to send—a true Holy Ghost Revival to the World.

I requested Orville H. to bring a dear holiness mother to see me. She answered him, "Orville, I am too sick to go; but I will send some scripture." She wrote down the verse of scripture on her daily devotional calendar: Leviticus 20:26—"And ye shall be holy unto me: for I the Lord am holy and have severed you from other people, that ye should be mine."

Think of that! Of all the verses from God's Word she could have sent me, Jesus had arranged everything so precisely that just this scripture should appear on her calendar at that date: ". . . I HAVE SEVERED YOU FROM OTHER PEOPLE, THAT YE SHOULD BE MINE." I was so thankful. I knew this scripture to be verification from God of what He had been showing me concerning my calling.

That very morning, this woman's daughter, Nora, had a vision. She lived about seventeen miles away in Roll, Indiana, and I had not seen her since she had sung for us at Oak Grove nearly four years before. But that morning she saw me standing before her. God spoke to her and said, "Go get your mother and take her to see Rev. Helm."

She hurried all the way to her mother's home. "Mother," she announced, "the Lord told me to take you to Rev. Helm."

She looked at her daughter and replied, "Why Child, he already sent for me, but I am just not able to go."

"I will dress you and take you," Nora insisted.

"I just don't think I can make it," her mother answered.

"Yes, you can." Nora said, "because God has told me to do it." She dressed her mother, helped her into the old car and brought her to see me. I still marvel that the very thing God had prompted me to work out earlier in the day, He accomplished perfectly, giving this dear mother and me a sweet time together in prayer. This was another encouragement to my heart that what I was going through in my spirit was of the Kingdom of God.

All during this time the Holy Ghost continued to fall upon me and move through me in waves of His love. He was so precious. About all I could do was praise God and give thanks to Jesus. In the days when God came upon me, slayed me, worked with me, and took out of me many things which were hindering His Spirit, I had to die out to everything. I could not do what I wanted. I had numerous responsibilities which seemed necessary and important, but I could do only that which God wanted me to do.

When He took me to the river of death, I saw that nothing mattered in this world but God's will. When I stood at the very edge of death, I knew that **nothing mattered at all but doing God's will absolutely.** Nothing else is going to last but what God directs, what He guides, what He initiates. **Nothing!**

And while God was bringing me into the depth of these marvelous revelations concerning His Kingdom and His work in the hearts of men, about all I could do was walk with Jesus and talk to the birds and the flowers. It was as if I were in another world.

God has taken us through many experiences, my friend. It is only by His grace that we have made it, for there were many pressures upon us—difficulties so immense that I am unable to share them. The pressure was this: would we bend to man or would we go with Heaven?

God will test you, dear one, to see what kind of person you are. He knows in the first place, but He is wanting us to discover it ourselves. Most people will not stand when they are put to the test. Most people have carnality, evil, and iniquity inside of them. God wants to remove that by plac-ing us in some difficult situations where we must submit everything to Him in order to make it through. But very few will press on into the struggle that God may inwardly cleanse them. Most persons will bend to the flesh and detour the path of trust, which goes right into the heart of the battle.

But if we submit, believe God, and press on in faith, He will cleanse the carnality and inner weakness out of us. It is only through Jesus Christ that we can survive the battle, and we must remain in that place of submission all the time for our hearts to remain clear, cleansed, and undefiled.

On the third morning that this precious handmaid had prayed at the altar of the church, she requested that Florence come and pray with her. This meant that I would have to care for our three children and see after the needs of the home. I was so in the Spirit, however, I couldn't do anything but walk with God and talk to Him. "Jesus," I said, "you will have to help us. I don't know what to do but trust you."

My wife went next door to the church to join this sister in prayer. (Years later this woman told us, "When Florence came into the church that morning, she looked like an angel to me." It was so important that she go to pray with her.) But how was I going to take care of our three children? Who was going to prepare the meals? How would I pay the light bill? I had no answer, I was just simply trusting Jesus to work out the situation.

Seated in a wicker chair outside on the porch at eight-thirty that morning, I looked up, and who should be driving around the corner towards the parsonage but Rebecca Pumphrey. As soon as I saw her I started rejoicing.

Rebecca stopped the car in front, came up through the yard with their little daughter, Barbara, in hand, and asked "Oh, Rev. Helm, do you need me? I'm not accustomed to the voice of God. I got up early this morning at six o'clock to wash our clothes, and I put a bucket of water in the tub to heat when God said, 'Go to the Helm's.' I put another bucket in, and the Lord would say, 'Go to Helm's.' The devil would say, 'Don't go. You have been over there every night for two weeks and have worn out your welcome.' "

As she told me I was happy. I was saying, "Praise the Lord!"

She continued, "You know, each time I put a bucket of water in the tub, the Lord said, 'Go to Helm's.' Finally I got Homer up and I said, 'Homer, pray with me because I am not accustomed to the voice of Jesus, and I think He is telling me to go over to Florence and Loran's.' He felt I should come over. I had to come. Do you need me, Brother Helm?"

I looked down at her with deep gratitude in my heart and said, "Rebecca, if ever a servant of God needed assistance, we surely need you today!"

God had told her to come just as she was, in her work dress. He knew that she was needed to look after our children. She was going to prepare the meals, purchase a few groceries, and drive in to pay the light bill. How very badly she was needed, and what a great help she was that day, no one will ever know.

The following day I was seated in the dining room looking out the window when I saw a tree—a beautiful cherry tree. It was round like the earth, and had fruits all over it just beginning to turn red. It was an early spring, way ahead of most springs that I can remember. I had never seen this tree so amply covered with fruit before, nor did I see it so afterwards.

I was lifted to a realm of a vision as I spoke out of my heart, "Jesus, that cherry tree is like the earth. As this tree rests on its trunk, the earth spins about its own axis. Oh, Jesus," I cried, "all these cherries are nearly developed fruits all over the earth. I can see them."

And He said to me, "Yes, that tree is like the earth. And as the cherries cover the whole tree, my Spirit covers the earth."

"But," I asked, "if your Spirit so richly covers the earth, why are men such spiritual skeletons? Your Spirit is so plentiful and abundant, yet we are starved."

That very second, a live dove flew into the middle of that tree. At the same instant, God spoke within me: "BY ME, THE HOLY GHOST, THEY WILL BE FED. ONLY BY ME, THE HOLY GHOST, CAN THEY BE FED." Then another dove fluttered into the tree beside its mate. God again spoke within me: "BY ME, THE HOLY GHOST, THEY WILL BE FED. THEY CAN ONLY BECOME SPIRITUAL, AS I, THE SPIRIT, FEED THEM."

He was revealing to my heart that **you and I cannot do anything without the leadership of the Holy Spirit.** Unless God begins something by His Holy Spirit, our labor cannot bring life to it. He was trying to help me see that His guidance, His leadership, His **will** was supreme above all our finest goals or fondest hopes. —"BY ME, THE HOLY GHOST, THEY WILL BE FED. ONLY BY ME, THE HOLY GHOST, CAN THEY BE FED."

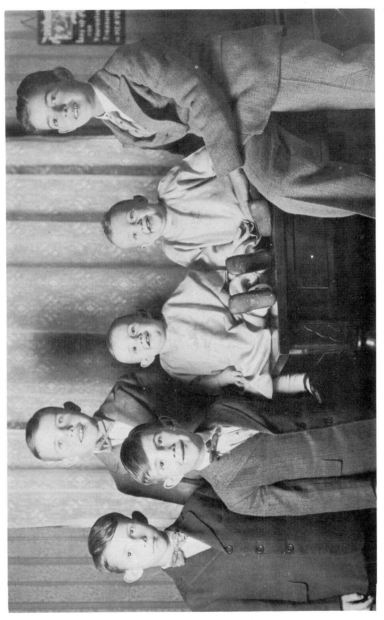

1927—Warren, Terrance, Richard, Edward, Edwin, and Loran.
Behind Loran's left shoulder a plaque which appropriately
reads: "Lay up for yourselves treasures in Heaven."

20 THE CALLING

At the baptism of the Holy Spirit, wave after wave of divine love came through me. This love of God was so marvelous that I am unable to adequately explain it. It was not worked up, it was a gift of Jesus through the Holy Spirit—the pure love of God to all men, even to my enemies.

If someone is persecuting you (and all who live godly in Christ Jesus shall suffer persecution), your reaction will reveal how much love of Jesus you have. If persons are telling lies about you, spreading rumors and tearing you to pieces with their tongues, then you find out how sufficient God's love is in your heart and how His love is flowing through you.

When you are in severe trial and battle, be encouraged. Many things will occur to let us see where we are within, for our reactions tell more about us than our actions. And when we are in great struggle, we learn the real condition of our hearts. If God did not let us know the weakness of our own natures, then we would not lean upon Him for all strength.

We all have our little tests and trials. It might be while eating breakfast at a fine restaurant: as you take the first bite of scrambled eggs, your teeth come down with a crunch on egg shells. So you say, "Praise the Lord," put that bite out of your mouth, and try another. Crunch!—And you discover still more egg shells. Now what is your response? Do you call the waitress over, tell her how terrible the egg shells are, declare your disappointment with the food, and make certain remarks about the cook? No—you simply praise the Lord some more.

Travelling in evangelistic work, we eat many of our meals in restaurants and homes. On one occasion we were dining in a fairly nice establishment when I ordered a lovely salad. I had taken but a few bites when I discovered hair in my mouth. Before long I found more hair in my mouth. Then my fork lifted a whole wad of woman's hair right out of the middle of my salad. What did I do? Why, by God's grace, I remained calm and undisturbed.

It is our reaction which reveals our heart. It is how we react to the little everyday things, when everything seems to go wrong, that tells us about ourselves. Our response shows us how alive Self is, for Self reacts. But if Self is denied, one can be joyous and victorious in Jesus through all experiences. You can say, "Glory! Praise the Lord!" in spite of circumstances.

Situations will occur to test us, to try our reactions. We were dining with two ministers and their companions when this precious waitress came from the kitchen with a tray full of food and accidently tipped it over on me. Meat, vegetables, and sauces tumbled down over the side of my suit coat and onto my trousers. "Praise the Lord," I said.

She was extremely distressed and ready to cry. "Don't feel badly," I told her; "it was supposed to happen."

While I was down on the floor trying to help clean up the food with towels, the manager came out and remarked, "Say, I would like to hire you."

"Oh, I have done this before," I told him. "I cleaned floors when I was a boy. These things happen to test us." I kept telling the waitress, "Don't cry, dear one, this can happen to anyone. Don't feel badly about it."

When things are hard, lift everyone around you. The self-denied life is taught this. Don't be grumpy and grouchy, making it difficult for people. Some individuals, you know, can become slightly irritable or harsh. But we are to keep

194

our hearts filled with joy and victory. We are to praise God in every test and trial.

When people are down-hearted and dark, praise God and let your light shine. Remember the song, "Hold out your light ye Heaven bound pilgrims"? Don't attempt to arrange places and events where your light could shine: merely let it shine brightly where you are. Rejoice and claim the victory for Jesus right where you live, in little day-by-day struggles and trials.

When everything goes wrong and nothing seems right, God wants us to deny Self and the reaction of the flesh. God wants us to die to that inner compulsion to complain, to retaliate, or to become angry. He wants us to be inwardly crucified. When the bus is not on time, when the train does not arrive, when the plane must circle the airport for an hour, when the car won't start—we are to "Rejoice in the Lord alway, and again I say, rejoice."

The factor which decides how we react in these situations is what we are in our hearts, whether Self has been denied or not. If Self is denied, it will be a dying, but this death will bring us to marvelous things. This moment by moment death will lead us to the glorious secrets of the hidden life in Christ.

These are but little things, tiny situations which are common to all men; but they can be used to prepare us for greater assignments. These are elementary lessons in the kindergarten of walking with God to prepare us for responsibility in His Kingdom months and years in the future.

It will be only by God's grace that we can react rightly. Self, you see, always reacts wrongly. Self will come short of a Christ-like response. We cannot praise God in ourselves. But to the one who has been obedient, God will send grace for the moment and give strength for the hour. We cannot, because we can only fail. But the Holy Spirit will undergird the trusting heart in the test. He will enable you; He will be with you and keep you. Yes, He will! Praise the Lord.

In those weeks and months that God was slaying me in the

inner man, I was learning this. All these reactions of Self had to be cleansed out of me before He could fill me with His Spirit. If God had done otherwise, it would have been dangerous. For Him to pour His power into an uncleansed vessel would be like putting high amperage electricity through weak and damaged wires: it could possibly destroy the wires and burn everything around them.

But when He baptized me in His Spirit, it was manifested by an overwhelming love from the Father for all men every-where. I believe that God wanted to send this same love to every heart in that community. And because God was truly trying to work through that village, Satan was raging. Few understood what was happening, but Satan was determined to destroy us and what God wanted to do through us.

As I walked through the streets of that village, I would feel as if there were lions wanting to tear me apart. The people of the village were very precious, just as precious as any people on earth, but the devil was raving to make them upset at us. When I stood to preach to my people, there was such love of Jesus flowing through me to them, but I felt as if some of their spirits would tear me apart.

A neighboring minister said to me during this time, "If people felt about me like they do about you, I would move out immediately."

But I told him, "Oh, Brother—God's men never run from a battle. When the battle begins to rage, God's men rejoice." I was as happy in the midst of this tempestuous struggle as if everyone were for me. Now it takes Jesus to give such happiness and rest when all around you is misunderstanding and discontent. This is far beyond man. It comes from God. Praise the Lord!

One person remarked, "I don't know what it is, but I want to go down to that parsonage and throw rotten eggs at it." I was informed by another friend that he feared some people would try to burn us alive in the parsonage. The Lord told me, however, if those dear persons would have started for our home with this in mind that they would never have gotten there, because God's angels were guarding us. We were unworthy of this; but you see, it was out of man's hands. We were in the hand of God, trusting Him like little children.

What had caused this great upheaval? Why was much of hell enraged against a youngster attempting to preach the Gospel?

I believe, dear friend, it was because of the Call which God had placed upon this unworthy servant's life. I believe it was due to the claims of the Kingdom of Heaven declared upon me while I lay on my bed for days, when God was slaying me, working with me, and talking with me day and night.

To help you better understand what I mean by this, I must share with you an experience in heavenly things which I did not include earlier. I trust you will receive it very prayerfully and with great appreciation, because it belongs wholly to Jesus, to the Kingdom of God.

You may recall that prior to this period of inner slaying and dying out to the world, I repeatedly told my wife, "God is calling us to something. I know that there is something that He is calling us to, but I am unable to discern exactly what it is." I knew that souls were being saved and sanctified under our ministry, the Lord working through us; bodies were being healed and dear ones were pressing to obey Jesus; but somehow within me I knew that the pastorate was not where God had called me. We were not striving to find out anything, we were simply trusting Jesus. We were not trying to work out anything, we were just waiting upon God the best that we knew how.

It was on the evening of the day the Holy Spirit baptized me that I finally understood the sacred calling which God had placed upon my life. That night I was still very much in the Spirit while in prayer upon my bed. I was looking to Jesus when suddenly I saw a saint of God standing before me in a beautiful light! She was a praying saint. "Jesus!" I said. "This is the Kingdom of God!" I was so humbled and felt my great unworthiness before God.

She vanished, and then there appeared before me a light not like the lights of this world. It was rectangular, approximately four feet long and two to three feet high, like the frame of a picture. Within this border of light I then saw words written in light. To my amazement I read the words: "I WILL LEAD THEE BY THE HOLY GHOST."

There was other writing in light as well, but I could not read it. God withheld it. All I could perceive was that God was going to lead me by the Holy Ghost, which was beyond my comprehension. Think how serious this is! I saw in light before me the message from God Himself: "I WILL LEAD THEE BY THE HOLY GHOST."

The other writing below was yet none of my business. I do not try to find out what I am not supposed to know. I only trust for whatever He wants to share with me. I am not worthy of even the very least revelation He has to give. It is only His great love and mercy that would ever permit me to know anything again. I am so glad that He taught me at the age of twenty-six not to try to find out anything, not to press to learn divine things, but just to trust Him: simply let Him teach me in His own way and at His own time.

When I saw the message, "I will lead thee by the Holy Ghost," I felt like Moses. I cannot explain to you how it was, but through my head, throughout my body, I felt like Moses trying to get the children of Israel out of Egypt—out of the wilderness, out of their wanderings—into Canaan.

Somehow God placed me into the life experience of Moses, and I was trying to get the church out of self-assertion into self-denial and obedience; out of the continous wandering amid forms and programs into a consecrated surrender to Jesus Christ. I didn't know this inner revelation was going to occur, but I felt it throughout all my body.

When this experience passed, dear friend, I was at once with Jesus. There was a great light above me, but high above

198

this was Jesus, the Son of God, the precious Christ of the God of Israel.

Suddenly I was standing with the apostles of two thousand years ago, with the inner circle—Peter, James, and John. They had already made the crossing to life eternal and were standing tall and straight, but I had not yet crossed over. Instead, I was pressed down with a heavy load upon my back. I was bent over with the weight of the churches, the load of the world upon my back. I was trying to look up at Jesus, but I could hardly see Him because my load was so great. The responsibility is so great in this world to help people be absolutely true and faithful to Jesus.

(After preaching one night in Saint Louis, I noticed that the pastor's wife was weeping. At the close of the service she told me, "Rev. Helm, while you were preaching I saw a big weight upon your back. I saw a load that you were carrying."

(I said to her, "That great weight was upon me the night God declared His call to me—the declaration of God to be His Apostle.")

As I stood with the apostles of Jesus, I finally knew what God had called me to at the age of five years when He said, "You belong to me. I will use you in my Kingdom someday." (God witnesses within me now as I share this with you.) I knew then that the Call was sacred beyond all the languages of men to express.

When this heavenly vision vanished, the powers of hell surged into that room in torrents of darkness. Demons by the multiplied thousands or millions (and the Holy Spirit tells me "millions") were over my head and calling me things that I cannot share with you. In the next few years these same accusations came through the lips of unbelieving people in various states.

But I wanted to be nothing but holy unto God. I desired to be a true man of God. I longed to be pure, without blemish, without spot, without wrinkle. I had to resist the devil with

199

all my might. "The devil is a liar," I said. "I am going with Jesus Christ!"

These demon forces came in upon me with great power and were trying to crush me. It seemed as if they put me in a vise and started to squeeze me to death. "You cannot answer this call," they hurled at me. "It is impossible to answer this holy call."

I cried out, "Oh God!—With all my heart I am coming!"

Satan began to flood my inner vision with pictures. I saw events which he threatened would take place if I followed Jesus with all my heart. "If you follow God in this sacred calling," Satan told me, "your wife will be taken from you. You will lose your babies. You will lose your parents, your in-laws. All the people will leave you." There is no way to convey the horror and hellishness of this satanic struggle.

I said with all my heart: "Good-bye loved ones—good-bye precious wife and children—good-bye Mother and Dad. I am going with you, Jesus. I am coming, God! With all my heart I am coming with you, God!" (Hallelujah! Oh, I feel the power of God operating all through me as I share this with you! I'm not just telling a story. This is of the Kingdom of God. I share this only for the glory of Jesus.)

I had to say good-bye to everybody on earth and to everything of earth. Satan told me that I would lose them all, but it has been the reverse. If we go with Jesus, He will give everything we need back to us sweeter than ever. I found it so. Praise the Lord.

The battle with the Powers of Darkness lasted for some time that evening, until God came in wonder to simply drive back the multiplied millions of demons. Since that night, much of hell has been against my ministry. From that moment till this, Satan has attempted to cast suspicion upon my life by spreading rumors and whisperings concerning me, especially among church leaders. False stories about me began to circulate throughout the states, reaching as far as Canada.

But, by God's grace, I loved everyone just the same, and

still do. The love of Jesus poured through me to all men alike. I loved those who talked about me as much, if not more, than my friends. I was not worthy of this marvelous love of Jesus, but He sent it through me anyway.

God is to be praised for this. He is the One we honor. In all that we share, it is only for the glory of God, the honor of Jesus the beloved Son, the praise of the blessed Holy Spirit.

Rev. and Mrs. A. E. Helm with Loran and Richard, 1918.

21 SPIRITUAL BURDENS

Since the declaration of my Calling in April of 1942 I had been anticipating and longing for the Holy Ghost Revival to the World which would precede the return of Jesus. The Lord had instructed me to wait upon Him, and in November of that year we began prayer meetings in anticipation and preparation for this mighty outpouring from God. Nightly we waited upon the Lord, trusting Jesus to direct as He saw fit by the Holy Spirit. We waited for weeks and months.

Night after night I was expecting God to pour out His Spirit. Out under the stars I would look up into the night sky and say, "Jesus, you are surely going to pour out your Holy Spirit tonight in the Great Awakening." My soul was longing for His presence and His power to move upon a sin-darkened and sin-crippled world. He had begun this Revival of the Holy Ghost in my heart at the baptism of the Spirit, and wanted to send it through every heart in that community to all the world.

But the Holy Ghost Revival was held back. In fact, the Lord revealed to me the person in that village who was the key to this community. Everyone respected and loved this individual. In depression times he would let a dollar bill fall in front of a man who had no money so that he might get something to eat. Going to him one day I said, "My Brother, if you will go with Jesus, put Christ first, do God's will, be at Sunday morning, Sunday evening, and prayer meeting services, in so many weeks there will be twenty men and their families in church. The wheels of God's glorious Kingdom will begin to move through this community."

He was behind the counter of his business when I shared this revelation. He merely looked at me and answered, "That might be." Those were the only words he said. It was the last God ever had me speak to him.

Jesus revealed to me that he was the key, but he did not sense how serious it was to hold such a position. It was not a position which he had specifically sought, nor was it an official office voted on by the people. It was a seat of high influence which he held by nature of his innate gifts, his personality, and his esteem among those who knew him. He may not have known it, but he was the primary leader of the community, though no official title had been given him.

Seldom do individuals of position or authority recognize the awesome weight which rests upon their actions and decisions. They have come to these places in the community because of the gifts and talents which God has placed within them. But they are not made stewards of these gifts for self-advancement alone—these are the investment of God for use in His Kingdom at His time. We need to pray for those in positions of leadership within our churches and communities that they will humble themselves to go with Jesus, for the cost of their disobedience and self-assertion will be great in eternity.

There is no way to tell how many souls were waiting on this particular man to give up his own desires in order to do God's will. If he had humbled himself and pressed to the cross, it probably would have touched many lives in that community. Then those lives would have perhaps influenced hundreds of others to be missionaries and evangelists. And, through the obedience of all of these, there is no way of knowing how many thousands or millions of lives all around the world would have been spared from hell.

You see, the responsibility of each person quickly becomes greater and greater. I tremble to think of the blood that will

204

drip from the fingers of those in eternity who have not used their influence while on earth wholly for the cause of Christ. The Word tells us, "To whom much is given, much is required." It is not popular to make these things known, but I must warn everyone how straight and narrow this Way is. From November, 1942 until June 7, 1943, we met almost every night to wait and pray for this mighty outpouring of God's Spirit. Jesus would lead and help us, talk to us of His Kingdom, and reveal Himself to us. Often we sang the mighty hymns of Zion. One song in particular spoke to my heart during this time. The stanzas read:

> Keep thyself pure! Christ's soldier, hear
> Thro' life's loud strife the call rings clear.
> Thy Captain speaks: His word obey;
> So shall thy strength be as thy day.

> Keep thyself pure! Thrice blessed He
> Whose heart from taint of sin is free.
> His feet shall stand where saints have trod,
> He with rapt eyes shall see his God.

> Keep thyself pure! For He who died,
> Himself for thy sake sanctified.
> Then hear Him speaking from the skies,
> And victor o'er temptation rise.

> Oh Holy Spirit, keep us pure,
> Grant us thy strength when sins allure.
> Our bodies are Thy temple, Lord;
> Be thou in tho't and act adored. Amen *

The cry of my heart was to be pure within. My longing was to be absolutely holy unto God; wholly cleansed and sanctified for His purpose. I yearned to be fully His in every room of my soul, every corridor of my heart, and in every fibre of my mind and body.

We have been trusting and believing for this Awakening now for nearly thirty years. By God's grace, our hope has not dimmed, our confidence has not slackened. These years of

* Words by Adelaide M. Plumtre, 1908, from "New Songs for Service," The Rodeheaver Hall-Mack Company, Winona Lake, Indiana, 1963.

waiting have seemed but a little while. My soul has been delighted to continue waiting upon the Lord, learning how to be led of the Spirit and how to obey His instructions.

The Holy Spirit was teaching me about burdens during this time, also. I didn't know what a burden was. I had heard persons speak of "burdens," but I thought they meant a concern for someone: a situation of trial or trouble with which they were acquainted. The Holy Spirit began to teach me, however, that a burden was actually a message about a need somewhere in the earth—a message of divine origin, not of my own understanding or knowledge. It was not an easy lesson to learn, for spiritual lessons are often grasped slowly.

I walked with God many years before I knew what a burden was like or where it was located in the earth. One night, as we were waiting for the Holy Spirit to be poured out upon the Church, a burden came upon me. I had no one to teach me about the inner operations of the Holy Spirit. I have learned this little by little, **over many years,** as I have walked with Jesus. God began to teach me as I waited hours a day on my knees. Some days I would wait only thirty-five minutes, other days five hours and longer. I did not know what this burden was that night, but I was so thankful that the Lord had taught me to recognize it as a burden for someone.

Many of the saints are burdened, have a heavy heart, and feel pressed in their spirits. This is a spiritual operation of the soul and the body. This cannot be explained in words; it can only be experienced by a person who will consistently deny Self and obey the leading of the Holy Spirit. Often when God gives some humble follower a burden, Satan will attack the mind or the nervous system with the accusation: "You have failed!"

But it is just the opposite: God has probably entrusted you with a burden. The need may be anywhere in the earth. It might be for one thousand people to be saved in the islands of the sea, or for the healing of a person a block away. The primary burden of the saints of God today is the professed church on earth.

Many times incidents will occur in your life and you will wonder why they have happened. Often God is seeking to instruct you through these circumstances, but Satan is attempting to confuse and camouflage the lesson. "See now," Satan will buffet and accuse, "you are having a hard time." If you walk with God, Satan will tell you that you haven't the victory, that you have committed sin, that you are not going to make it to Heaven. We must resist these thoughts, for he is a liar and the father of all lies. Jesus would never tell us such things. And if thoughts are not of God, we simply must resist them, no matter how reasonable they might appear.

God has revealed to me that many saints of His are being buffeted and don't know what to do. They need a shepherd somewhere to pray with them and say, "Get hence, Satan! This soul belongs to Jesus!" God's people need to be encouraged. They need to be lifted up and strengthened.

When a true follower of Jesus is a recipient of a burden, he may feel heavy-hearted, somewhat nervous, or even upset. The Holy Spirit is attempting to communicate to that heart a need somewhere on the earth and use him as an instrument of intercession in the Kingdom of God. But Satan is also there to buffet, hurt, and accuse. Many of you possibly have been buffeted in the last few days.

We can be alerted to Satan's voice by the fact that he tends to accuse us in the mind, bringing a number of failings or shortcomings to our attention at once, in order to cause confusion. On the other hand, Jesus speaks gently and lovingly to the heart, focusing our thoughts on a single place where we have failed in order that we may ask forgiveness and not do that certain thing again.

When this burden came upon me, I began to pray for the church, the community, the people near me, on and on. Finally I prayed for my father's brothers and sisters. When

I came to Peter C. Helm, the power of the Holy Spirit witnessed. I knew this was my burden.

The body is the temple of the Holy Spirit. If you are completely yielded, the Holy Spirit possesses all of you. The body is like a piano or a typewriter. God can say many things through it if you will only be yielded to His hand. It will take many years of waiting upon Him and walking with Him before you will begin to learn to recognize what an "a" is like or a "b" is like. But God desires to teach us if we are willing to wait.

However, one cannot expect to read the Hebrew language in a short while. Each lesson must be mastered in sequence in order that we understand properly. If we miss a lesson, our comprehension will be lessened. This is how we learn to walk with God. As we obey the Holy Spirit moment by moment, day after day, He brings us gradually into the place of understanding, by His gifts and His Spirit. (By "gifts" I mean the gifts of "discernment" and of "helps" as discussed in First Corinthians 12:10,28.)

I must again underscore the fact that **we do not study to learn these mysteries of God.** They are not wrested from their hiding place by intellect or by human insight. These mysteries are revealed unto babes, as Jesus tells us in Matthew 11:25; "I thank thee Father, Lord of Heaven and earth, because thou hast hid these things from the wise and the prudent, and hast revealed them unto babes."

Spiritual secrets are given unto those who fear God—to the meek and lowly of heart, the child-like in Spirit, the self-denied pilgrim. They can only be trusted to the crucified heart, for only the heart dead to the earth and its goals will give back to God all the glory. Only the broken and contrite spirit will permit God to use these gifts and revelations as He sees fit and at His own time.

I began to pray for Uncle Peter Helm that God would strengthen, encourage, and deliver him. I was so thrilled! You see, when the power of God fell all over me, I knew for the first time how to locate my burden! God taught me. Now don't become discouraged if you do not understand all that God is doing with you. I had to walk with God for years before I knew what a burden was. Then I continued to walk with Him in order to be taught how to locate my burden. One is taught these lessons best as he obeys humbly each leading of the Holy Spirit and remains childlike in his heart.

The glory of God fell as soon as I came before the Throne with the exact petition which God willed that I pray. I was delighted! When the power of God fell all around, the dear ones with me received the blessing as well.

The following evening we expectantly made our way to see Uncle Peter C. Helm. "I want to ask you a question," I said to him. "What were you doing last night around seven-thirty to eight-thirty?"

Looking at me, he answered, "Loran William, after a difficult day I was sitting in this chair by the stove wondering: 'Lord, have You had Loran William pray for me?'"

I was rejoicing! "Uncle Pete," I explained, "I had a real prayer meeting for you last evening. The Holy Spirit gave me the revelation of your situations. He privileged me, through Jesus, to pray to God for you!"

Uncle Pete and I were thrilled. It was my first experience of locating a burden after walking with God for nearly ten years. It took many years before I knew what God was wanting to do with me. It's by God's grace that I will ever know again. It has often been my experience that when I say "Amen" as I finish prayer, the Lord reveals for me to pray on. This is when real prayer begins, for the Holy Spirit prays through me then, revealing burdens in the church, in the nations, in bodies, in the earth.

The Lord will possibly burden you for some need in the future. Always be thankful for it. The more appreciative you are, the more He may lead you. I believe that God leads in proportion to our delight and our trust in Him. People become so excited about new clothes, new homes, and new cars. But I am more delighted over the leading of the Holy Spirit and the things of God's Kingdom. Often our lack of praise prevents us from receiving something we have long desired. But if you truly revel in the things of God, He will give you the desires of your heart.

Since 1941 I have not desired any earthly thing more than I have longed to do only God's will. Over the years He has been merciful to instruct me concerning His revelations, and I am only in the kindergarten learning my ABC's (John 16:13). After these years of instruction He is able to tell me whether my burden is for a need of the soul, for healing in the body or the mind, for storms, earthquakes, or for situations and conditions upon the earth: peril, darkness, danger, accident, evil, iniquity, war, struggle between nations, or whatever.

There is no need to think this strange or unprecedented, for Jesus told His disciples in John 14:26: "The Comforter, which is the Holy Ghost, whom the Father will send in my name, **He shall teach you all things,** and bring all things to your remembrance, whatsoever I have said unto you."

There is a tendency for us to relate this scripture only to the disciples who were hearing the promise from the lips of our Lord in person. However, God has demonstrated to His children time and time again that He wishes to instruct us daily in the mysteries of His Kingdom. **In fact, unless the Holy Spirit Himself instructs us, we will not really know anything about God's Kingdom. We will only be supposing and guessing.**

It is only as He leads and directs us day by day that we can truly be used in His Kingdom work. All our attempts at spiritual endeavors are still strivings in the flesh, and Paul tells us very clearly in Romans 8:8 that "They that are in the flesh cannot please God."

The fact that God desires to teach us was stated by Isaiah (54:13) and given absolute authority when Jesus told his questioners: "It is written in the prophets, and they shall be all taught of God." (John 6:45) It is imperative, therefore, that we be instructed how the Holy Spirit leads—how He checks us and how He talks to us about needs throughout the earth.

Now for some who have accustomed themselves to analyze spiritual processes and construct rational explanations for every phenomenon, the fact that God would burden a saint for some need far across the ocean could appear strange. I am certain that some would be tempted to ask also, "Why would God have someone pray about storms or earthquakes?"

I would not attempt to explain the "why" of God's marvelous love toward us. That He sent Jesus to die for us is so immense a display of self-giving that my limited mind is not able to grasp it, even forty years after my conversion. But I do know through considerable experience that God shares a few of the countless needs around the earth with those who are in tune with Him, because He has somehow allowed us to be included in the working of His great and mighty Kingdom here on earth.

There are a number of passages in God's Word which are not immediately obvious in meaning; but, at the same time, I am certain that God has veiled volumes of insights and understandings within the pages of this sacred Book which our dull hearts have been unable to perceive. In my walk with God I have not insisted on a specific interpretation of certain scriptures and then searched for facts to substantiate my belief. I have simply believed God's Word as it stands, looked to Jesus for all things, and sought to obey Him continually. As I have followed, He has taught me a fragment of His love and of His wisdom. I have been delighted to also discover along this path of obedience, that He demonstrates within me and through me the truths of His Word in ways that surpass my thoughts about them.

This is to be expected, of course, for the apostle Paul reviewed the prophet's words to the church of Corinth by saying: "But as it is written, eye hath not seen, nor ear heard, neither have entered into the heart of man the things which God hath prepared for them that love Him. But God hath revealed them unto us by His Spirit: for the Spirit searcheth all things, yea, the deep things of God."

These verses plainly indicate that what God has for us in this life—things both spiritual and physical—is beyond any-thing we ever imagined. Many feel that this verse refers primarily to our heavenly reward, but Heaven is beyond "things." "Things" are of the earth. Paul was endeavoring to alert Christians to the little-known fact that all about them in the earth are waiting marvelous things. We receive them one by one as we trust God, deny Self, surrender our own ideas of how God's Kingdom should operate, and obey the Holy Spirit continually. They are already prepared for us; but if we do not wait on God, following patiently under a cross, we will pass by these hidden treasures and never know it.

They are not perceived by great talent and ability. They are recognized only by the help of the Holy Spirit's revelation. Some of these treasures will concern spiritual secrets; others will be jewels of His family whom He will permit you to meet along the trail. At other times they will be surprises of a more temporal nature, such as clothing, furniture, a home. One is always unworthy of even the smallest gift, but we can praise God all the more for providing one so unworthy with that which was needed.

We know that the "Spirit searcheth all things," for God knows the tiniest detail about all things which exist in, around, about, and through this earth, this galaxy, and the galaxies beyond. It is not unreasonable that His heart of love would long to share some of the earth's sufferings with His beloved sons and daughters that they might pray and intercede for divine intervention. And if it still appears to be beyond the realm of reason, by God's grace, I can tell you that it is a fact.

The other morning I called one of my dearest brothers before he could leave for work. His precious companion answered the phone. "Oh, Brother Helm! How glad I am that you called. R. is so burdened down."

When R. got on the phone he was so exhausted that he

could scarcely talk. "Brother!—" he managed to say. "I don't know what is the matter with me. I came home from church last night and I could hardly make it to bed. Now, even after sleeping all night, I don't know whether I can manage to work or not."

As I began to pray, the Lord revealed to my heart that He was burdened for the sanctification of many souls in the professed Church of God in the earth. The moment we discerned the intercession which God wanted and lifted that petition to the Throne, his burden lifted like a cloud. His strength revived and he felt like a different person.

"Brother!" he exclaimed. "This is the most rest I have had in several hours. I feel as if I have had a vacation!" It was because the burden had lifted. He told me later that the glory of the Lord was all about him that day at work.

While recovering from surgery in Logansport hospital in November, 1970, the Holy Spirit spoke to me very early one morning, revealing that I was to call a young couple in Tennessee. By God's help, the nurses permitted me to call out of that hospital from my bed at five-thirty in the morning. J. answered the phone and said, "Well, praise the Lord! B. hasn't been able to sleep all night. She has been in such turmoil and struggle."

I began to pray and found thirty to forty burdens which she was carrying for storms, earthquakes, bodies to be healed, persons in mental upheaval, souls to be convicted, converted, reclaimed, cleansed, and sanctified all over the earth. The needs were many, but the Holy Spirit led us to locate each burden and lift it in prayer. J. and B. could discern in their hearts each burden along with me, by the witness of the Holy Spirit. B. said, to God's glory, that after the revelation and prayer, it seemed as if she had received a night's rest.

Many times in the past years the Lord has been gracious to help me pray for burdens which saints of God have been carrying. It is only by His gifts and His love that this could be done, and I thank Him for every privilege He gives me.

213

One morning I had only a few minutes to accomplish several matters of business: I wanted to get to the post office, visit the Chevrolet garage, and transact business at the bank before it closed. As I started for the bank the Holy Spirit spoke within me: "Don't go to the bank. Go to Sister W's." That meant the bank would be closed before I could get there. What was I to do? There was only one thing to do— go to this home and forget everything I had planned. When God leads to stop what I am doing, the Lord helping me, I proceed no farther.

This dear saint of God opened the door that day, looked into my face, and sighed, "Oh, Brother Loran, how did you know I needed you this morning? I am so pressed down I don't know what's the matter with me!"

"Praise the Lord!" I encouraged her. "Be glad. You have a burden."

"Is that what's wrong with me?" she asked. We began to pray, and the Lord revealed that her burden was for four souls living within a radius of four to five miles of Parker who needed to be saved. We lifted her burden to the Throne of Grace, the power of the Spirit came, and the burden was gone. She was so thrilled. She knew God had undertaken because the heaviness, the weight, lifted as soon as we prayed. She felt pressed down because God wanted the burden of these four lives to rest upon her long enough in order that she could lift their souls to Jesus.

God wants to lead all of His children. He wishes to teach us the movings of His Spirit; to reveal the various ways He leads and directs, helps and instructs. **And He can do this only as we wait upon Him, as we deny Self second by second, and as we press to the cross joyfully in consistent obedience.**

The question naturally arises: "How do I recognize a burden?"

First of all, we must review that we do not seek a burden. We do not strive to be used by God in specific patterns or in special ways. Among you dear ones who believe my explanation of the mystery of burdens to be true, a certain number will immediately have a desire: "Oh, teach me, Lord! Lead me. Help me to know how to bear burdens!" But our seeking to be led will be misguided by the flesh. I have never endeavored to be led. I have merely sought to love God and worship Him. As I waited in His presence, He began to slay out of me hindrances in my nature. These had to be crucified in order that there would be no earthly intrusion of the mortal mind to prevent God's will and His revelation.

Do not strive to be led. Simply wait on the Lord and let Him refine you. If we begin to seek for something, we may get a result, but it well might not be of God. Our assignment is to simply trust God, obey continually, praise Him often, and love Him for Himself alone. Do not seek any specific type of experience. Strive only to be filled with His love for all persons. He will send to you what you need at His own time.

Secondly, do not try to look for burdens or situations which need prayer. We are not to look for troubles, problems, faults, or difficulties, for we will quickly discover much more than we could possibly handle. According to the exhortation of Philippians 4:8 we are to think only on things true, honest, just, pure, lovely, and of good report. Be consistent in reading the Word, in talking with God, in witnessing, and humbly obeying the Holy Spirit. Fill your life with much praise and God will reveal to your heart the burdens for which He wishes you to pray.

If any problems of loved ones, friends, or persons of your acquaintance attract your attention, do not dwell on them. Simply lift the need immediately to God and leave it there. Neither brood over situations nor mull them over in your mind. Let Jesus carry the load, for you will not be able to bear the griefs and sorrows of even one little village, let alone the world.

Thirdly, you may recognize that Jesus has entrusted you with a burden when you feel pressed down for no certain reason. Satan may attempt to tell you that you have sinned or backslidden; but you are to resist him. Search your soul and ask God to bring to mind any place where you might have fallen short of His will. Ask Him to forgive and cleanse from your heart anything that might have grieved or hurt Him.

If the heaviness does not lift from your heart and the joy of Jesus is not within your soul as you once experienced it, it could be that the Holy Spirit has entrusted you with a burden. This operation of the Spirit might be for any number of needs around the earth: for souls to be converted in Africa, for bodies to be healed where you work, or for a storm in Europe. We can know what the spiritual operation means only by the witness of the Holy Spirit.

Many persons are striving to learn the secret of intercession by reading books on prayer or attending prayer retreats. These activities are fine, but the fact is that we can agonize and labor in prayer for months and not once prevail with God. **The key to actual prevailing prayer is praying the exact petition which God desires.** And it is as we wait upon God in adoration and praise that He can more quickly lead us to that petition which it is His will that we make.

Because of His gifts and the precious instruction of Jesus through these many years, when a burden operates within me, I pray over the possibilities among the many concerns. When I reach the correct one, the Holy Spirit witnesses to my heart that this is the burden. Then I lift my heart in intercession until He helps me to know the exact petition which He desires. Often I can tell in my heart, by the witness of the Spirit, when the correct petition is made. The burden then lifts, or He tells me of another which needs further prayer.

Do not become confused by trying to locate the burden exactly. After many years of humble obedience you may be able to learn more in these sacred areas of prayer. In this precious beginning, however, simply present the situation to God. Lift the need by saying, "Jesus, here is this burden.

You know what is is, Lord. I give it to you." As you continue to pray, I believe the burden will lift, and that you will sometimes know when you have reached the appropriate petition. God will teach you little by little.

Most of us are impatient. We want to understand immediately all that is to be known. But God does not work that way. He moves very, very slowly; yet, He moves as rapidly as our trust will permit Him. **We learn swiftest by simply trusting and not seeking answers or insights.** This is one of the great secrets of walking with God, but few will hear it.

Many think that you should be able to read a book and learn how to walk with God. They want the steps laid out— one, two, three. But God knows how little able we are to take part in such a sacred work as His Kingdom without much dying out to pride, Self, and love of power. He knows how weak we are once we learn something. Our tendency is to think that "we know it" and forget that it was only by God's infinite grace and mercy that He stooped to reveal such a wonderful mystery to such an unworthy servant.

This is the reason God's men are slow to share what God has taken years to reveal to them over the course of a patient and hidden walk, traversed in lowly submission to His will day by day. **Unless we have been slain and crucified day after day for many years, it is unlikely that we will appreciate the great cost and suffering which brought us to these marvelous gifts of God.**

I have found my walk with Jesus to be truly filled with thrills, romance, and adventure. Sometimes I ask my precious wife, "Honey, do you know anyone who is having a better time in this life than I am?" She lives with me and knows me as I really am. If you could ask her this question, I believe she would tell you that she doesn't know of anyone who is more delighted in walking with God than I have been.

But this delight is because I have not sought for gifts, insights, unusual revelations, or mighty power. I have simply tried moment by moment to love God with all my heart, exalt Jesus in all that I do, and humbly obey the Holy Spirit in everything that He tells me.

I urge you to "seek first (which actually means 'continually') the Kingdom of God and His righteousness (that is simply God's will, His way, His character), and all these things shall be added unto you." God will never come short of this promise which Jesus made. In fact, He will far exceed your expectations.

22 LEAVING ALL

On May 23, 1943 we officially left the pastorate to embark on this wonderful adventure of absolute trust in God. Naturally our parents were quite concerned about us. But I was as happy as a lark in a meadow, fish in a stream, and children at play. Very few understood us, yet it seemed as if I had many with me. There was joy in my heart and great peace in my soul. Who could give this but Jesus?

If you had a precious wife, three daughters, no salary, no idea where you were going to live—all you had was faith in God, the Word, and prayer—what would you do? Would you be downcast? Would you fret yourself with the questions: "Oh, Lord, what shall we do? Which way am I to go? What is going to happen to us?" Oh, no. You rejoice, look to Jesus, and trust Him more. If it had been our own personal decision to leave everything and live wholly by faith, we would never have lasted. But since it was the Holy Spirit who had called us to follow Jesus and trust Him entirely, we knew He would provide for us.

Our folks, and most of our friends, were asking, "Where will you go?"

I answered, "I don't know. I am going with Jesus."

"Where is that?" they questioned.

"I don't know."

"You have a wife and three children. How are you going to live?"

"I am going to live by faith."

"What are your plans?"

"They are in the hands of God," I answered.

My wife's father came to me and quietly inquired, "I would like to ask you one question, Son." (Now if you had an only daughter married to a young man who didn't know where he was going to live, didn't know where he was going to get a loaf of bread, had no idea where his children would go to school the next day, and was thought peculiar by nearly everyone—how would you feel? Would you be a little concerned?)

I said, "What is it, Dad?"

"I would just like to ask you," he continued, "if you think you will be able to make a living for your family?"

It took a lot of courage for him to approach me with this question. He would never have said a word if someone had not persuaded him to ask me, for he and I were very close friends. He was one man who believed me. Whenever I told him something, he knew it was a fact (and I can sense that now within me as I tell you about it).

I said, "Dad . . . ," and began to share with him how God had called me when I was a little boy; how He spoke to me in my heart at the age of five years, saying, "You belong to me. I will use you in my Kingdom someday." I told him how God had led me, how He had called me to leave everything to follow Him in simple trust.

After I had given him the story, he looked at me and declared, "That is good enough for me. It is nobody else's business, and I am for you." Those are the only words he ever said regarding the matter, and he never questioned me again after that. He was always my friend.

My own parents at that time were crushed and deeply hurt. (My mother no longer remembers this, but some of my brothers recall it vividly.) They had worked and sacrificed to provide me with a fine education. They had prayerfully hoped that I would someday become a pastor of a large urban church and be recognized within the religious world. Now it looked as if their twenty-seven-year-old son was throw-

ing his entire future away. Theirs was not an easy assignment. Nearly all parents would not have understood, unless
it had been revealed by the witness of the Holy Spirit.

When I left everything to go with God, my father asked,
"Son, how will you live? How will you have any finance?
You're not going to have a job. You don't have any meetings
scheduled. You mean to tell me that you just plan to read
the Bible, pray, and wait?"

I answered, "Well, Dad, I'm going to trust Jesus. I don't
know about the future; I am simply going to believe."

"Son," he replied, "I think that within two years you will
come to ask me for financial assistance."

I told this one that I loved so very, very much: "Well,
Father—I am going to trust Jesus."

That was in February, 1943. To God's glory, and only
by His grace and mercy, I can say that I have never asked
my father for one cent since September, 1937—almost six
years before the time he made the statement that I would
come to ask him for assistance. Through Jesus, I didn't need
to ask my parents or my wife's parents for help, although
either one of them would have gladly assisted us if I had
asked. I was penniless many times, but I did not tell anyone. I simply trusted God to provide.

It is only by God's infinite mercies that this was possible.
He did miracles to look after us. When it looked as if there
was no possible way for us to make it, God provided what we
needed without my asking people or telling anyone. It would
require a small book to share all the precious ways He has
provided, and we know that we are unworthy of the least
thing that He has done for us.

I began the process of locating a home for my family.
Houses were scarce during the war and in village after village
I could not locate a home. After eight days of seeking a
home, I was informed by the treasurer of the church, "The
District Elder has called and said that you must know about
a place to live today."

The pastor who followed us, Frank Y., however, let us know that he was not pressing. "You don't have to worry, Rev. Helm," he assured me. "We don't have to leave our present home until a week from next Tuesday."

"Yes," I told him, "but I don't want to be an imposition. When we move out of this home I want the floors mopped and everything cleaned. You won't have to do anything but move in." (Of course, that's the way a Christian tries to leave a home or an apartment he is vacating. He tries to leave every place better than when he first arrived, whether it is a home, a filling station, a restaurant, a church, or a school.)

I called the Earl E. Agency and spoke to Herschel, the brother of our former Sunday School Superintendent's wife, who worked there. He told me, "Brother Helm, we have had fourteen requests for rentals today and there is nothing in sight. One can hardly find anything to rent anywhere." So I rejoiced anyway. My wife and I again sought to look for a home in the surrounding area, but found nothing.

When we returned to the parsonage, Florence was rather disheartened. You would have been, too, if you were being pressured to get out of your home and had no place to go, no tangible assurance of immediate income, and less tangible promise of future finances. But Jesus gave me courage, peace, love, and light within my heart, just as if we had a lovely home already. God continuously gave this wonderful assurance in my heart that He would take care of us.

Florence wasn't actually discouraged either, by God's grace. She simply felt the pressure of the situation and would like to have had an idea of where we were going. It is natural, isn't it dear ladies, to want ten or twenty dollars or more a week to buy groceries and things? But my wife didn't know whether she was going to have two dollars, six dollars, or none. She had no guarantee of even having a roof over her head and a bed on which to sleep.

222

Together we prayed. The Holy Spirit showed me when we were first married that whenever there was a difficulty, whenever there was a trial—and we all have our little tests and trials—the first thing we must do to keep the victory was to get our arms around each other immediately and pray. God someway helped me to know this, because no one gave us this counsel before we were married. Through the years I have tried to encourage young married couples and older couples to get together with their arms around each other and pray right away when there is a difference, a trial, or a struggle.

When we had our little tests, I would get Florence in my arms and suggest, "Honey, let's pray."

She would remark, "Here?" We might have been in the kitchen while she was doing dishes, in the bathroom, or in the living room. It was often not convenient, but I would say, "Let's get on our knees and pray now." So she would put her arms around me and we would bombard Heaven, crying out to God until the darkness was passed and it seemed as if we were in our courtship days again.

Now the flesh and the devil are against couples doing this, but there is no other way to keep the victory. Every couple has struggles over money, homes, neighborhoods, children, relatives, personal life, and work. But if each partner will be willing to resist Satan immediately, lift the shield of faith, then go to prayer together at once, the darkness will be driven back and the joy of Jesus will lift you above the trial. **This is one of the secrets of a victorious marriage, but few have been willing to put it into practice consistently.**

Of course, Florence and I were not in a struggle ourselves at this time, but we were praying about the grave situation which faced us. While I was praying, the Holy Spirit revealed to me that I should go to Taylor University by way of Hartford City. Hartford City was about eight to ten miles north of Shideler, and Taylor was located at Upland some ten miles northwest of there. I rejoiced and told my wife, "Honey, let's

223

get started. God has told me to go to Taylor." When God gives me an assignment, I want to get going. No matter where it is, I love to go where God directs me to go. By God's grace, I am always thrilled.

We got into the car, turned west, and stopped at the stop sign before turning north. Now we have places to eat, places to sleep, places to study, places to play. Why not have places to pray? Since January of 1939, I have made stop highways a place for me to pray. While I was stopped, looking both directions, I offered a simple thanksgiving to God: "Thank you, Lord, for providing, keeping, guarding, guiding."

Driving north into Hartford City we turned left at the corner of Washington and Walnut. Just as I started to turn west I received word from Heaven. "Stop right here in this filling station on your right, Son," the Holy Spirit said.

I had no time to tell my wife what I was doing. I suddenly stopped the car, pulled the emergency brake, and went inside as quickly as I could. "Do you know of a home that I can rent?" I asked. "I have a wife and three children." Of course, I didn't know a single person in Hartford City.

They were unprepared for such a question, and didn't know how to answer it. Then one man said, "Say, just a minute. In three weeks there will be an apartment of three rooms available."

"Thank you very much," I replied. "That won't be sufficient. I need more than three rooms. Thank you for your kindness." And I started to leave.

"Wait!" he called out to me. "Have you inquired at the D. Agency?"

"I am sorry," I answered, "D. Agency? Where is that? I am a stranger in this town."

"That's the realtor up here," he explained. "They may have help for you."

I asked, "Where is it?"

"A block east, half a block north," he told me.

Locating the D. Agency, I inquired, "Do you have a home in this town for rent?"

"Oh, no," they advised me. "We only sell homes. It is difficult to ever find a home to rent."

"Thank you very much. I appreciate it," I said, turning to leave.

"Wait just a moment!" they called out. "Have you tried the News Times yet?"

"News Times? What is that?" I asked. "I'm a stranger here."

"That's our little newspaper," they informed me; "our evening publication."

"Where is that?"

"Half a block north, a block east, back half a block." It was just like I was going up stairsteps. Praise God!

Into the News Times office I walked and spoke to the woman behind the desk. "Pardon me. Do you know of a place in this city for rent?"

And without referring to her files, a list, or anything, she replied, "Yes, Sir. In an hour-and-a-half our edition comes out, and in it, 301 East North Street is advertised for rent. Marion G. passed the Army exam and he decided to rent rather than sell. This property will be advertised in our paper in one hour and thirty minutes."

"Praise the Lord!" I shouted in my heart. I was so thankful to hear this news. The praise was really sounding wonderfully within my soul!

She told me how to get there, and when we arrived we discovered a lovely home only eighteen months old. We were to find that it had hardwood floors, a shower downstairs, a bath upstairs. In the kitchen were beautiful cabinets and a double sink. We never had enjoyed such modern cabinets or sink, nor had our parents.

When I had asked my wife in the Fall of 1942, "Honey, will you be willing to leave everything and trust God for all things?", she asked, "Do you know anyone who ever really did this?"

"No," I answered, "but I know there are those who have done it, because the Bible says so."

"Where will we go?"

"I don't know," I answered her, "but God will give us a hut or a cottage somewhere." I pled with her to let our bodies be mattresses for our children, if need be, and go with God entirely.

In two days she declared, "I am ready to go." By God's grace that settled it. She never worried any more about it. "God will look after us," she affirmed, and believed right along with me.

Wasn't that wonderful to have a companion willing to go with me and trust for all our needs? Praise the Lord! My companion, which Jesus had called to help me (and the Holy Spirit moves in my heart when I tell you this) has been such a precious help and encouragement all through the years. In the trials and battles which have faced us in this wonderful walk of trust, she has never wavered or turned aside. She has been like a rock by my side, by God's grace and help.

I have tried always to encourage wives to be more thoughtful of their husbands, because there is more to a woman's assignment in marriage than washing dishes, preparing meals, mopping floors, and raising children. Too many wives have forgotten their husbands. Any man who is going with God today is having a more difficult time with evil than any woman could ever know. It would eliminate many troubles and temptations if wives were striving lovingly and enthusiastically to take care of their husbands.

Likewise, husbands need to be kind, gracious, thoughtful, and tender with their wives. Husbands should be loving and stimulating, working gently and easily with their companions toward a mutual fulfillment of the love relationship, not simply the satisfaction of his mortal desires.

The demon powers influence wives to make them cold and unloving to the husbands, and at the same time affect husbands to make them attracted to other women. Our men need to be so cautious in all their behavior with women who are not their companions, and wives need to pour more love into their husbands so that they will not be so severely tempted away from the home.

Walking to the door of 301 East North Street, I knocked. Marion G. opened the door. "I am Rev. Helm," I said. "I have just heard that your home is for rent and I came to inquire."

"Oh, certainly," he replied. "Come right in."

When I walked in, his wife remarked, "Why, I remember when you married my cousin and your brother."

"July the sixth, 1941," I added.

"Yes," she said. "I remember you." (Think of that! God had taken us right to someone who knew us!)

After they had shown us through their lovely home, I told them, "Let us pray about this and we will be back."

We left the house and got back into the car. While we drove around, my wife said to me, "I can live here and not be frightened. When you must be gone, I will be thankful to stay home. I know God will take care of us while you are away."

I had no idea where the money was coming from to pay for the rent. In fact, I didn't know where any money was coming from, except for five dollars a week which one man promised us. Five dollars didn't go far, but it went a little, and we were very thankful for it. But I needed thirty-five dollars a month for the rent alone. Thirty-five dollars then would be over $125 a month now.

Returning to 301 East North Street, I stopped the car in front, got out, and stood by the car door praying. What were we to do? I prayed, "Jesus—see those electric wires up there? I don't have anything in this world, Lord. I am trusting you absolutely. I am alone with you. Please send two doves up on those high tension wires in so many seconds, and I know it will be a sign that you will provide for us in this home."

(Now I wouldn't advise anyone else to do this. Some people hear me share how God has led me, and they pattern their own lives along the same lines. I was never led to pray this way before, nor have I been led to pray this way since.)

As I waited with my eyes closed in prayer, I was standing by our car on the driver's side rejoicing and praising the Lord. In thirty to sixty seconds I heard the flutter of wings. I opened my eyes, and there they were!—two doves sat right where I had asked God to place them! "Look, Honey," I cried. "I just asked Jesus to put two doves on those high tension wires if He was going to help us here, and there they are!"

I hurried to the door and knocked. When Mr. G. opened it I announced, "We will take it!" and gave him the rent for two months with money that was back salary which had been owed us.

In just a few minutes people came from over the city and around that area asking the owner, "Why didn't you call and tell us you were going to rent your home? Why, we are your friends. We wanted this place."

"We didn't know," he told them. "We just advertised it in the paper."

Our parents and many others asked us how we ever found such a lovely home. The answer was very precious: before the newspaper even was off the press, the Lord Jesus had led me there wonderfully by the guidance of the sacred Holy Spirit. And instead of a hut or a cottage, He gave us a very nice home. Praise the Lord.

23 WAITING ON GOD

It was June 8, 1943, when we moved into this lovely dwelling at 301 East North Street, which was to be our home for the next sixteen months.

The Holy Ghost had called me to wait upon Him in the Word and in prayer, and that is what I began to do. I would try to read ten to twenty chapters a day in the Word. Some days I would read more, some days a little less. I also tried to spend from one to four hours a day on my knees waiting before God, although some days it was less than an hour. This was not a rigid pattern I set up out of a formal sense of duty. I was delighted to wait before God, to talk with Him, to praise Him, and—most important—to listen to Him. The longest time I ever spent on my knees in prayer within a twelve-hour period was a little over eleven hours.

I think I had one or two revivals that first year. Of course, I could have sent out announcements to many churches that I was available for evangelistic services. But the Holy Ghost revealed to my heart: "You may go out in evangelism, but if you go, it will be your doing. If you wait until I send you, it will be Mine; and what I begin, cannot end."

Waiting on God is paramount and indispensable. It is as urgent to true Christianity as breathing is to the body. Our waiting on God must be continuous and unbroken, as the breathing that maintains life. If we do not breathe, we die. If we do not wait on God, we come to spiritual night and barrenness, to spiritual poverty and death.

The deep need to wait on God lies first of all in the very nature of man. His first sins were disobedience, pride, and trustlessness. Man wanted his own way. He chose to do something God had commanded him not to do, relying on his own judgments rather than those of Almighty God. Man wanted to trust in himself rather than in God, and he desired knowledge to make this self-reliance possible.

Since disobedience took us away from God, the path back to fellowship with Him through Jesus is by obedience: by doing what God leads us to do—what He assigns and what He orders. The difficulty, however, is in humbling ourselves to do His will. The struggle comes within our nature, which is unwilling to surrender, to be submissive, to comply to God's design and His order.

You see, there is a crisis here. **There is a matter of vision. We must somehow get the vision that only what God leads will last.** Some fifteen to seventeen years ago I was communing with God in the prayer room when the Holy Spirit revealed to me, "What God begins never ends. There is no end to any one thing that God begins." In direct contrast, all that we originate, master-mind, or motivate has no life in it. Anything and everything that we touch ends in death. We are of the earth, and the earth has received the condemnation of death.

There is life only in Jesus. Life comes only from God. **Only as God works His will on earth through the Holy Spirit can we have any spiritual life.** This is what He revealed to me in April, 1942, when He said, "By Me, the Holy Ghost, they (all men) will be fed. Only by Me, the Holy Ghost, can they be fed." But the Powers of the Air fight to prevent this simple, inviolable, fact from reaching us. Unless we wait on God sufficiently, we will not so much as be aware that we simply cannot participate in the Kingdom of God until He leads us and directs us.

Because of this simple and primary fact, **the most important activity in the earth is to learn what God wants in our life—**

230

what is His word from Heaven; what is His will for me? And the choice of my heart must be to will God's will.

Because of our innate disobedient tendencies, we must wait in order to be taught how to receive our instructions; for the truth of the matter is that God has quite a bit to do with us before we are ready to follow the instructions. There is much to be done within us in our waiting before we are prepared to start on the assignments of God's Kingdom.

God can work through only the individuals who wait upon Him. He cannot operate through a person who arranges things by his own ideas or for his own convenience.

In waiting upon God we first experience spiritual observation. We observe the Person of God: we observe His Word; we look to the Son of God; we look to the Holy Spirit. Then the searchlight of His love starts in the inner man. We begin to observe what we are, who we are, how small we are, and how limited we truly are. In waiting, we learn spiritual observation. We become dimly aware of the things which God wants to do through us, if only He can remove from us the carnal traits in our natures which hinder and hurt others.

There is, in waiting before God, a spiritual refining, a spiritual crucifying. Sometimes we must wait before God quite a while before we see a number of things within us that are in the way, that are hindering Him and stop the flow of the Spirit through the church. There are many veiled characteristics of the self-life in individuals which will not allow the Holy Spirit to flow through a body of believers. That body, therefore, is barren. Very little divine power flows through a church when the organs of that body are not willing to comply with the spiritual law of the Word of God. But while each member of that body waits in prayer upon God, the Holy Spirit searches him and then begins the refining process where Self is crucified.

In our waiting before the Lord we see ourselves as we are. Isaiah said, "In the year that King Uzziah died I saw also the Lord . . . high and lifted up . . . " A great prophet of

God confessed: "When the King died ... I saw." Now as we wait upon the Lord, He begins to crucify the kingly elements of our lives. That is the "I" business, the ego, the self-reliance: what we think we are; what we think we can do. He begins to reveal to us our uncleanness, our naughtiness, our jealousies, our wrong incentives, our selfish motives, and our warped attitudes.

As we wait upon Him for a few months or a few years He reveals more to us concerning some spirit of strife, resentment, or malice in our lives. We will not be waiting long on our knees before the Lord will reveal to us that we have analyzation that must be eliminated from the inner life. It's a natural thing to want to know "why?" But He cannot work through us if we want to know answers to all the questions. He can work through us only as we will submit ourselves **to become the answer** as Christ lives in us a life of obedience, surrender, and trust.

At the place of prayer, God meets us; and in His presence we become aware that it is expedient for us to be crucified. With great agony of soul we acknowledge that all carnal traits must be removed, obliterated, and cleansed out of our heart and mind by the blood of Jesus. This isn't an easy time. It is severe. You will think you are dying. You will be dying; yet you will be coming to life. God will be slaying you; yet you are more alive, because He is working through you.

We are not able to do this ourselves. We cannot arrange this or accomplish this on our own. God can only perform this through individuals who are willing to remain in His hand, willing to wait in His purpose until He is able to cleanse from them these weaknesses; until He is able to take from them all things that mar, deter, hurt, crush, and cause the Holy Spirit to be grieved with us.

As we become quiet, the Lord begins to break us to pieces. It requires quietness to attain a clear vision. As we see God clearly and view Jesus Christ in His beauty, we begin to see why we should be broken; why we ought to be purged, cleansed, and filled with the Holy Spirit. This experience of brokenness is but a part of the beginning of divine surgery. No minister or layman can serve victoriously in the church until he is broken and subdued. Oh, he can be laboring and, like the disciples returning to their earthly interests, toil all night and catch nothing. He can work and work, but there will be no divine joy or heavenly victory.

Most persons will not wait upon God. They proceed with their own plans, arrange their own lives, and later say, "I don't understand why we are having such a difficult, disappointing time." Often if we are not willing to wait, God leads us to the waiting by severe experiences. If we do not wait on God, we will be stopped somehow. The gears of circumstances will grind us to pieces. If we are not willing to wait on God and let Him have His way, there will be something that will halt spiritual progress. It is preferable to wait in the beginning, until all is set in order, so that we can move in the right direction. Otherwise, we miss God's objectives.

Once we begin in proper order, we are to go slowly, for in the Kingdom of God, the true saint never moves rapidly— he goes slowly. Often the individual who is long in getting started with Jesus, wants to go full speed ahead. This is spiritual immaturity. The mature saint goes very slowly and carefully. He is quite cautious in his behavior and with his decisions. This is discovered in a life of waiting on God.

When God revealed to me that He wanted me to wait upon Him, I didn't understand all that He wanted, but I was glad to wait. Day after day I would pray and wait. It was primarily my listening in. Occasionally I would pray with vigor and energy for half an hour to an hour, then wait an hour or half an hour. I would listen in to see what He was teaching me, to learn His revelation. He had many things to teach me.

I had a number of carnal tendencies within me, which He first needed to remove before He could enable me to help someone else. You see, if I were to try to assist some person by means of my own insights and suppositions, I could easily discourage or injure him. But when God leads me, all are benefited. **(If we could only perceive this, it would be worth the entire book.)** I am still learning.

Many people in the church will try to tell you what to do. As a rule, a spiritual man never seeks to give counsel to anyone. He never informs the pastor what his programs should be. It is usually a ·carnal person who insists on giving instruction to the minister. Anyone who thinks he knows all about spiritual things hasn't waited enough as yet. If he waits awhile, he will learn that he knows very little and that only God knows the necessary information. This is among the first lessons we learn as we wait on God.

Did you realize that the things we know——our seeking to understand, our theories, our insights——have many times gotten us into a great deal of trouble? The Word of God exhorts us to "trust in the Lord with all thine heart, and lean not to thy own understanding." Needless to say, there is no premium on ignorance. But many persons have been depending upon their own understanding rather than trusting God (meaning——leaving the leading and the planning to Him).

The spiritual person never dictates what followers of Christ should do. Individuals call me from all over the United States asking, "What does God want me to do? Which way shall we go? Does God want me over here? Is this the work? Is this the right choice?" Many are seeking counsel. I cannot answer according to my own personal opinion or in response to my own ideas. I must have the guidance of the Holy Ghost. I must pray to discover whether Jesus would be pleased to reveal His guidance to my heart.

Most counsel is of the flesh (and I can tell by the opera- tion of Jesus in my heart that this is true). Very little counsel is of the Holy Spirit. God's Word says: "Blessed is the man that walketh not in the counsel of the ungodly, nor standeth in the way of sinners, nor sitteth in the seat of the scornful."

The counsel of the Holy Spirit comes to the person who consistently obeys and waits upon God. The first few years he is on his knees, this lowly heart will learn the seriousness of giving counsel to anybody. He will learn how cautious he must be, how he needs to be just what Jesus would have him to be, so that God can work through him what He wills. I have prayed now for twenty-five to thirty years that I could be, by God's grace, close enough to Jesus that God can speak through me the very words which the people need. To Jesus' glory, He has done this on a few occasions.

I recall talking to a man in a filling station when unexpectedly I said, "Claude, I have the leading that you should retire today and go home." He was rather surprised and wondered what it meant. I didn't know I was going to say it myself. It just came out of me. In seven days he had his heart attack and was forced to rest. God was wanting to use this limited servant to spare this man needless suffering and loss, but he was not able to recognize that the words I spoke were more than my own.

In waiting on the Lord we are brought to brokenness, if we can remain steady and quiet long enough. Sometimes it takes a long while to break us up. It comes by waiting upon God. To wait on God is worth more than all the gold in the land, all the pearls in the sea, and all the diamonds in the earth. **This is the secret of revival in the church,** for if the people of the church are willing to wait upon God, it won't be long before they are confessing their criticisms. Tender hearts will be confiding to neighbors: "Oh, you didn't know it, but I criticized you a year ago. It grieved God's heart terribly and I am sorry." Repentant souls will tell pastors: "I talked about you to my companion and I can see now I was out of divine order. Please forgive me."

If you say one critical word about anyone, you have grieved the Holy Spirit. (Rom. 2:1; 14:13; Mt. 7:1) If I were to criticize or find fault about any person to my wife—in any way, at any

235

time—I would grieve the Holy Spirit. He could not use me in God's Kingdom until I repented of that.

Someone may ask, "How do you keep from criticizing?" The only way is to have the spirit of criticism removed and cleansed out of us by the blood of Jesus. Another may say, "I just find myself complaining about this person and murmuring about that problem." It is because a fault-finding spirit is in your heart. This must be taken out of the inner life, for it will damage the church, causing it to be barren, dark, and unattractive.

Some people claim to be filled with the Holy Spirit, but they find fault with others. The Holy Spirit does not live in people who criticize and find fault with anyone. He is grieved with them. The Holy Spirit lives in a gentle, broken, obedient heart, which loves Jesus with all its strength. **If people in a congregation find fault with each other in secret, God cannot bless them in worship or anywhere else.** I know this is not popular to say, but we must know the truth, because the truth will set us free.

Whenever there is a conflict in a Christian group it is because of a carnal spirit. The Holy Spirit does not lead along the lines of contention or argument. The apostle Paul clearly indicates this when he admonished young Timothy: "And the servant of the Lord must not be quarrelsome— fighting and contending," the Amplified version puts it. "Instead he must be kindly to every one and mild-tempered, preserving the bond of peace; he must be a skillful and suitable teacher, **patient** and **forbearing** and **willing to suffer wrong.** He must correct his opponents **with courtesy and gentleness** . . . " (II Timothy 2:24-25) The Holy Spirit is always grieved when there is division, conflict, or fault-finding in a so-called Christian fellowship.

God will soon reveal to all waiting souls that we must not criticize or murmur about anything or anyone, for He said in the second chapter of Philippians: "Do all things without murmurings and disputings: that ye may be blameless and harmless, the sons of God without rebuke, in the midst of a crooked and perverse nation, among whom ye shine as lights in the world . . . ''

One of the primary sins that has caused the church to be barren (which indicates that the power of God is not in her midst) is this spirit of criticism or finding fault. This grieves God. Whenever you find yourself picking at people, remember that this is carnal and you need to be cleansed from it through the Holy Spirit and the blood of Jesus Christ. God cannot live in a life that is critical, hateful, impatient, jealous, angry, or spiteful. We learn this in depth only as we wait upon the Lord.

God absolutely does not want us to criticize or find fault with each other. If Satan can tempt two or three persons in a congregation to murmur or complain about one another, the demons are laughing in hell, because they have that church right where they want it. I repeat: **the spirit of criticism must perish.** It must be removed out of us in order that we may see revival and be used of the Holy Spirit.

How can we rid ourselves of these evil tendencies? Well, we cannot. It is not in us to do it. It is only by the Holy Ghost who lives in us. We are lifted above the critical spirit by obeying every leading of the Holy Spirit; by trusting the Lord with all our heart; by reading the Word daily, praying faithfully, and praising the Lord frequently. By His Love, we surmount and resist criticism. When our heart is filled with love and holiness, a critical spirit is a stranger. In the humble, broken, and contrite heart, the spirit of criticism is unwelcome and resisted.

In this School of Waiting we also learn adaptability; how to adjust ourselves to the conditions we are in; how to follow Christ with wisdom.

When I first found Jesus, I wanted everyone saved immediately. I have since learned that often I must wait for a long period of time before I am permitted to say anything about salvation to certain individuals. There are people in my home town to whom I haven't spoken about their souls for forty years. I want to say something, but I cannot.

By the help and leading of the Holy Spirit I have been privileged to see a man saved at a filling station within fifteen minutes. In a motel I helped a precious person find Jesus in twenty-five minutes. I have seen persons saved in my car in various states. But in my home community I must keep quiet, because in each case I am to adapt to the situation.

I am not free to talk about spiritual things to a number of persons in my home community because they place me under certain pressures which all true servants of God experience. Jesus said, "A prophet is not without honor, save in his own country, and among his own kin." For twenty to forty years I have prayed for many in our locality, and we have seen a few genuinely converted. However, I can tell that the great majority do not want me to talk to them about their salvation. A number are disturbed when they hear me praise the Lord at worship or about the town. On the other hand, I am thankful for the few with whom I have had Holy Spirit fellowship.

Some dear and earnest Christians will speak exactly what is on their minds, simply because they feel that the Bible instructs us to witness. But unless God is leading, the dear ones we are attempting to reach do not appreciate the sharing or the precious exhortation. Instead, they resent it and are driven farther away from the victory which we long for them to experience. If this dear Christian pilgrim could have prayed, trusted, and obeyed a few days, a few months, or longer—the Holy Spirit would have arranged the appropriate time for the witness or the sharing. Conviction would have pierced that cold heart, and God would have brought him into the Kingdom by His might and power.

I have learned that when we are in a church where there are a number of lukewarm church people, unless the Holy Spirit really puts the praise in our hearts to be said aloud— unless the power really works it out of the inner man—it is

238

better to praise God inside. Otherwise we will lose our influence with the dear ones who are far from the sacred will of God. If we praise God audibly in the flesh, those who stand far off from Jesus are offended and draw back further. Now if Jesus praises God through us in the Spirit, though it may cause some stir, it will only intensify conviction, for the Holy Spirit has led it.

Something else happens as you wait upon God—your faith is placed on exhibit. You begin to see your faith in operation. You perceive how much you are in need of the Faith once delivered to the saints. You find in waiting that your faith is tried, tested, measured, balanced, and explored. In waiting on God you discover the strength of Jesus' Spirit within you. You learn your own personal weaknesses and your utter dependence upon Him. In waiting upon God your faith is renewed, enlarged, and increased; your usefuless is multiplied.

Some have the failing of talking too much, and others do not talk when they should. It would be wonderful if we could encourage those who get out of divine order and speak in the flesh to hold silent; and to persuade the shy, backward souls to speak out when God prompts them. The talkative person has many times damaged his influence by speaking too frequently, whereas the timid person can still be wonderfully used for Jesus. However, Satan tries to attack them with such fears that they will not open their mouths when God is urging them to obedience.

Many earnest Christians could be used of the Lord, but they have hurt their influence by moving or speaking out of order. They didn't wait long enough to find out how to react to the situation; they went on in the strength of their own well-meant ways and their influence has been marred. But God desires that we wait until He can teach us when to speak and how to follow Him. By learning at His feet, we are less liable to cause injury to anyone, but can assist in carrying their burdens.

If we could only persuade people to be willing to wait on

God: to let God take out of us, through Jesus and the work of the Holy Spirit, those things which cause us to be jumping ahead of His leading. We go too rapidly. We want to bring spiritual things to pass too quickly—far ahead of God's time.

The Lord revealed to me a few years ago while in the pulpit of a precious congregation that we in the church are in the garden where the seed of the Word has been sown, as the parable of the sower describes it. The seed has been sown and tiny tender plants (precious souls) are waiting to be brought to life by proper sunshine, moisture, and loving care.

However, if we in the church are not trusting, if we have not sufficiently waited on God to receive His instructions, if we have not learned what Heaven wants in every situation— then we are blind. We mean well; we want to do good; we desire to serve Jesus. But because we are proceeding in the flesh and not by the leadership of the Spirit, we are blind and cannot see where the plants are growing. Instead of nurturing and assisting these tender souls, we are actually trampling them down. As the seed in the parable of the sower was trodden down, we in the church are many times hurting the souls we deeply long to see born again. We bruise the souls who could be brought to spiritual maturity.

In our earnest endeavors we are crushing people with wrong motives, by our words spoken out of order, through harsh preaching. In the trustless body of believers we tread under foot all the things we are trying to accomplish. **Unless we are inwardly cleansed and crucified, we will be crushing the souls which we want to be won to Jesus.** They will be hurt by a little carnal strife, some fault-finding, theological argument, impatience, or petty jealousies.

I was a very impatient person before I was cleansed. God had major surgery to perform on me. I did most all things fast: drove fast, walked fast, talked fast. God had to slow me down. In order to be in divine order I had to remain lowly at the feet of Jesus daily to be constantly slain and purged.

240

On the other hand, my wife is very slow. Thirty-seven to thirty-nine years ago as we prepared for church I would say, "Honey, hurry up, we are going to be late." The more I talked the more behind she was. My urging only confused her. After Jesus sanctified me, however, many times I could carry her shoes and hose to her, help bathe the children, and get them dressed. Of course, she did about all the housework and caring for the children, but occasionally I could assist her.

God puts a slow person with a fast one to teach the slow person to speed up and the fast one to slow down. He puts the talkative individual with a nontalkative one to teach the one who doesn't talk to speak up a little, and the one who talks too much to quit talking so much and listen more. Sometimes a husband will be untidy: his trousers are left lying over there, the shoes are over here, his belongings scattered everywhere. The wife, on the other hand, likes everything in the house arranged in an orderly fashion. God puts a tidy one with an untidy one to teach them both lessons of longsuffering and patience.

Oh, how we need to wait on God and let Him make us ready for the battle. He has much to teach us and much to develop in the inner life. We will be always learning of our limitations and inabilities. We will learn that we need His knowledge, His strength, and His wisdom. Many precious people are seeking to be filled with the Holy Spirit in order to have more spiritual power. **But true spiritual strength can only begin when we recognize our inner poverty and come to the end of depending upon ourselves.**

In spite of this fundamental admission, pride will often prevent a person from forsaking his own ways and acknowledging his limitations. Hidden deep within us we often have so many stubborn, prideful ways that are unwilling to submit to the ways of God. We have lovely homes, good jobs, plenty of luxuries; but within the interior heart the life is drab, dark, and empty. There is no glory of Jesus, no radiance of divine joy.

It is sometimes because of a spirit of arrogance, a spirit of self-reliance: that defensive voice which says, "I am as good as anybody else." I felt that way before I met Jesus. But after I began to wait upon Him, He helped me to see that I was the least of all servants. I felt myself to be on the bottom. I wasn't on the second rung of the ladder: I was absolutely on the bottom.

Now if you are happy at the bottom, you are happy any-place. When you are glad for a little bit of nothing, then you are thankful for anything. You may have nothing much of earthly value, but you are so thrilled because you have Jesus in your heart, and He is everything. When we begin to realize that we are unworthy of the least thing that God does for us, when we discover that we are unworthy of the tiniest crumbs of His love and His revelations, then we are coming close to the bottom in humility.

We are not able to reach this bottom place by simply deciding to be lowly and seeking to be humble. It is the Holy Spirit's assignment to strip us of the carnal dependencies and superficialities which insulate us from the terrible knowledge of our wretched spiritual bankruptcy. Our self-sufficiency and our own good works have blinded us to the true poverty of our souls. We are already the least of all things; we are already empty of any redeeming value; we are at the very best "unprofitable servants"—we simply aren't aware of it yet.

The Lord often lovingly begins to make us aware of this spiritual bankruptcy by taking from us all the earthly props which lend us the illusion of our own self-sufficiency. At the very beginning He took from me the understanding of my Elder, my father, my friends, and my relatives. He took away my human sources of comfort in order that I would look to Him alone for strength and guidance. He removed my earthly supports so that I would begin to trust Him in actuality, not in word only.

242

You see, our great tendency is to lean on a friend, rely on respected opinion, depend upon certain situations, and look to established groups or accepted ideas. We want help from the pastor, from parents, from teachers. But God desires us to come first to Him. He wants us to seek for help, counsel, and succor first from Him. He wishes to be all things to us. But we will never find Him all-sufficient and all-providing until we discover the abject poverty of our own resources.

When He begins to remove those things which are artificially holding us up, we will begin to learn how weak we actually are. We won't know how weak we are for a long time. It may require many years to learn how dependent we are upon God. But because God knows that we will never truly be fulfilled until we are trusting only in Him, He will teach us about our inadequacies and our limitations. He will demonstrate how prone we are to speculate, to waver, and to wander.

When God brings us, then, by His mercy to the end of our meager resources, there is nothing left for us to do but fall helplessly into the arms of Jesus. This, finally, is trust. Trust is resting only on the promises of God. **Trust is walking not by our own insights, our own deductions, or our own ideas—but wholly by His Word and by His revelation.**

This way of trust is so simple, but it has been missed by most people since time began. It's so simple we have overlooked it. We preach about trust. We sing about it and teach it. But how long will it take before we actually begin to apply it in the interior life?

While we are waiting upon God, He is working within us miracles for His glory which we cannot observe or describe. You may think that you are not making progress. You may feel that you have waited too long and time is wasting, but often you are moving fastest with God while you are waiting in secret. You are approaching the goal which is not gained by speed.

A hymn, deeply loved by my wife and me, has well expressed this truth to our hearts over the years.

> Not so in haste my heart!
> Have faith in God and wait;
> Although He linger long,
> He never comes too late.
>
> He never cometh late;
> He knoweth what is best;
> Vex not thyself in vain;
> Until He cometh, rest.
>
> Until he cometh rest,
> Nor grudge the hours that roll;
> The feet that wait for God
> Are soonest at the goal.
>
> Are soonest at the goal
> That is not gained by speed;
> Then hold thee still, my heart,
> For I shall wait His lead.
>
> —Bradford Torrey, 1843-1912

While you are waiting, God is rooting you downward in His love and His likeness. He is planting your feet upon the solid Rock, Christ Jesus. The roots of your experience, your insights, and your abilities are sinking deep into the crevices of His purpose; they are reaching deep into the cool streams of His hidden designs. The soul is casting off the garb of earth's religious values and is being robed in the righteousness of Christ alone.

As you go down in humility, God lifts you in revelation. While your roots are sinking down in lowliness, the spiritual branches are mounting upward. God brings us upward to give us a glimpse of His marvelous Kingdom. We may see far-away horizons of His many, many purposes in the earth. These are but a few of the sweet delicacies of His love which He shares with those who wait upon Him.

I recall one day when I had waited in prayer for a few hours. All at once the lovely fragrance of blooming roses permeated the air. I knew that there were no flowers in the room; still it was as if I were in the midst of a rose garden. I had often sung of a beautiful garden of prayer, but this was the first time God ever permitted me to experience one. Another time, after waiting a long while, it was as if I were in a room full of gardenias. This is beyond earthly knowledge indeed. One may pray for years and years and never have this experience. I wasn't expecting it, but Jesus sent it. It required a few years of prayer to get there.

I experienced a similar gift of God's love while with Rev. Robert Morgan and his wife in Marion many years ago. We were privileged to have fellowship day after day, sharing the things of the Kingdom of God. One night about midnight, while in prayer together, we were suddenly in a garden of lilies. "Do you smell lilies?" they asked.

I answered, "Yes, I do!" Oh, how happy we became!

What people will receive by waiting on God! You will enjoy more than flowers, as wonderful as they are; you will get more than perfume: you will possess the loveliness of Jesus within you. His compassion will come into you, along with great tenderness and gentleness. His love will begin to flow through you to all people everywhere.

In waiting, God teaches many things about Himself, about the Kingdom, about His work, about His love; but He teaches you mostly about yourself. He acquaints you with yourself. Many people are seeking to know themselves through various methods of analysis, but this knowledge is of the earth. God will make plain your true person as you are able to yield that newly discovered individual to Him continually.

While we wait upon God, He somehow takes the blindness from our eyes. We see Christ in a new perspective, and in His purity we see ourselves reflected as we actually are. As we view His marvelous majesty and holiness we will know for a certainty that "in us dwelleth no good thing." With loud voice we will witness to the fact that we are indeed "no-thing". We are as dust. And when we really know we are nothing, then He becomes everything; He becomes all.

In nothingness there is no jealousy, no anxiety, no self-ishness. You have no plans, no schemes, no programs; everything is in the hands of Jesus. You are merely trusting. Until you are brought to nothingness, you will not truly trust God.

There is a unique quality in the trusting heart: it is filled with much praise. In hard places, when things are going wrong, when the food burns, the tractor stalls, the water heater breaks—the trusting heart can still rejoice. And as we meet in secret daily with our beloved Lord, we will be taught the lesson of adoring God and praising Him much more.

God has shown me that praise is the very breath of trust; and where there is no praise, trust is choked to death. Now praise is dependent upon the joy in the life of a true son of God, and joy is dependent upon his obedience to the Holy Spirit. Where there is obedience, joy flows like a river.

Don't be discouraged when you don't know how to pray. Simply wait on the Lord and He will teach you little by little. Through the years we have endeavored to have family scripture and prayer regularly, and sometimes after my wife and the girls were asleep I would be on my knees trying to pray. I would wait and let the Holy Spirit reveal to me what He wanted me to pray. I have wept for joy sometimes when I was so happy it was beyond description. Upon occasions I have wept as I have waited in prayer so that some may have thought me sad, but I wasn't: I was thrilled. I was so delighted I hardly knew what to do. I would rather like to cry sometimes, but seldom am I permitted unless the Spirit comes upon me and I can see the wonder of God's love for me.

One night between midnight and two in the morning I was crying out to God when, in the Spirit, I could see Him on the Throne and Jesus Christ by His side. I could see how God's heart was grieved with us mortals because we had come so far from His will. It seemed as if I looked into God's broken heart. The glory was so great within me and around me that I wept. My heart was broken because He was so grieved with us mortals. Yet, in the midst of my weeping, I experienced an ecstasy of joy because the revelation was so marvelous.

Jesus was a man of sorrows, but He was not sad or morose. He sorrowed because He could see the potentials of the men about Him. He could see that mankind had been working around in the rubbish when He could have brought them to the garden of His purpose. His heart is still broken because we are missing so much. We are living on the marginal when He would have us at the center of His will. We are gnawing on the bones of the "good" when He would offer us the rare delicacies of His "best." He would continually give us lovingly of His best, if only we could daily in our hearts live the words of this prayer hymn:

> My times are in Thy hand:
> My God, I wish them there;
> My life, my friends, my soul, I leave
> Entirely to Thy care.
>
> My times are in Thy hand,
> Whatever they may be;
> Pleasing or painful, dark or bright,
> As best may seem to Thee.
>
> My times are in Thy hand;
> Why should I doubt or fear?
> My Father's hand will never cause
> His child a needless tear.
>
> My times are in Thy hand;
> I'll always trust in Thee;
> And, after death, at Thy right hand
> I shall forever be.
>
> —William F. Lloyd, 1791-1853

In this chapter and throughout the book I am able to share only a tiny, tiny bit of what is involved in walking with God. But He will teach each follower of Jesus as he denies Self to wait upon Him, trust Him, and obey Him. What God has given me in the hours, days, weeks, months, and years of waiting upon Him in prayer and in the Word, I would not exchange for anything in this world.

And yet, I did not begin to wait on Him in order to get something in return. I went daily to meet with Him because that is what He called me to do. I waited upon God because He invited me to commune with Him, to love Him, to worship Him. Waiting did not come naturally to me—I had to press daily to meet with God. He called me to serve Him for Himself alone. I know of no higher privilege for man.

It is still a marvel to my heart that the Lord could teach me as a young man of twenty-six the urgency of waiting **only** upon God. Remember—I may be only in the vestibule of waiting and trust. Dear one in Jesus, be encouraged to press onward to the goal.

24 HOME BUILT BY FAITH

In September, 1944, we were obliged to leave 301 East North Street because the house had been sold. But God miraculously led us to another home just at the last moment. (There are many marvelous guidances of the Holy Spirit which I could not include in this book due to insufficient space. Perhaps, the Lord willing, they might be included in a companion volume some time in the future.) About two years later the couple owning this home then wanted to move back from Ohio to again take up residence in their home, which meant that we would need to move once more. I had no idea where we could locate a suitable dwelling.

When my wife's father and mother learned that we would need to find another home, they visited us. "We want you to come to our house," they said. So we went over to be with my wife's father and mother for what we thought would be two or three days, and stayed almost seven years.

It is a common opinion that two families cannot live under the same roof without a little conflict. To make our stay with Mother and Dad Spence slightly more involved, we had three daughters with us as well. It is not an easy assignment for grandparents to live with grandchildren. In addition, my wife's parents believed in correcting children simply by talking with them. They did not especially want anyone to correct children with a switch. On the other hand, I was a strict disciplinarian. Whenever I chastened our children, I took them into a room by themselves so that our precious parents would not be hurt.

Mother and Dad Spence were so helpful to us. By God's grace we got along wonderfully. There was never a difficulty or conflict. And when two families can live under the same roof—when grandchildren can live with grandparents without upheaval or turmoil—it requires the Holy Spirit. When we left there, they loved us more than when we arrived. We want to praise Jesus for this, because it is only through Him that our love for one another after these seven years was even greater than when we first came. My dear wife and I are so thankful for this precious memory, and for the help of God which made it possible.

When Jesus revealed to my heart in 1934 that He would someday build us a home that would be a demonstration to all that God provides for His prophets today as He did of old, I did not start asking, "When is it going to be? How is it going to be done?" By God's grace, I never once pressed to know more about it. I simply left it in the hands of God.

On one occasion, while preaching in our first pastorate in 1937 or 1938, without premeditation I suddenly said, "If I am faithful and true, win men and women, boys and girls to Jesus, God is going to lead in the building of a home for my family some time in the future. It will be a home built by faith." My congregation simply looked at me. I received a similar response from other dear people as I would share this from time to time throughout the years. It was a little difficult for them to hear what I was saying or to believe that God would actually lead in the building of a home.

In 1950 I met a man of prayer who wanted me to come to his precious congregation for services in Grant City, Indiana, as soon as the Lord would lead me. When he did not hear from me for many months, he felt that perhaps God might never send me. At ten o'clock one night he related to God in prayer, "Well, I guess Your servant isn't coming to our little church. Perhaps our congregation is too small. I'll just turn this whole situation over to You, Father." About four hours later the Holy Ghost revealed that I should call this servant of God to inform him that Jesus was leading me to be with him in just a few days.

The Grant City revival lasted for three or four weeks, during which time this humble servant of God and I enjoyed several times of prayer together. I learned that this minister was a real prayer warrior. In fact, his son-in-law, Warren Cox, informed me that when the doctor examined him, he found thick calluses on his knees: calluses resulting from waiting so many hours a week before Almighty God. I have been privileged to be with him and a few others together in prayer many times through the years. During those services we once prayed until midnight. On another occasion we prayed until four-fifteen in the morning, and another time we were together in prayer all night. He would talk to God with such devotion, earnestness, and childlikeness.

During the third week of the revival, he and I were the last to leave the sanctuary following the Sunday morning service. I was sharing with him how I had left all to follow Jesus and had known what it was like to have the moving van back up to our door with no place to go; yet, how I was as happy as if I had everything.

I had studied the scriptures, but until I left all to go with God I didn't really realize the significance of Jesus' words: "There is no man that hath left house, or brethren, or sisters, or father, or mother, or wife, or children, or lands, for my sake and the Gospel's, but he shall receive an hundredfold now in this time, houses, and brethren, and sisters, and mothers, and children, and lands, with persecutions, and in the world to come eternal life." (Mark 10:29-30)

I was declaring to this loving brother how I had trusted Jesus to one day build a home for us, and that I had been waiting many years to really pray with someone about the home to be built. "I'll be glad to pray whenever the Lord leads," he said to me as we put on our overcoats and started for the door. Mother C. already had a lovely lunch waiting for us at her home a few miles from the church.

251

Just as my hand touched the church door, the Holy Ghost operated within me to inform me that it was now time to pray. We had waited fifteen years and eight months for this leading. Turning to this precious servant of God I said, "Brother Field, I know lunch is waiting, but we will have to go back to the altar and pray."

"Wonderful!" he rejoiced. "Wonderful!"

Soon two men who loved Jesus more than they loved to eat were in earnest prayer at the altar. We had just begun to pray when, caught away in the wonder of intercession, Brother Field and I suddenly realized ourselves to be with Abraham and Isaac on Mount Moriah! My brother was praying as to the scriptural account of Isaac being sacrificed on the altar which Abraham had just built. It was as though, in the Spirit, we were close by observing in prayer this marvelous event. I have seldom experienced anything like this in prayer before or since.

The lad's voice was heard to ask, "Where is the sacrifice, Father?" And Abraham answered, "The Lord will provide, my Son." (The scene was so real. I cannot explain how vivid it all was through the Holy Spirit.) Abraham bound the hands of the boy whom he loved as his own life and laid him upon the sticks of the altar. He raised the knife overhead to plunge it into the tiny body, when the angel's voice spoke, "It is enough!" I saw the patriarch turn and behold a ram caught in the thicket by its horns. At that moment the Holy Ghost witnessed to me: "YOUR HOME IS AS A RAM CAUGHT IN A THICKET." It was a thrilling moment of sacred revelation.

The following summer my youngest brother, Edward, assisted me in revival services at the Friends Church in Shirley, Indiana, by leading the singing. To express their appreciation for his assistance the congregation wished to take up an offering for him. As the plates were being passed Edward leaned over to me and asked, "Would it be alright with the Lord and with you if I just take this offering and start a fund for the home to be built by faith? We could call it the 'Ram Fund.' "

I said, "Brother, that would be wonderful!"

The beginning was sixteen dollars and a few cents. When the idea of a "Ram Fund" was shared with dear ones who prayed regularly with us, it seemed to touch the hearts of a few saints. We began to search for a place where the home might be built, but every possibility was blocked by Satan. (I know of few things in my experience which the devil fought more severely than he did this home to be built by faith in Jesus. My words can never describe to you the many battles and struggles which we passed through to accomplish God's purpose in this project. It has been only by God's grace and mercy that it came to pass so beautifully.)

It was during this time that the Lord revealed to my heart early one morning, "You are going to Texas to pray with Rev. Pumphrey regarding two issues: the Holy Ghost Revival to the World, and your home to be built by faith." The next day God brought a man twenty miles to give us the seventy dollars for the journey.

When our twin daughters heard of my intended journey they said, "Daddy, here you are going on a trip of about twenty-two hundred miles and we need shoes. We only have one pair of shoes apiece and they are nearly worn out. Our playmate has two or three pairs of shoes, and you have told us now for several weeks that one of these days God would provide us a new pair." All I could tell our girls was that I was trusting Jesus to supply the need.

That night Florence and I took our three daughters forty-two miles one way to visit my parents and other friends. During the course of the evening we had three or four prayer meetings, and when we returned home we had four five-dollar bills which had been given to us: two dollars for Jesus and eighteen dollars for the girls' shoes. God had provided! Praise the Lord.

When we knelt to have family prayer that evening a great burden moved upon my heart. It was still on me the next morning and I was unable to locate it in all the parishes I had ever served or among the people I had known. I did not comprehend what all was involved in this spiritual operation—I simply entrusted it to Jesus.

My route to Texas was different than my accustomed itinerary, for the Lord had made it plain that I was not to go directly from St. Louis to Waco, Texas; rather, I was to take a train from St. Louis to Hearne, Texas, then go by bus the sixty miles from Hearne to Waco. I didn't understand this round-about route, but I didn't try: God simply wanted me to follow.

Along the course of the journey Jesus permitted me to witness to a few persons. When I arrived in Waco I was privileged to preach in Homer Pumphrey's congregation, where God gave me a few friends. The following day I enjoyed wonderful fellowship with a man who loved the Bible dearly and knew it remarkably well. The Spirit of the Lord was upon me, and during our first hour together a cowboy came into the room and stayed for two hours. At the close of the fellowship he said, "You would be welcome in my home any time." I learned later that this fellow generally disappeared in five minutes every time a minister came around. But God gave me favor with this precious man. A short time later I was privileged to be with him when he came to Jesus.

As we returned home that night Homer asked me, "When are we going to have the prayer meeting that God told you about in Indiana?" Just as he asked me that the Holy Spirit spoke within me, revealing: "I am with you. I will lead you." I told my brother that Jesus would arrange it.

Not many minutes later I was down on one knee in their kitchen telling them how God had sent my wife and me to the Smoky Mountains for rest in 1951. We were heading for Gatlinburg to find a motel, but my wife was becoming ill. I realized that she wasn't well and needed to lie down as soon as possible. Nonetheless, in spite of her illness, I said to her, "Honey, we must find the right place to stay."

Stopping at the first motel, I was shown a lovely room which would have cost us only five dollars a night. The Lord revealed, "Don't stay here." So we went to another motel. This room was also lovely, with fresh linen, towels, hot water, and soap. A king could have lived in that room and felt comfortable. Jesus helped me to know, however, that we could not stay there either. We went to the third place, and again God told me that this was not His choice. By this time my wife informed me that she was feeling worse, so I cried out, "Oh, Jesus—help my wife! Encourage her, strengthen her!" And through Jesus' help, my precious companion was able to sit up and go a while longer.

It was not an easy assignment for me to see my companion suffer, but there was only one thing to do and that was follow the leading of the Holy Spirit. The human tendency would have taken the first motel room in order to get my companion quickly comfortable. But I was to make the choice for God's will rather than for my wife's immediate comfort.

Whether you know it or not, you are continually under the observation of God. He is noticing whether you are going to do His will or not. He was looking then to see if I was going to let this sickness bend me to the choice of the earth, or if I would press on to His holy plan. Most people will not do God's will under stress. They will pamper the flesh and bend to the pressures of man. They will choose that which appears reasonable or expedient. Because of this, God's will has seldom been followed continuously and consistently in all the ages. **But all followers of Jesus must press to do, not their own will, but God's will at all times.**

We found a fourth motel but it also was not the place. However, as I walked up the steps of the fifth motel, the Holy Spirit said, "This is the place."

I spoke with the manager, mentioning that I was a minister. "That's wonderful," he said. "My father was a minister."

After we had talked a few minutes he remarked, "You know, I have the feeling that you are going to stay with us." (I rather wondered how he could have known that. I'm sure the Lord had sent me this way to help answer the petitions of his minister father which had been prayed some forty to fifty years before. How God wants to order our steps to answer the prayers of His children.)

This man showed us to cabin number six. On the way I saw a woman coming towards us with a shining face. "Praise the Lord!" I greeted her. She responded with, "Glory!"—and we had a meeting right there in the yard. This was just the beginning of many marvelous events, too numerous to include in this volume, which took place in later years because of God leading us to this particular motel.

In three or four days our money was gone; so we packed to start back home. Stopping at the office to return the keys before finding a place to eat breakfast, I told Sister T. and Sister C., "I want to thank the Lord for the privilege my wife and I have had of being here these days with you."

One of the women remarked, "Brother Helm, you haven't sung for us yet."

"That is right," I agreed and called for my wife to come into the office. I have seldom seen my wife as hungry as she was that morning, for it was almost noon and we had not yet eaten. Nevertheless, she cheerfully accompanied me to the grand piano, and together we sang:

> There's a Rose that is blooming for you, friend,
> There's a Rose that is blooming for me;
> Its perfume is pervading the world, friend,
> Its perfume is for you and for me.
>
> All in vain did they crush this fair flower, friend,
> All in vain did they shatter the tree;
> For its roots, deeply bedded, sprang forth, friend,
> And it blooms still for you and for me.
>
> —H. R. Palmer

Then, as we began to sing "I walk with the King," the glory fell upon us. Until ten minutes till two in the afternoon we preached and sang with the anointing of God on our souls. When the glory of God was falling the sweetest, one sister turned to the other and asked, "Have you ever felt the power of the Holy Spirit like this in your life?"

The sister replied, "Only one time—when Gypsy Smith was in a meeting at Decatur, Illinois."

And just that second, while I was sharing this experience with Homer and his wife in Waco, Texas, God spoke to me, saying: "You are now before the Throne concerning the two issues for which I sent you to pray."

We rejoiced! For five to ten minutes I pled with God for the outpouring of the Holy Spirit upon all the earth (and the Holy Spirit bears witness now as I tell you). I cried for Him to send the mighty refreshings of His Spirit that fell long ago. And He said, "I hear your prayer." Then we came before Him concerning the home to be built by faith, for we had no idea where we would be able to find a lot, nor where the first foundation block or the first studding was coming from.

The next morning as I sat on the bus which was to take me the sixty miles out of my way to Hearne, Texas, to board the train to St. Louis, a young lady asked if she might occupy the seat next to me. I told her that she might. When she put her handbag on the rack overhead I said to her, "This is a wonderful day the Lord has given, isn't it?"

Jesus whispered in my heart, "You be quiet and I will tell you what to say."

I answered, "Yes, Father."

So I was still until God told me what to say. I spoke and waited for His instruction. Soon He had me sharing more, until the glory of God began to fill that old bus. I was revealing to her the joys of salvation as if I were talking to a crowd of one hundred persons. I was explaining how to make one's way to the Straight Gate, wherein if a man would confess his sins he'd be saved, transformed, lose his darkness, and receive the inner joy of Jesus.

Looking over I saw her face was bright; it was all aglow. "Sister! Did you just follow me in the instruction?" I asked.

She nodded, "Yes, I did."

"Then you have peace and joy in your heart?"

She replied with sweet assurance, "I have!"

I rejoiced. My, I was happy! Within seconds I saw beckoning hands in a vision. I said, "Oh, Sister—I see that there are those calling you from foreign lands as well as home lands, saying, 'Come and tell us the story of Jesus.' Sister, you are a missionary. You are called to preach the Gospel of the Lord Jesus Christ."

As this was announced to her by the Spirit, I saw big tears in her eyes. In a few moments she answered, "I had wondered what I was to do. I had asked for help, and God has sent it."

Half-a-mile to a mile farther down the highway toward Hearne, Texas, the Holy Spirit spoke to my heart: "Do you remember the burden you had on Friday night and Saturday morning before you left on this trip?"

I replied, "Oh, well do I recall."

God said, "The burden you had, my Son, was for the woman just saved whom I have called to be my missionary."

Sent by the Lord of all Heaven on a journey for prayer concerning the home to be built by faith, we found a priceless soul called to declare the Gospel of Christ. What a marvelous privilege.

After returning from Texas I was very thankful that God had heard prayer for the home which He was going to build, but I had no idea how it would be done. However, Jesus had His own plan, which I was simply to wait upon.

One day a minister friend and his wife visited us. She was under heavy burden. When we prayed to locate what God was revealing to her, the Holy Ghost said, "Her burden is for your home. You are to get started."

"Glory to God!" I nearly shouted. Jesus had given the signal to start. Her husband accompanied me as I went to speak to Mr. Thornburg, my banker, about lot number seven of the W. E. Baker Addition of our village—a lot which the banker himself owned.

"Well, Loran," he said cordially, "first of all I'm so glad that you and Florence have decided to stay here in this community with us. But as far as that lot is concerned, a number have already wished to buy it. What will they think of us if we sell it to you? And, we have likewise thought of someday building there ourselves." I explained to him that he simply would have to meditate about it and decide what he felt best. "Who is going to help you build this house?" he inquired.

I said, "God."

"That is wonderful," he replied, "but where is the money?"

"God is going to build this home," I reiterated, and began to share with him how God had revealed to my heart in 1934 that He would some day provide for us a home which was to be built by faith in Jesus.

"That sounds good," he told me kindly, "but how about the money for the materials and the supplies?"

"Well, God knows where it is," I answered.

"Don't you have a backlog of savings or cash to start the building?" he asked.

I said, "No. There are a few brothers and sisters in the prayer band who have sacrificed to help us. .They haven't much, but we are trusting God to supply."

"You come back tomorrow," he told us. "I will talk to my wife to decide whether or not we can let you have lot number seven."

"I would like to have prayer before we leave," I mentioned.

"That would be fine," he agreed. And if they never had anyone down on their knees in the council room of that bank before, they had one that January day of 1952. When I said, "Amen," the banker said, "Amen," for he was a precious brother: a man faithful to attend church and also prayer meeting when he could. He was my friend then and still is now.

The following day, accompanied by another minister friend, I made my way back to the bank. As I opened the bank door the Holy Ghost fell through my body pleasantly. My banker friend inquired how I was getting along, and I answered, "I am trusting." He asked if I had yet acquired a backlog of cash or assets. "No," I acknowledged, but I believe God will provide. This home will be built by God. The Lord is going to do this."

"That sounds good," he said with warmth and concern, "but I would hate to see you get a few studdings up in the air and not be able to complete it." Mr. Thornburg lived just across the alley from lot number seven and he had more than simply a professional interest in our home being completed if it were begun. It is remarkable to me that this precious man was so gracious and understanding when there was little justification from a business point of view for even considering our request at all.

"Brother," I told him, "I believe that is where faith will come in."

He looked at me, then said kindly, "That's fine—you may have the lot."

I was on my knees in that office as quickly as I could get there, thanking God in Jesus' name for this miracle!

When I left the bank that day I made my way in a slight mist of rain to lots number six and seven on South Fulton Street. My brother owned lot number six and had been gracious to promise us fourty-four feet of his property if the banker would sell us lot number seven, making our lot ninety-eight feet by 132 feet.

I was rejoicing, for this least servant had been waiting many years for this day. I got down on my knees in that mist, looked up, and prayed, "Oh, Lord God—this lot is Yours. Sanctify it from side to side and end to end." And

God sanctified that whole place to His name's honor and glory. He has told me since then, "This place is mine. This belongs to me." Seldom has He told me this about lands or buildings across the United States.

In a short time about six or seven hundred dollars came into the "Ram Fund." This was enough to purchase the lot as well as the cement, the sand, the gravel, and the blocks for the footing of the foundation. A friend had volunteered to bring his bulldozer and prepare the lot, but we had no idea how we were going to continue building. We were simply trusting and rejoicing.

Some six to eight days after the banker had sold us the lot, my father-in-law knocked on the door of our room (for we were at that time living with my wife's parents) to inform me that someone wanted to see me. I had prayed until one or two in the morning and was still exhausted. Instead of putting on my robe to come out to pray with the visitor, as was my custom, I asked my father-in-law to send him into the room while I remained in bed.

Presently into the room came a timid, gentle man leading a small boy by the hand. They entered quietly and sat in a chair across the room. "I am Horace Reynolds," the man quietly stated. "I have heard of the home to be built by faith." From where I lay on the bed I could see moisture standing in his eyes. "I just wondered," he continued very slowly, word by word, "if you would accept the trees in my woods for the materials of your home?"

I tell you, I was out of that bed and on my knees, saying, "Thank You, Jesus! You have provided the lot; You have sent in finance for the footing and the foundation; and now You have given us the wood for the floor joists, the ribs, and the rafters of this home. We praise Thee, our Father, for doing this!" I sanctified the trees right there on that bedroom floor. To say that I was happy would not express the deep joy and thanksgiving in my heart for God providing like this.

Thirty of Brother Reynolds' eighty acres comprised a fine woods, which appeared as if stock had never grazed in it. When I took a sawyer friend to view the trees he told me in his delightful Swiss accent, "Loran, these are quality trees!" But the woods was far back on the property, with many dense thickets of smaller trees all around. I knew that it would take a miracle to get the large trees out after they were felled.

We had additional difficulties in finding someone to cut the trees. From about January tenth to March nineteenth we looked for a man to do the cutting. One person agreed to do it, but when it came time for the job, he said that his hands were swollen and he wouldn't be able to work. It seemed as if the devil was fighting severely, but we continued to seek and to pray.

After over two months of diligent search I located a Christian man willing to fell the trees. In a bank barn on a rainy afternoon I met with him, having a little prayer together. He told me, "Rev. Helm, I'll cut your trees down the day after tomorrow—March twenty-first."

"Praise the Lord!" I exclaimed with thanksgiving. God had provided the man we needed after this long delay.

On March 21, 1952—five years to the day that we had come to live with Mother and Dad Spence—I wakened early, put on my old clothes, and left the house so thrilled that I forgot to take any sack lunch with me. All I could think about was getting the trees ready for the home. The day was sharp and cold. Brother Reynolds got me his old Army hat to cover me up better, for I'm a cold-natured person. That hat covered me down to my chin. I still wear it sometimes in the winter when I go out to burn the trash.

When the workmen felled the first tree they said, "Now Brother Helm, we would like for you to take hold of this saw and cut the first log for the home built by faith." It was the first time I had ever taken hold of a saw like that. What a thrill it was to see it cut down through that first log for the home which God was building for His glory.

It was soon time for lunch, but I had failed to bring my food. Therefore I was trying to slip off into the woods so that the men wouldn't notice. "Here! Rev. Helm! Where are you going?" the foreman called out. I told him that I thought I would go on the other side of the woods while they ate. But he said, "Oh, no. You come back and share a sandwich. I want you to have grace before we eat." I tried to tell them that they had worked hard and that I was not worthy to have any of their food, but they insisted.

I got down on my knees beside them, took off that old Army cap, pulled my coat around me, and looked up toward Heaven to ask God's blessing on this humble lunch. As I started to sanctify those little sack lunches I suddenly entered into a heavenly banquet hall. The glory of the Lord came down and I was as happy as if I were in a king's palace. The joy of the Lord was all around us and within us.

Opening my eyes I looked at the man sitting on the far log—a man who had told me earlier in the day that, to his shame, he knew more gamblers and drunkards than anybody in New Castle—and his face was all aglow. The tears were coming down his cheeks. Right in the midst of grace for the table, he was close to the Kingdom of God and was about as happy as I was. Because God, not man, had ordained that this home be built, He just sent a little of His Kingdom into the woods on the first day that the trees were being cut for the ribs and joists of the home to be built by faith, and softened a hardened sinner's heart. Praise the Lord!

In those seven days one hundred trees were felled, a total of 24,400 square feet of quality white oak, red oak, bass wood, and other varieties. When the trees had gone through the sawmill and the lumber had been delivered on the lot, several men of our community marveled at it. "This is the best bunch of timber I've seen in many a day," one precious man said. Another was amazed that it had so few knots in it. Brother and Sister Reynolds had given us the best of their woods, and my prayer was that God would, in turn, give the best of everything back to them. I still call him every once in a while to tell him how deeply I appreciate his obedience in giving us the fine trees of his woods.

On March twenty-eighth the last tree was cut—a red oak 138 years old: which meant that it had been a small sapling when my great, great-grandfather helped build the church in Windsor over one hundred years ago. It was being grown then to become a part of the home which God would build for his great, great-grandson, who was going to walk with God. Praise the Lord!

When we had started to cut the trees the lane had been filled with water; but the weather had so wonderfully changed that by the end of the week we could drive the car back to the woods. Climbing into the car with the three men who had cut down all this beautiful timber I said, "Brothers, now that you have finished your labor, would you allow me the privilege of just talking to Jesus for a moment?" And as I thanked God for all those trees I began to weep. It was precious how God visited us in that car. They drove me up to the barn lot, where I gave them the two hundred twenty dollars and some cents which God had provided for this work. We were so very thankful for all that had been done for us in every way.

Before I left the farm, Brother Reynolds and his son, Philip, got into the car with me. We had another prayer meeting; then I was ready to start for home since I had revival services that night. But the Holy Spirit said, "Wait—don't move."

As we waited in the car, Brother Reynolds began to tell me about a certain man. He had not shared long before I interrupted. "Why I know him! He was converted in Greens boro when I was there!" And I began to relate how Jesus had wooed his heart and drawn him to the cross. Soon I was shouting, Brother Reynolds was weeping, and as I turned to look at Philip in the back seat I saw the light of Jesus all over his face. "Philip," I asked, "did you just find Jesus?" And he answered, "Yes."

Still rejoicing that a soul had been saved, I again thought, "Surely I must be on my way." God again said, "Wait— don't move." Isn't it wonderful that Jesus could tell me not to leave that place? God has shown me that if we in the church don't wait on Him enough, we won't be able to discern His will: we won't perceive Him when He operates with us; we won't understand what He is showing us.

We in the ministry and the laity need to wait on God in order that He can teach us how to proceed and can reveal to us what He wants next. If we don't know what God wills to do in our daily lives and in our church services, it is like trying to have school with teachers who don't know their ABC's. If we try to have church without first waiting on God long enough that He might teach us His ABC's, how can we expect to have His Kingdom in our midst?

Please try to observe what God is teaching us here about the seriousness of really walking with Him. I wanted to go home. The trees were cut down. I was ready to get started. Do you see what I would have missed if I had gone?—I would have missed the conversion of this precious boy, who has been a minister of the Gospel now for a few years.

God has much for us to do if He can get us quiet enough. But He had to slay me for months and years before I could understand His guidances and His operations. I had to walk with Him for years and wait before Him on my knees hundreds of hours while He taught me how to listen to and obey Him.

We do not need intellectual attainment and aesthetic sensitivity in the church today as much as we need a genuine humbleness of heart. I know that we need education, but we need far more a brokenness within, a desire to wait upon God and love Him for Himself alone. God wants to teach us of Himself, but too often we prefer, instead, to follow the patterns of men.

One fact will never change: **to be taught of God will crucify the natural tendencies and the reasonable plans of the fleshly mind.** Very few have ever been willing to follow the path to

God which daily crucifies what we want to do, how we want to do it, and the time schedule in which it is to be accomplished. The path which leads to a true fellowship with God leads directly and inevitably to the Cross. One cannot bypass it, or he steps off the Narrow Way.

I was wanting to go, but God had instructed me to wait. I asked, "Jesus, what is it?" The Lord spoke in my heart, "It is the boy's eyes. Philip has trouble in his eyes."

Ten seconds after Jesus revealed this to my heart, Brother Reynolds, in his quiet way, spoke very softly, "My son can't see very well." Opening my Thompson Chain Reference Bible I turned to the thirteenth chapter of Hebrews and held it for the boy to read, but he could not even read the large type.

I reached back over the seat, put my thumb and index finger of my right hand on this young man's eyes, and called to God. I prayed once and then again. When I started praying the third time the Holy Ghost came into my arm with great power. This had never taken place at any time in my life before. My arm shook with the power of God going through it. I knew beyond a shadow of doubt that this boy was going to see.

When I again held up my Bible, Philip not only read the large type, he came right down and read the small print where Paul says: "Remember them that are in bonds, as bound with them; and them which suffer adversity, as being yourselves also in the body." His daddy was weeping with thanksgiving and I was rejoicing. This man had given the best of his woods to God's least servant, and on the day that the last tree for the home built by faith was cut, God saved his son and opened his eyes. Glory to God!

One of my brothers in Jesus sent his partner, John L., with his bulldozer to clear a path for the trucks to reach the woods that we might haul the logs to the mill. This dear man, who was to find Jesus a short while later, returned home the first day with the report, "I have never seen so many preachers in one woods in all my life!"

266

Many were assisting us in loading logs on the truck by means of skids, chains, and a tractor. We were inexperienced at this type of work, but the Lord helped us move eleven loads of logs to the mill some three-and-a-half miles away. Everything was going fine on the twelfth load as each log was secured by chains and pulled up the skids by the tractor. A man on each end of the log guided each piece into its proper position. Just as the men hooked onto the last log of the twelfth load the Holy Spirit spoke to me. "Wait a moment," I called out. "Something is wrong!"

"What do you mean?" they asked. "We're doing it just like all the other times. It's not any different."

"But Jesus tells me something is not quite right," I told them again. "There is danger."

"We can't see it," they said.

"I know it," I agreed, "I can't see it either. But you men stay away from the ends of the log. Don't follow it up, because something is wrong."

They believed my report and stood aside as the tractor started pulling the log up the skids. When it was just about eleven inches from reaching the top of the load and easing into place, the chains suddenly broke and that log came hurtling down with a crash! If it had not been for the Holy Ghost warning us, those men could have been crushed to death. How we praised God for His guidance!

After my dear friend had bulldozed the lot, we were preparing to lay the footing and foundation. A man by the name of Forrest J. brought the sand and gravel for the beginning work, and God gave us a Holy Ghost meeting with him. When he dumped the sand and gravel he said, "Don't worry about what this costs. I have been blessed more than these materials are worth." God had given us a rejoicing time over the sand and gravel that made up the footings of the home. Praise His wonderful Name for making a way where there seemed to be none.

We had many prayer meetings in each section as the home

began to take form in the rough; for as we began to see God's revelation to my heart come to pass, we were humbled and so grateful. The Holy Spirit began to move upon the hearts of his people. A man in the North, whom I had led to Jesus by the help of the Holy Spirit in 1946, said to me, "You need some help. We have a burden for you." I told him that we were just trusting the Lord and he replied, "Here is two hundred dollars and a check for five hundred dollars. In a few days a check for a thousand dollars will come and in so many days another thousand will come." This sacrificial act of obedience permitted the carpenters to begin erecting the frame of the house.

During this period a number of persons in our little village were conjecturing, "That home will soon be stopped. It can't be done." One person spoke to a minister friend about us at that time saying, "Well, the boy has gotten along pretty well through the years, but building this home by faith is a mountain he will never cross. He can't climb over this. It's too high." Of course, I couldn't have gotten over anything. But I had an Elder Brother who was making the path and leading the way. His hands were mighty to deliver. His hands were beautiful to save. He could reach around the universe to the end of all things. Glory to God!

The entire project was far beyond anything I had ever dreamed, for we did not make the choice of the home which was to be built. My wife and daughters were to look over various plans for homes, but none was right until we came to this specific one. It included two stories with living room, dining room, kitchen, prayer room, foyer, utility, hallway, bath with shower, and garage downstairs; upstairs—four bed-rooms, hallway, and complete bath. This home was so large that when we contemplated building, it seemed to me as if I were actually trying to climb over a large mountain. I didn't know where all the labor and supplies were going to come from, but somehow the Lord gave me the sweet as-surance that He would take care.

One day, after they had brought a load of lumber to the lot, I went with a friend to the restaurant in Farmland for lunch. We had just finished the blessing when I saw this man seated at the counter. The Lord said, "He has back trouble," revealing to me the location of the difficulty. I spoke to the man just a few feet away saying, "My Brother, do you have back trouble?" And he said that he did have. "Is it right here?" I asked, pointing to the place Jesus had shown me.

"That is where it is," he admitted.

"Would you give God all the praise, all the honor, and all the glory if He would heal you right now?" I asked him. He said that he surely would; so I asked God in Heaven to send His power into this man's back, to put all the cartilages and bones into place for His glory. When prayer was finished I asked him to lean over and touch the floor, which he did! God had healed him instantly. He was so touched by Jesus' love that he went to services the same evening and began his affiliation within the church. The owner of the restaurant told me some time later that this man had not had that trouble in his back since.

While we continued eating lunch that day, we were talking about the town of Shirley, Indiana, where my friend lived and where, also, my father was then pastoring. As we talked, such a terrible burden came upon me that I told my friend, "My brother, I have such a burden for Shirley, Indiana. It is severe! I have to pray." I quietly began to plead, "Oh, God, take care of this town. You know about the situation that's coming. Take care and drive back whatever this is." I cried and pled until I was relieved. "You'll know when you get home what this means," I told my friend.

That evening Florence, the girls, and I were away until late, and upon our arrival home Mother Spence informed us that someone had phoned several times while we had been gone. When I returned the call, I discovered that it was my friend from Shirley. "Rev. Helm," he related with excitement, "do you remember how God dealt with you today at the restaurant about this town of Shirley? Well, I want to tell you that I came home and was standing out in my father's back yard telling him about the wonderful things God has been doing, when we saw this tornado coming into Shirley from the West. It was a terrible thing!" (My father saw it and told me afterwards that he never again wanted to see anything like it.)

But do you know what God did? He permitted the tornado only to damage the lumber yard a little before taking the fury of the storm right up in the air, where it blew apart. Not a single person was killed. God was so good to answer prayer and deliver.

For one year the raw timber in the floor joists, the ribs, and the rafters needed to stand exposed to the elements in order to cure. The home in the rough was not a very attractive sight with naked timbers standing starkly against the sky. Some persons rather ridiculed it, calling it "the barn." But the rough timbers which made our home then appear ugly also gave it such unusual strength. My dear friend who works with huge earth-moving equipment told us that he would not be afraid to run his heavy crane right over the second story. If you had seen the huge white oak floor joists, you would really begin to understand that God gave us the very best materials for this home (though it will be only by God's help and protection that our home could be kept safe in all types of situations in the future).

Other dear ones felt led of the Lord to offer us assistance. (May I say that I did not ask anyone at any time for help unless he had first asked me what he could do to assist me.) One man said to me, "You need help. Come over to see me." He took me into a bank and gave me five hundred dollars to buy doors and the plyscore sheathing for the sub-flooring of the entire downstairs. When we needed windows and siding, the Lord marvelously laid it on a man's heart to give the finance needed. As it came time for the roof to be put on, God miraculously provided for us. Step by step

Jesus was bringing His revelation to pass before our eyes, and we sought to thank Him much for every loving gift and kind assistance.

In 1952 I had had the privilege to lead a young boy to Christ and see his sister get back to God (oh, that they would remain faithful to the blessed Saviour). Their father was so thankful for how God had used us to encourage his family that he called us one day. "I want you to bring your wife and daughter and come to see me in the next couple of weeks," he said. So we made our way there. Just as we turned off the road to enter the long lane leading to their lovely home God spoke to me from Heaven. "Oh, Honey!" I said. "God is revealing something wonderful to me as we arrive at this precious home."

Once inside their home we began to share things of the Kingdom and pray. Finally Brother Campbell asked, "Rev. Helm, what is the need of the home? What do you need now?"

I was thankful to the Lord for his asking me. "Well, Brother," I told him, "we need rock lath for nine rooms, two halls, and two baths." That was quite a huge item.

"I'll tell you what I'll do," he said. "I'll send it to you."

"Do you mean that you'll provide all the rock lath that we need?"

"I'll send a truck load," he declared, "enough lath to do the whole thing." I tell you I thanked the Lord. I praised God! "What else do you need?" he asked me.

I was still thanking God for the rock lath and he was asking me what else we needed. "Brother, we need a water heater," I managed to tell him.

"I'll give you a check for that," he said, and wrote me a check for three hundred dollars. One hundred was to purchase our water heater and the other two hundred was applied to our bill at the lumber yard. My, how we did praise God for the way He was working!

After the rock lath had been put on, we needed to pray concerning the plaster for these same nine rooms, two halls, and two baths; a project that I had heard would cost at least fifteen to eighteen hundred dollars. At that time I had no money, had just closed a revival in a small country church, and had been fasting three days when I received three letters: the first contained ten dollars; the second was a letter from this little church stating that they felt led to send us more money from their Sunday School treasury; and the third letter was from Mrs. Campbell saying, "My husband will be at your home this afternoon with the plaster contractor from Richmond, Indiana." We rejoiced that morning because God was helping us. We felt so unworthy of everything.

When Mr. Campbell and the contractor arrived that afternoon I showed them the walls to be finished and asked, "Sir, how much will it cost for the plaster, the insulating material, and the labor for this home?"

Just as I asked the plasterer this question, Mr. Campbell spoke up: "Rev. Helm—don't worry about the cost. We'll look after that."

I fell on my knees in that dining room and cried, "Lord, you have been making the way day after day and time after time. When we haven't known what to do, you have taken care." I sanctified all the plaster, materials, and labor the best I knew how, trying to thank Him and thank Him and thank Him in Heaven for providing the needs of this unworthy servant.

You see, dear one, this to me is a miracle story because we weren't instigating; we weren't arranging; we weren't scheming; we weren't pulling for this or asking for that. We were only trusting and waiting. It is a simple thing to talk about trusting God for all things, but something far different to experience it, believe me.

In a few weeks the plaster contractor had sent a crew of five men to our home. I would be talking first with this man about Jesus, and then I would tell another about answers to prayer. As they worked I would try in my limited way to tell them the good news of Christ. Some time after they had completed their work in our home, the foreman of this plastering crew, an excellent craftsman, was eating lunch in a restaurant when something happened in his body and he died in a few hours. Mr. Campbell said it seemed as if he was living just long enough to reach the home built by faith that he might receive a lift, a little help of some kind. It was very important that I shared with these five men the things of God while they were in our home.

With a dwelling the size of this one, I wanted a gas furnace. But many in our village were of the opinion that we would never be able to obtain a gas permit, because several from the town had already tried and had been refused. "What are you going to do?" they asked. All I could tell them was that I was trusting.

I made application for the gas permit in the main office in Muncie with Mr. H., the chief engineer, and was told that I would have an answer in three weeks. When the three weeks had passed, I knew that my request had not been granted. I felt that I should go back and inquire again, but just as my hand touched the door of the gas company the Lord of Heaven said, "Don't enter this place at this time."

"Oh, Jesus," I cried. "I want to go in and find out about the permit."

"Not now," he counseled me. So I went on down the street, although in my flesh I wanted so badly to go in and find out the situation.

Days went by, then Jesus led me to go back. As I entered, people were ahead of me speaking to Mr. H.; therefore I stood and waited, the last in line. When it was my turn I said, "Sir, I am Rev. Helm. I am interested in obtaining a gas permit," and explained to him the particulars.

Mr. H. informed me, "It will be six months to two years before we will have any permits available." I thanked him and started to leave.

During the last few moments of this conversation a handsome, black-haired man had come out of his private office

273

and seated himself at a big double desk just opposite the desk of the chief engineer. As I started to leave, he spoke: "Just a minute."

"Yes, Sir," I answered. He then asked me two questions and I told him about the home built by faith. I learned later that he already knew of our home from one of his men who had been in a restaurant where the owner had a gallon jar full of water in which customers could deposit loose change to help purchase a gas furnace for a home to be built by faith. I learned that the man to whom I was talking was the head man of that particular office. God had brought him out of his private room and set him down at this desk just at this precise moment so we might meet. In all the times I was back in that building, I never once saw this man again. "You plan on the gas furnace," he said.

"Do you mean that we can have a gas furnace?" I asked. He said, "You plan on it."

Glory to God! The Lord answered prayer and took care of it when it seemed impossible! "Thank you, Brother!" I told that man, and went my way rejoicing. We still have that gas permit on file in our home.

The day Florence and I went to the tile and marble company to make our first selection for the tile to be used in the shower base and the hearth of the fireplace, I wanted to have prayer with the man and his wife who owned the business. They were in his car as we were leaving, and when I began praying he started the motor. I thought he was going to pull the car away as we prayed. The second time I returned I felt led again to have prayer with the owners. On this occasion the husband simply left us and walked away into the kitchen. He was a very backward and timid man.

Our choice of tile had to be changed twice; so when my wife and I returned the third time to the tile company, this man's wife began talking with us. Soon we were sharing of our walk with God. In all her years she had never known

274

Jesus; but that rainy afternoon she took a little trip to Calvary and met the wonderful Saviour of all men. The salvation of this precious soul is connected with the tile in the shower base and the hearth.

The day that her husband came to lay the tile he told me that the job would cost ninety dollars. Though I had not asked him for any deduction, he said, "I wouldn't do it for anyone else for that price, but I will for you." When he stepped inside our home and began to look around he was so astonished. "I wasn't expecting to see a home like this!" he remarked.

I told him, "It's not us. The Lord Jesus has made the way for us. Everything you see is because of Jesus and for His honor. He's provided and made the way. I don't know what to do, but He does."

When he finished the work that day, I took him upstairs, showing him various rooms. He was appreciative. "This surely is a wonderful place," he told me. And I again tried to praise the Lord for providing.

Then I said to him, "Now, Brother, here is the ninety dollars that I owe you."

"You don't owe me anything," he declared.

"You told me it would cost ninety dollars!" I exclaimed.

"That's entirely alright," he replied. The Lord had touched his heart.

In January, 1953, when the house was ready for finished floors, I went to the phone to order the flooring, but the Holy Ghost would not let me call. I could have ordered the hardwood from many cities, having it delivered within days. But every time I would go to the phone to call, the Holy Spirit would check me.

My girls were anxious for the floors to be finished, for they had not had a room of their own for many years. In fact, the five of our family slept in one room for some time. Four of us, then, slept in this same room for almost seven years. Our daughters would keep asking me, "Daddy, have you gotten the flooring yet?" When I would tell them that I hadn't, they would ask, "But why?" And I would try to tell them that I was simply walking with the Lord and could not go ahead until Jesus permitted me.

We kept wanting to order the flooring through January, February, and March. Each time I went to the telephone, however, the Lord checked me. My girls repeated many times, "Daddy, we want to move into our rooms. They're all ready except for the floors. Can't you order the flooring?"

And I would explain to them, "I would like to girls, but you see—I walk with God and He reveals to me that I can't order the flooring yet."

On the last Monday of April, my wife and I were in the northern part of the state with a man who showed me two pieces of red oak select flooring, which came from Bowling Green, Kentucky. He said, "Rev. Helm, if you like, I can get this for you and you may pay for it as you are able with no interest. Take ten or fifteen years to pay for it if need be."

When he told me that, the Holy Ghost operated in my heart. Turning to my wife I said, "Honey, there is more involved in this than just the floors of our house."

Some days later, on May sixth, I was informed that these three hundred thirteen bundles of red oak select were waiting to be unloaded from a large truck. I went to the lot in order to help my brothers and another man unload these bundles weighing fifteen to thirty pounds each. None of them knew that I had been fasting for three days concerning the Holy Ghost Revival to the World. It was not long before my strength left me. I had to excuse myself and rest. I came back to carry for awhile, then had to rest some more. I weighed only about 145 to 148 pounds. "Lord, give me strength for these remaining few bundles," I prayed. And every time I reached for a bundle, the power of God would assist me.

By the time I had lifted the last bundle, I was under the anointing of the Spirit. I found myself looking into the face of the man who had brought this flooring from the South, and I was telling him about a Friend of mine. The power of God fell on that truck and he didn't take his eyes off of mine. He told me that he had heard of Christ but that God had never called him. Before long I was down on the street preaching up to him as he stood in the truck.

I then took him over to see the lovely new car God had provided me through ten or fifteen families. I was telling him how I had had it only three days when a big stone truck had backed out from the curb the wrong way and simply ripped the front fender back. I told him what peace had been in my heart when I heard the noise of the accident, and how I had come out of the restaurant where I was eating and praised the Lord in spite of my new car being damaged. While I was telling him of this experience, I asked, "My Brother, do you have the call of God in your heart? Is your heart throbbing?"

He answered, "It is."

"Would you give your heart to Jesus today?"

His eyes left me for the first time since the anointing came upon me and his head went down. "I am ready," he declared. We started in prayer together and soon found the Cross, where his sins fell off and he became a new creature in Christ Jesus. The man who had brought the hardwood flooring for the prayer room and the upstairs of the home built by faith had found the Master on May 6, 1953.

I recall being outside one day when Rev. Luke M.'s future son-in-law drove up. We had just closed a revival at this pastor's church a few days before, and we had been praying that God would truly come upon this young man with old-fashioned conviction. Coming up the walk that day he remarked, "Rev. Helm, I can't get along with anyone. I can't even get along with myself."

We came right inside to the unfinished living room, spreading some newspapers on the floor. He knelt down facing the south, I knelt down facing the west, and we began to bombard

Heaven. The blood of Jesus was applied to his heart and God took all the blackness, the darkness, the sin, and the iniquity out of him. He wrote his name down in the Lamb's Book of Life and made a new man out of him. He was laughing, he was crying, he was shining. Praise the Lord.

Because of God's leading me way back in 1937 to take the least pastorate offered us, I was led to Homer Pumphrey. This leading then took me to several churches in Texas many times. It was in one of these congregations that Brother Homer S. was wonderfully converted and his wife miraculously healed as well. I only wish it were possible to give you some small idea of what all God has accomplished for His glory because of that single leading in 1937: the souls saved on the trains going to and from Texas; the bodies healed; the victories won for Jesus. Only eternity will reveal it for the Holy Spirit has led it all.

Homer S. was Brother Pumphrey's lay leader, a concrete engineer who owned and operated a successful business. When Jesus healed his wife, the Lord laid it on his heart that he should temporarily leave his business, his men, and all his work to travel a distance of over one thousand miles back with me from Texas to pour the concrete for the porch and walks of the home built by faith. Needless to say, he really surprised me when he suggested that he wanted to do this for us. I was deeply thankful for God laying this on his heart, and for his obedience to come.

While Homer was finishing the work, he took such a pain in his heart. God privileged me to pray for him and he was healed. A few hours later my daughter, Nancy, came running in. "Oh, Daddy!" she cried. "The rain is coming and is going to ruin the porch and the walk! Come out and ask God to stop the rain till it is all dry."

I ran outside where the men were still doing the finishing touches, lifted my hands, and prayed, "Heavenly Father, I know that Thou art faithful. I just pray You'll not let it rain on this walk and ruin it. Stop the rain, Father, and we'll give Thee the praise and the glory." And God just stopped the shower. It didn't rain any more until the concrete had set.

Later that evening, when all six of us brothers came over to my parent's home to sing for Homer, he was hurting so severely in his hip that he could hardly stand on it. We had another prayer meeting and God took out all the pain. Our song fest that night was just for him, with Florence playing the piano and the six brothers singing. Homer has never forgotten it. He told us later, "I've hunted bear in the mountains of Colorado; I've caught fish in the streams of Mexico; but the most wonderful trip I have ever made was to Parker, Indiana, to pour the porch and the walks of the home built by faith." Jesus alone could have done this.

December, 1953, the home which Jesus had shown me in my heart as a light in 1934, was dedicated. About 175 people were seated in the living room, the dining room, in the kitchen, in the prayer room, up the stairway; they sat on the beds in the bedrooms, stood in the halls and in the bathrooms to help us commemorate this precious moment when God's promise to an unworthy eighteen-year-old was fulfilled through the good grace of Jesus and the faithfulness of His people.

I was especially grateful to Jesus for letting my wife's father live to see this home dedicated; for if you recall, he asked me but one question when I took his only daughter with me to live wholly by faith: "Do you think you will be able to make a living for your family?" He believed me when I told him how God had called me to trust Jesus. But for him to be able to see God provide his daughter and son-in-law one of the nicest homes in that village spoke more to him of God's faithfulness and the true calling of God upon our lives than words could ever say. Thank you Jesus.

You see, when I fell in love with my wife, I fell in love with her parents as well. I loved them and made over them just like I did over my own father and mother. In the late forties

the Lord told me, "Love them much, for their time is short."
On June 10, 1947, in a dream I saw my wife's father dying
in his rocking chair. And in 1949 Dad Spence said to Mother
Spence, "Grace, I'm slipping. I won't be here very long."

I went to my bedroom and began to cry out to God to
extend his days. I prayed, "Lord, when Jacob was with Laban,
you blessed his household. Let Dad Spence live a little longer.
Make him well. Extend his years!" The Lord helped me
pray him through his sixty-fifth birthday to the time of the
dedication. Not long after, he went Home, and I was privileged to pray him through the gates of the City.

Some fifty to one hundred men worked on this home from
the cutting of the trees in the woods to its completion. By
God's grace, I never asked one person to help me, unless
he first came to me and asked if he might assist me in some
way. And, to God's glory (to the best of my knowledge),
among the fifty to one hundred men who worked on that home,
not one thumb or finger was smashed. Ordinarily inexperienced workers will hit a thumb or hurt themselves in some
way. But, because of Jesus, the precious Holy Ghost, not
one man was hurt while working on the home which God
had built.

A few dear ones were fearful that we would not be able
to keep such a large home going, for a home involves much
care and upkeep. But one of my brothers told them, "If
God is able to provide them a home, He is able to keep it
as well." How true this was we have found out over the
years, and for every single blessing and help from God we
give Him honor.

We moved into this lovely home on December 20, 1953.
From that day until this, God has mercifully seen fit to save
a few souls, encourage hearts, and heal bodies within these
walls. One day Rev. G. brought some friends to see the
home. While we were passing through the dining room God
said, "Pray in here." When I knelt to pray, God revealed
that the man from Peoria, Illinois, to whom I had just been

introduced, could get back to Him today. I began to pray for this fellow whom I had never seen before, and soon he was weeping. He got back to God that very hour! The joy of the blessed Saviour came into his soul. He was happy and we were rejoicing with him.

Mrs. W. E. Baker was a precious Christian woman who had helped us on several occasions, and we had wanted her to visit our home ever since it had been dedicated in December. But she had not been able to come until the following May. As she sat in the living room, I was sharing answers to prayer and a few of the marvelous things which had taken place during the building of the home. A knock on the door interrupted our conversation, and the man who picked up clothing for the laundry came in. "May I see you a minute?" he asked. I told him that he surely could, and took him into the prayer room.

He began to pour his heart out to me. "I prayed last night as a sinner that I could get through this terrible fix that I am in," he confessed to me. "I asked God to lead me to one of His disciples who could help me. When I saw this woman in your front room, I knew that I was in the right place." Wasn't that wonderful? Here we had wanted Mrs. Baker to be with us for weeks and months, but God sent her by on just the right day.

I began to tell him how to find the Narrow Way. I got down on my knees and prayed and then asked him to pray. When he finished he said, "Rev. Helm, from the time I started to leave this chair until my knees hit the floor, I felt like shouting. I tell you, I really got it! Can I tell your family what Jesus has done for me?" The Lord had already heard him tell me all his burdens; so He just took his darkness, his cares, and his sins from him before he could even kneel to pray.

Going to the north porch he told my wife and her mother, "Do you see that water tower up there about four squares? I would like to be on top of it today telling everyone what God has done for me." As he went out the front door he looked up at the sky and declared with great joy, "What a wonderful day!" It was cloudy and looked as if it might rain any time, but there was sunlight in his soul. Three years later he called to say that, through Christ, he had won seven souls to the Lord.

I was going for prayer one day when I was called back home sixty miles. When I entered the house I found this young woman who told me, "My fiance has cancer of the stomach and the doctors give him no hope. What can be done for him? Is there anything you can do?"

I prayed for a time to learn the counsel of the Holy Spirit, then answered, "If you will both repent of all your sins, all your neglects, all your wrongs—I believe Jesus will shrivel that cancer in his body."

Suddenly she cried, "Am I having a nervous breakdown?"

"No," I told her, "the Holy Spirit is calling you." Her heart was throbbing with such force that she didn't know what was happening to her. I explained, "This is the power of God speaking to you, saying, 'Give Me thine heart.'" She was converted, he was reclaimed, and the cancer dried up in his stomach. That was eighteen years ago.

A call came to our home one day and a man's voice said, "I am in some trouble." I told him that I could hear it in his voice. "Do you have time for me?" he asked.

"Certainly," I replied.

"Are you sure?" the voice asked again.

"Yes," I assured him. I learned that he had a friend and that they both were in trouble; but when his friend had gone to see this one servant, he continued to look at his watch much of the time, making this person feel as if he wanted to be elsewhere instead of talking with her. "When do you wish to come?" I asked.

"When is it best for you?" he said.

"Let's turn it around," I suggested. "When is it best for you?" He didn't want to be an imposition, but I wanted to make it as easy for him as possible. When he arrived, I heard that he was in a hard, terrible place. I spent two hours with him, and when those two hours were over, beloved, he went out a new man in Christ Jesus.

I was just ready to leave the front door when the Holy Spirit revealed, "You cannot leave." In four minutes a car drove up and out stepped a man with a shining face whom I hadn't seen for three or four years. "My Brother, I'm so glad to see you," he rejoiced, meeting me at the door. "I have been trying to get here for two or three weeks and I knew I was to come today." When I shared with him that God had stopped me or I would have been gone, he praised the Lord.

He began to tell me of his trials and struggles, which I found to be very serious. For three years he had been passing through a desperate battle of the soul. During this period he had been going from place to place seeking help, but no one knew what to tell him. I was able to say to him, "Rejoice, Brother! You're going into the deeper things of God." I would not have known how to counsel him had not God led me through this same deep river, a similar dark area of testing, some years before. "As you go into the deeper things of walking with God you will experience great struggles at times," I was able to share with him. "Sometimes the enemy fights very severely." We began to pray, the glory started to fall, and he was delivered. God be praised for all His marvelous operations and holy workings.

If I had the privilege of taking you from room to room in this home which God has so graciously provided us, I would try to point out where one woman was reclaimed in the prayer room. Another woman with gall bladder trouble met the Saviour and was healed not far from where this other woman found the victory. In my room, our youngest daughter came to a real transforming knowledge of Jesus at the age of twenty-four. Not far from where she met Jesus, just several months ago, another young woman was sanctified. Also in this same room, my nephew of twenty-six years, who had been in very deep sin, was marvelously saved a few weeks ago on February 12. He is now so happy in Jesus. It was in the foyer where God spoke to me one night, along with several of the prayer group, about a missionary in Bolivia who was in danger. We later found out that he and his family were being stoned at that time in their home. God delivered them through prayer.

We could go on, if Jesus would permit and help me, to recall the many things which He has accomplished for His glory in this home: but there is no end to anything which God begins. Our words are too feeble to convey the deep thankfulness in our hearts to Jesus for the way He has provided this home and for the way He continues to bless many who visit it.

We know that we have been unable to mention, nor do we actually know about, all who helped make this revelation a reality. There is no way that we could adequately express our debt of gratitude for each and every person who contributed to the building of this home with their finance, their gifts, their talents, their time, and their prayers. It could not have been accomplished without the obedience of God's people.

I know that the investment of those dear ones who had even a tiny part in building this home will receive precious rewards, for this is not an ordinary home. It is the fulfillment of a divine revelation. It is an expression of the will of God. It is a monument to this village and to this age that God provides for His servants today as He did for His prophets of old.

We rejoice to share with you that subsequent to the first two editions of this humble pilgrimage, our first precious son-in-law, Jack, gave his heart to Jesus in the livingroom of our home early in the morning of October 1, 1975 at approximately two o'clock.

25 WARNING FROM A WATCHMAN

"So thou, oh son of man, I have set thee a watchman unto the house of Israel; therefore thou shalt hear the word at my mouth, and warn them from me . . . if thou dost not speak to warn the wicked from his way, that wicked man shall die in his iniquity; but his blood will I require at thine hand." — Ezekiel 33:7-8

I feel constrained to cry out concerning one of the issues of the time. In the last few years a style has gained increasing popularity which encourages girls and women to expose their bodies. I believe that girls and women who expose their bodies from a little below their knee upward subject every normal man to severe, difficult temptation, the aftermath of which may result in serious penalty at Judgment. The Judgment, of course, is in the hands of God: but being one of His servants, I feel that it is wise to mention it gently and rightly, with caution and carefulness.

In all the writings of leading ministers today—though they are very fine men—I have never read one warning about this matter. Yet, every man of God to whom I have shared my concern has affirmed that what I believe is true. I am certain that our precious women would want to know the seriousness of the clothing styles which they select, for any man who is truly going with Jesus today is undergoing more severe temptation in this world than any woman could possibly comprehend. I know that every handmaid of Jesus would desire to only help men of God rather than place a stumbling block in their way.

Jesus has revealed to me another serious concern of this age, indicated by Paul's words to Timothy: "Charge them that are rich in this world, that they be not high-minded, nor trust in uncertain riches, but in the living God, who giveth us richly all things to enjoy; that they do good, that they be rich in good works, **ready to distribute** . . . laying up in store for themselves a good foundation against the time to come, that they may lay hold on eternal life." (I Timothy 6:17-19)

The Lord has laid it on my heart that I am to lift up my voice in love to all those of any wealth, for Jesus very plainly indicates that it will not be an easy assignment for the rich to enter into the Kingdom of Heaven. He compared the rich man's assignment to persevere to Heaven like that of a rope (as I understand from certain Bible scholars) going through the eye of a needle. It is possible to work a rope through the eye of a needle by separating it first into strands, then dividing these strands into even finer fibers, but it takes much labor and determination. However, Jesus gives encouragement to those who can be classified as wealthy when He added, ". . . But with God all things are possible."

We in the United States can easily conclude that Jesus was talking about millionaires and those with family fortunes when He said, "How hard it is for them that trust in riches to enter into the Kingdom of God!" (Mark 10:24) But when we consider the great poverty which grips numerous small nations and many of the islands of the sea, it is simple to see that if we have a roof over our head, carpet on the floor, and a car to drive, we are actually very wealthy individuals.

I know that it is not popular to mention finances, but as God's servant I must lovingly warn all who have any amount of wealth or I will be responsible for their blood in Judgment. Jesus said that the rich have had their consolation. This has stirred my heart that I would not fail to warn every precious person that we must be certain to pray about where God wants us to place our finance, so that we won't be found wanting when we get to the Judgment.

The Lord has shown me that many people of considerable means—dear ones who have savings, stocks, bonds, or investments of one thousand dollars or more—tend to give to God's work in the proportion of the average wage-earner. Many have rested on the assumption that a tenth is all that God expects us to give of our means. But when I inquire of the Lord, He reveals some very serious facts about those having several thousand dollars in their control.

I must urge every dear person to seek the guidance of the Holy Spirit about how his finance is to be invested in God's Kingdom. The more that I have, the greater proportion of my income God will want me to reinvest in the Kingdom. As I joyfully give it back to Him, He could increase the returns even more. Earnestly seeking God's will in the matter of giving is much more serious than I can tell you.

I wish to make perfectly clear that I deeply respect and appreciate each person who has managed his earthly possessions well and has accumulated some wealth. Such individuals are greatly needed. In fact, it is possible that the abilities which permitted success in the area of finance are gifts from God to be used primarily in the vital areas of financing His Kingdom work.

If we are not sensitive to the Holy Spirit, we'll not press on to discover what God wants us to do with our wealth. If we love God more than we love our possessions, we will be anxious to learn God's will and give gladly what He reveals. But if we love our possessions more than we love God, it will place a great bind on our soul to persevere to God's perfect will and share what He requires.

I do not know how much Jesus will ask of each of you. But God has clearly witnessed that I must warn those who are rich that they not come up to Judgment and discover that they have kept too much for themselves and shared too little for God's work. (And when I tell you this, God says, "I lead thee by the Holy Ghost.") I want to be true and faithful to all people everywhere.

A PRAYERFUL REQUEST

If I might make a humble request, I would like to encourage each of you who read this pilgrimage, if you are suffering from a particular sickness or affliction, to simply have faith for God to heal you. I am not a healer. There is no power in me. However, my faith is that if God wills, you can be healed even as you read these pages. I believe some will be healed as they read these experiences which God has done, at His direction, for others. Please give Jesus all the praise always. If He delays your healing, simply trust and be thankful. If it isn't His will to heal you, be faithful and true just the same, maintaining a right spirit in Jesus by God's grace and help.

The promise of James 5:14-15 is also fully available to every follower of Jesus: "Is any sick among you? let him call for the elders of the church; let them pray over him, anointing him with oil in the name of the Lord: and the prayer of faith shall save the sick, and the Lord shall raise him up; and if he have committed sins, they shall be forgiven him." Each of you may request elders in your local area to anoint you and pray for your healing.

I share this with you because I recognize that many may wish to call me in order that I might pray for their healing. But unless the Holy Spirit leads me, I am unable to pray for anyone. It may be God's will that your pastor pray for you, or the elders near you, or that one of your brothers or sisters in Christ petition Heaven on your behalf.

On the other hand, the Holy Spirit may lead someone to ask me to pray for them, and I would not want to miss a single divine appointment. But, if you are certain that God is leading you to contact me, I would ask that you please grant me the liberty of seeking God's guidance concerning your need.

It is such a high privilege to pray for God's people, and when the Holy Spirit leads I am lifted and strengthened in my soul. If God is not leading, on the other hand, it demands much more strength to pray, for I am not able to get through to the Throne without the Holy Spirit leading and helping me.

I trust that each of you will accept this small request in the spirit of love in which it is given. I need your prayers more than any of you can realize, unless the Lord Jesus reveals it to you by His love and purity.

26 THE BEGINNING

"Then Jesus said to His disciples, if any one desires to be My disciple, let him deny himself—that is, disregard, lose sight of and forget himself and his own interests—and take up his cross and follow Me (cleave steadily to Me, conform wholly to My example in living and if need be in dying, also.) — Matthew 16:24 (Amplified)

This book has not been written to draw attention to myself, nor has it been compiled primarily to inspire God's people. It has been created only at the direction of the Holy Spirit to be a Voice Crying in today's Wilderness of religious thought and practice.   It is a call away from the popular religious forms, away from the competing calls of denominational churches, away from the claims of all earthly ties.   It is the same cry that has distinguished all of God's servants through the centuries.   It was the message of Jesus Himself: "Repent, for the Kingdom of Heaven is at hand."

Every true man of God has called for individuals to prepare for the Heavenly Kingdom.   And God's Kingdom on this earth is simply **His will being done** by those of us in earth, as Jesus clearly told us when He taught His disciples to pray: "Thy Kingdom come.   Thy will be done in earth, as it is in Heaven."   God's "Kingdom come" equals His "will . . . done in earth as it is in Heaven."

You may remember that the first message God gave me after calling me to leave everything in 1941 was Romans 12:1,2: "I beseech you therefore brethren, by the mercies of

God, that you present your bodies a living sacrifice, holy, acceptable unto God, which is your reasonable service. And be not conformed to this world: but be ye transformed by the renewing of your mind, that you may prove what is that good, and acceptable, and **perfect, will of God.**"

He was leading me from the wilderness of man's finest and most earnest attempts of religious service to that rarely experienced realm of **God's perfect will.** Jesus consistently demonstrated that God wanted more than legal fulfilment of duty. He desired to walk with men and lead them according to His own plans and wishes. Even the divine Son of God did not do His own will while on this earth—He submitted joyfully and continually to His Father's will. **This, then, is Christ-likeness: to actually do God's will.** This is what it really means to be a Christian: to actually do what God directs.

As we read of the first Christians in the book of Acts we are made conscious of how earnestly they sought the leadership of the Holy Spirit before they moved along a specific path of action. When we note how often the Holy Spirit gave them literal instructions, it becomes obvious that much of that intimate fellowship with Jesus in the Person of the Holy Ghost has been lost from our present-day Christianity. These early Christians were true **followers of Jesus** in the Person of the Holy Spirit.

In these nearly thirty years of walking with God He has made it increasingly clear to my heart that His desires and His requirements for His followers have not changed. Every man or woman, boy or girl, who claims Jesus as Saviour must likewise press on to experience Him as the absolute Lord of his life. Conversion is only the very beginning in the Christian life, like unto a newborn infant's first little cry. We then begin the adventure and high privilege of walking with Jesus: going where He goes, stopping where He stops, speaking what He speaks, holding silence when He is silent. We are to learn **to actually follow Him day by day.**

But dearly beloved—God has revealed to my heart that seldom in all the ages have men done this. Rarely have persons pressed on from conversion to learn how to walk with Jesus, how to hear the Spirit's voice, how to learn His checks and His guidances. To **follow** someone's instructions, you must first **receive** the instructions.

The great missing link in Christianity through the ages is simply this: **we have not learned how to get our instructions from God.** We have failed to discern God's will. We have forgotten that God has His own ideas and His own plans and have gone along with our own conceptions of how His Kingdom should be run. Terrible to say, but either by choice or by ignorance we have said with our lives concerning Jesus: "We will not have this man to be King over us!" We have instead chosen to be our own rulers. We have become the architects of our own tragically crippled "Kingdom of God."

This is why the power of God does not operate in our midst. We have not waited to receive His instruction and have wandered along a path that seemed right but which proceeded from an earthly origin, not a heavenly one. Only what God leads will stand in Judgment. Only those things begun in the Holy Ghost will reach into Eternity. Any and everything begun in the flesh, no matter how beautiful or apparently sacred, cannot please God. The Word tells us that "they that are in the flesh cannot please God." Can we hear that?—**the flesh cannot please God!**

Jesus was the only man who ever pleased God the Father entirely. And it is still His Son alone who pleases God today. It is only the life of the Son of God living in us that can please God. And Jesus lives in us and dwells in us only as we do His will. It is very simple. Jesus makes this clear when He tells us in Matthew 7:21: "Not everyone that saith unto me, Lord, Lord, shall enter into the Kingdom of Heaven: **but he that doeth the will of my Father which is in Heaven.**" Now Jesus Himself tells us this. He informs us that we will not enter Heaven unless we have done the Father's will!

My loved one—and I love each one of you reading this book with the divine love of Jesus in my heart—can we possibly begin to grasp the tremendous seriousness of what Jesus is telling us? He is saying without question that to truly belong to Him **we must actually do God's will.** We must learn what He wants and follow His directions. We must in actual, everyday life follow the living Lord Jesus Christ. We must learn how to hear the voice of Jesus that we might receive our instructions.

You see, to actually be a follower of Jesus is much more than just having a conversion experience and thinking that is all we need to make it to Heaven. Having our sins forgiven is marvelous and miraculous, and we are unworthy of the tiniest drop of our Saviour's blood. But this is only the very beginning, howbeit, a glorious beginning! My burden over the years has been that very few continue on from conversion to discover how truly marvelous walking with God can actually be. And I know that I have just a slight glimmer of what God has for us here on earth if only we could receive it.

Since God's ways are not our ways, and since His thoughts are far above our own thoughts (even the very best of our converted thoughts), how then can we possibly learn what God wants and discover what He is saying to us? How can we learn to walk with Jesus as the first Christians did? How can we discover this link which has been lost from the Church through the ages?

A portion of the answer, I humbly believe, is to be found in the words of Jesus our wonderful Redeemer when He said: "If any man will come after me, **let him deny himself,** and **take up his cross,** and **follow Me.**" These words are recorded in some form in Matthew 16:24; Mark 8:34; and Luke 9:23: "**If any man will . . . ,**" Jesus said. My heart has often been made heavy by that little word "if," for God has found few in all the centuries who will truly, whole heartedly believe Him and obey Him. But in His precious love He opens the opportunity to "any man."

292

The call from Heaven is for us to "come after" Jesus, to follow His footsteps, to pattern after His example, to be filled with the Holiness of God, without which no man shall see the Lord. We are to be filled with those divine qualities which His sweet Spirit brings forth as fruit: love, joy, peace, long-suffering, gentleness, goodness, faith, meekness, temperance. But in ourselves we are blocked from these priceless virtues by a raging ocean of Sin. We stand on one bank of this angry sea which sin has made. On the opposite shore beckons the priceless rewards made to those who will overcome by the word of their testimony and the blood of the Lamb. There is no way we can reach these rewards by our own insights, our own methods, our own achievements. Jesus was able to walk upon the waves, but alas—we quickly sink in spite of our fervent aspirations.

We would be lost in despair if Jesus had abandoned us to the condemnation of death which bruises everything of earth. This sense of hopelessness is reflected in the response the disciples made to Jesus when He stated the divine require-ment: "Except ye eat the flesh of the Son of man, and drink His blood, you have no life in you." The majority of those who had followed Him cried out in anger and amazement: "This is a hard saying! who can hear it?" When God's standards surpassed their own ability to achieve, they turned back to their own ways and followed the Son of God no more.

"It is the Self-life in man which is brought to despair by God's standards of holiness". There is no fleshly wisdom, no human philosophy, no noble earthly aspiration able to form an acceptable bridge to God's holiness. We are under the con-demnation of death which cursed all that belonged to earth. We are of the earth earthy and can only bring forth death, no matter how noble our intentions nor how high our purpose.

Our only hope is Jesus. He is the Bridge reaching from death to life. He is the Path, He is the Bread along the Way, He is the Water to quench our thirst, He is the Prize towards which we reach. Since we lost all in disobeying God in the

Garden of Eden, our path back to God is in Jesus through obedience. And in order to obey, we must first receive a command which we can obey. To "come after" Jesus means that we obey Him. How then do we learn to obey Him?

The simple, but monumental, first step in following Jesus is found in the next phrase of His command: **"Let him deny himself . . ."** This is wonderfully simple, as are all of God's truths, yet it will take the help of the Holy Spirit for us first, to clearly perceive self-denial; and second, actually begin to apply this to our daily lives.

Our comprehending self-denial is similar to our great, great-grandparents of a hundred years ago asking, "How can I get from the East coast to the West coast in only ten hours?" Most of their friends in the horse and buggy era would have answered, "It's impossible!" But to the one who had been given the vision of the jet airplanes which so numerously criss-cross our modern skies, the reply would have been as simple as "let him deny himself"—"let him fly," he would have answered. (Habakkuk 1:8)

The spiritual fact of "let him deny himself" is marvelously simple; but its practice in everyday life is as staggering to our contemporary understanding as the jet plane would have been to a Civil War soldier. The idea might seem splendid, the possibilities almost inexhaustible: but how on earth do we actually accomplish it?

We learn how to deny Self and obey God by following a remarkable law which governs the Kingdom of God, and that law Jesus clearly stated immediately after telling us about denying Self: "For whosoever shall save his life shall lose it; and whosoever will lose his life for my sake shall find it." He is telling us that the earth, as man knows it and tries to operate it, is going in reverse to the law of God's Kingdom. In order to be the greatest, Jesus tells us, we become the least. In order to gain, we lose. In losing all, we find all.

Now this is the milk and meat of the Gospel. This will help awaken tired spiritual muscles and put a spring in our step if we will pull our chair up real close and chew every bite well. Too many times, I fear, we prefer to have a little sweet cake of blessing and dismiss ourselves from the table. But there'll be plenty of divine calories in this meal if you will keep pressing on in love and appreciation.

God wants to come down and walk arm in arm with us in the garden of our heart, just as He did with Adam. Adam chose to disobey God, which threw us into death by sin. Jesus brings us to life by His shed blood, His death, and resurrection. But to receive this life we must come low in brokenness and humility.

The Bible tells us that "The sacrifices of God are a broken spirit: a broken and a contrite heart, oh God, thou will not despise." (Psalms 51:17) And the promise of God to all men is that He ". . . is nigh unto them that are of a broken heart; and saveth such as be of a contrite spirit." (Psalms 34:18) However, most of the time we want to get up from this place of contrition and assume a place of recognition and respect. **The secret of beginning and continuing a walk with God is to remain at the bottom in humility always in your heart.**

It is not the nature of man and woman to go this way, however. The path of humility is absolutely contrary to our nature because of the carnal spirit and the carnal mind which we acquired in the Fall. This carnal mind takes us to death, according to the apostle Paul (Romans 8:6,7), and is likewise enmity against God, for "it is not subject to the law of God, neither indeed can be." This same mind is born into every living child.

Jesus was the only person born of woman without the carnal nature, for this nature is inherent in Adam's seed. Babies get their blood from their father. But, praise God, Jesus didn't have an earthly father. He came by the divine Father, the Holiness of God. His sacred blood was from God Himself—undefiled, holy, and pure. Jesus Christ was born of the virgin Mary, and He was without sin: perfect! He was the only one ever born in this earth without sin, without this terrible carnal nature. And He became the propitiation for our sins, that we sinners could be saved. I am only a sinner saved by grace. Bless the Holy Name of Jesus.

It is this inbred carnal nature which refuses to acknowledge the right of God to reign over our lives. It is this carnal mind which resents, resists, and rejects anything of that divine mind which was in Christ Jesus. Therefore, this carnal mind must be dethroned. The carnal nature must be slain in order that God can replace it with His own nature, with the mind of Christ. He wishes to give us His Spirit, but He can only give His Spirit to those who obey Him. To do otherwise would be dangerous. (I Cor. 3:1-3)

There is so much carnality in us: much more than we are aware of. We are angry, envious, spiteful, resentful, critical, contentious, argumentative, foolish, and jesting. Some people are willing to relinquish part of their carnal selves, but retain five or ten percent. God wants to slay this carnal nature out of us absolutely.

The reason sinners don't want to have much to do with the church today is because there is carnality in most who claim to be Christian, and sinners want nothing to do with that kind of "Christianity." We pray good prayers, sing fine songs, preach commendable sermons, but the persons who live around our churches seldom attend. Why?—because Jesus is not often seen much in those who are praying and preaching and singing.

Oh, my friend!—Jesus wants to live in us! He wants to work through us in little humble ways of holy love and self-less giving. **But we are trying to have Christianity without the Cross.**

The Cross is simply God's will. The Cross is where the carnal nature is nailed and crucified. The carnal nature is put to death on the cross. As Jesus voluntarily went to His Roman cross, we must volunteer to put the carnal nature on a spiritual cross. We must voluntarily bring our evil natures

296

and submit them to the hand of God. This is what it really means to be sanctified wholly: it is to be crucified with Christ in the inner man. We cannot do this in our own strength. God alone can slay us.

This carnal nature comes wrapped in a brilliant package called "Self." When we deny Self we are continuing to hold our carnal natures to the cross. Jesus could have come down from His cross any moment He chose. He was not there against His will. He volunteered to endure that agony, that pain, and that ridicule "for the joy set before Him." **As we follow Him, we also must volunteer to remain on the cross in self-denial that this carnal nature may be crucified, buried, and His divine nature resurrected within us.**

We cannot dictate how this carnal Self will be crucified. Self will not want to die. If we ever get close to death, we will try to live. He will slay us as we wait before Him. (We have tried to describe the absolute imperative of waiting in chapter twenty-three.) It is our nature to get busy and "do" things. But the Holy Spirit has revealed to my heart that in our "doing" religious things which appear good, we have undone the true work of the Kingdom and have missed God's best. If we are willing to wait on God consistently and lovingly, He will then bring us to the best at His own time and in His own way.

The speed of our progress in being led of the Spirit is dependent upon our submission to His will. God moves us ahead as swiftly as He can **in the proportion that He can trust us.** The walk with God, therefore, is not so much our learning techniques of how to be led of God. The primary concentration is pressing in the interior life to submit to God's will so perfectly that He might be able to trust us with a greater measure of His Spirit.

My friend, are you really determined to wait on God until He finishes the work He has begun at conversion? Will you let Him slay out of you that selfish, prideful, jealous, murmuring, fault-finding, analytical, self-sufficient spirit? He wants to uproot these poisonous weeds so that He might sow in us the seeds of His divine nature. But most people are unwilling to wait for God to produce His precious fruit. They want all that God has for them immediately. Most everybody wants a victorious, overcoming life in Christ; but often they want the prize without the race. They desire the ends without the means. They wish to read a book and find out in a few hours how to walk with God.

We live in a society of so many modern conveniences. We push a button and our clothes are washed. We press another button and our meals are cooked. We turn a handle and hot water pours out in abundance. Growing accustomed to ease in our earthly lives, we want convenience in our Christianity as well. We think it is owed us. But that is not the way God brings us into His likeness.

Spiritual understanding never comes this way. It comes little by little, step by step, through much suffering (Acts 14:22). **We have been trying to manufacture some wheels of our own inventiveness in order that we might reach the goal more swiftly and more easily.** But without the suffering we would not properly value God's mysteries. We would think lightly of divine secrets most sacred, and God would not be able to trust us. The more you suffer to get something, the more you treasure it when you have it. Of course, often the suffering that you will pass through will not be physical: it will be in the interior life, hidden from the eyes of those around you. The suffering of the Cross is secret and personal. And the more that one suffers in self-denial, the more he is willing to be slain.

The suffering of the soul is terrible, yet it is wonderful. It is agony, but it is the way to all Life, because in the life of losing yourself you are going to find everything. Oh, you will have battles, burdens, struggles, heartaches, and many difficulties—but you will have everything in Jesus. (And the Holy Spirit witnesses in my heart when I tell you, "You will have everything in Jesus!" You see, these are not just human ideas I am telling you. God is witnessing to my soul from Heaven that this is true. This is worth all the money you will ever see and more if you could hear these simple truths and bind them to your heart forever.)

It is going to take most of us who have been on this Christian journey a while, a long time to get back to the life of self-denial. It will be a tremendous adjustment to consistently, continously deny what we have been accustomed to do, in order to do what God wants. He doesn't want us simply denying Self occasionally to do His will—just going hit-and-miss, once today and twice next week. No. God wants to walk with us from the very beginning. In fact, I do not actually walk with God unless I have denied Self at every step, because in order to follow I must take up the cross, which is God's will.

In order to perceive His will I will need to die out to all those carnal things which keep me from hearing His voice. We are attuned to hear God's voice only as we deny Self and obey His guidances. Unless Self is consistently denied, our spiritual hearing is impaired and we cannot receive God's message.

We return to the cross from a life of disobedience by first confessing our neglect, disobedience, and failures. If we are just converted, we are able to begin at the same place: at the foot of the cross. The heart then turns its attention from the attractions of earth to the eternal goals of Heaven. It is not an easy assignment, for our natural tendency is not to look to Jesus in faith: it is to look to ourselves by reason. We learn to trust God little by little as we humbly read His Word, talk to Him in prayer, witness to the miracle of Jesus saving us, and strive with every bit of energy we have to obey the Holy Spirit.

When we begin our walk we are but tiny babes, no matter what our earthly age; and God lovingly treats us exactly according to our needs. He will teach us gently, but as swiftly as He can, about following His guidances. He will attempt to prompt every Christian to some small act of obeying His voice very soon after conversion or after returning to the cross. He will ask him to say, "I love Jesus," in a church service. The Holy Spirit may impress him to ask forgiveness from a neighbor for getting angry at him last week, or ask him to apologize to his wife for being stubborn the night before. It will be little things in the every-day life that God will lead you to and through. Seldom will God's request come naturally to the flesh, for the cross of Christ is an instrument on which the flesh is crucified.

It is impossible for us to discover this new life in Christ until we get rid of the old. God actually wants us to "die" to the earthly ambitions and desires in order that we might be raised with Christ to a heavenly preoccupation while still living in this world. Paul indicates this paradoxical living while yet "dead" in Colossians 3:1: "If ye then be risen with Christ, seek those things which are above, where Christ sitteth on the right hand of God. Set your affections on things above, not on things on the earth. For **ye are dead,** and your life is hid with Christ in God."

Now if each new convert will faithfully determine in his heart to do exactly what God lays on his soul to do, the marvelous walk with Jesus will begin. A new life actually **in Christ** begins to happen. But every step will be proceeded and accompanied by denying what Self wants and what Self wishes. **Self must never be permitted to make another decision in your life.** You must settle it forever and fix your will like a rock: "Jesus is now Lord of my life. He sits on the throne of my heart. I will seek His advice on where I am to go, what I am to do, how I am to dress, what I am to speak." Your life will become very simply "no longer I, but Christ."

I say "simply," and yet it is by no means effortless. It will take all the energy you possess, all the determination, all the crying and pleading for God's help and mercy to let you day by day, moment by moment, breath by breath, and yes—second by second—resist all evil and the demands of the earth to wait upon God and do humbly and consistently in love only what He directs you to do. All hell is against this kind of intimate walk with God, and it will only be by God's grace that any one of us will be able to continue. But praise be unto God, we will discover with the apostle Paul that in our own weakness He is made strong.

The devil and well-meant counselors of the earth will try to tell you that by waiting on God you are losing time and wasting time. They will tell you that there are souls to be won and many things to be accomplished. But the secret of life is in waiting upon God. While you are waiting on God you are learning to love Him, you are learning to praise Him, you are learning to commune with Him, you are learning how to recognize His voice. Sometimes as you wait you will be praying; often you will be listening; occasionally you will be shown a need in your heart, a glaring weakness of the soul which is hindering His Spirit from working through you. Then you may adore Him even more and meditate upon His suffering, His sorrow, and His heartbreak over a lost and dying world.

While you are waiting you are actually climbing in His own purpose. You may not be permitted to observe it, but He is lifting you to His own likeness as you go deeper in humility and in the knowledge of your own unworthiness and nothingness. Quite to your surprise, you will discover that from time to time this new-found Friend will direct vou to a needy soul. When you least anticipate it He will have you in the right place at the right time, and some precious heart will be converted because of Jesus working through you; someone may be healed or a dear soul lifted up. You will be so thrilled and filled with joy because Jesus did it! He was the one. You were simply privileged to be there and have His Kingdom work through you. Oh, glory to the Lamb of God, even Jesus!

Here is where the true adventure begins. In fact, God will give you such surprises in His fellowship that you will wonder why so few have gone this path before. The earth will be seeking pleasure in games, fairs, parties, and sensual experiences; but you will be so overjoyed with the work of the Holy Spirit in leading, in cleansing, and in instructing that people will say, "What is wrong with them? It looks like they don't have much of anything, yet they're carrying on as if they had everything."

But we are not to seek for adventure, for miraculous events, or even to be led by the Holy Spirit. We are simply to pour love back to God, honor Him, adore Him, and try to praise Him for His name's sake. We are not to become tense or nervous about how to die out, how to be slain, how to be crucified, or how to obey. We are to relax like a little child, remain right down at the bottom in brokenness, and simply trust God for all things.

You see, there are wonderful promises to those who actually trust God. The one which opens to every good and perfect gift is found in Proverbs 3:5-6: "Trust in the Lord with all thine heart, and lean not to thine own understanding. In all thy ways acknowledge Him and **He shall direct thy paths."**

Since the God of the entire universe has promised to guide us as we relinquish our own authority on our lives, give up our own limited views of life, and turn to Him as the only source of life and joy—we can rest assured that He will do exactly that. As we wait, He will teach us about self-denial in little humble ways. He will actually begin to direct our lives. And when He begins to take control, then we must gladly abandon our own plans to follow His command.

Throughout this pilgrimage I have tried to share but a few instances of self-denial: where my plans and my wishes had to be laid aside, and what God suddenly told me to do then became my plan.

I recall leaving our home in Hartford City several years ago to get a quart of milk, some bread, and meat. I hadn't gone more than four to five hundred feet when Jesus spoke to my heart. I had not simply been sitting around waiting for God to tell me something to do. I had been on my knees in prayer and in the Word—watching, waiting, crying, and praying hour after hour and day after day.

God said, "I want you to go home, get dressed to travel, take the bus to Muncie, and go to Parker City to visit T. L. Smith." What I had planned for that day had to be forgotten. My plans ended and God's began.

After getting the groceries I took what little money we had, walked down to the bus station, boarded the bus to Muncie, then took another bus to my home town. Coming into Parker I passed my wife's parents' home, and I always liked to stop there because I loved them like my own mother and father. But this morning I was not able to stop to see them or even my own folks. Self had to be denied. I was to do what God had told me to do.

When I walked into Tom Smith's little store his wife exclaimed, "Oh, Brother Helm! I'm so glad to see you. Tom has been sick. He's swollen in his tonsils and is feverish. He has been praying all morning that God would tell you to come."

And God had done just that. I give Him the praise for this. But I could not continue what I had planned for that day. I could not remain in the Word and prayer. Self had to be denied in order to do what God had said.

Going back into this man's bedroom where he lay ill, I fell on my knees, looked up into the face of Jesus in Heaven, and He came by the power of the Holy Ghost to take the fever out of this precious man. In a short while Tom was out of bed, dressed, and getting a haircut at the barber shop. That night he went to prayer meeting and told them what God had done for him. I didn't plan it or arrange it. The Holy Ghost was the Leader and Guide.

Even before God called me to leave everything, He was teaching me about walking with Him in self-denial. It was 1939. I had entered a store and had taken but three steps when the Lord told me to stop and go to a certain man's home. I ran to the car, drove to his home, and found that he had just returned from the hospital. I didn't understand all about the situation but I knew that he was very sick. "Jesus has brought me and I want to pray," I told him. In my feeble way I started to pray, and God became so precious to us that it seemed like Jesus came down in a white robe and stood a few feet from me to the left. Thrilled, I said, "I can go now, Jesus has heard my cry."

His insurance company had insisted that he undergo more tests at Robert Long Hospital in Indianapolis, and there the doctors gave him certain tests and X-rays, just as the physicians had done in our county hospital. After a few days, seven young doctors and one older doctor filed into his room and stood around his bed observing him. "We want to ask you a question," one of the doctors said. "We have the X-rays from the hospital in Winchester which clearly show a growth the size of two fists. We would like to know the name of the surgeon who performed this delicate operation and removed this growth. We cannot find a scar where he cut it out or where he sewed you up. Would you tell us, please, this surgeon's name?"

The man looked up from his hospital bed into the face of that physician and declared, "His name is Jesus the Christ."

God had done this. He had stopped me at my own affairs and sent me on an assignment of His Kingdom. The work which He accomplished was a miracle of His grace and power. But He could work through this poor, limited, unworthy servant only because I was obeying **His** command and doing **His** will.

Do you see what I would have missed if I had not forsaken my plans to do what Jesus bid me do? Oh, my friend!—How much have we missed in the past years, months, and days because we have failed to deny self? Because we have failed to wait on God that He might teach us how to hear His voice and be led of the Spirit?

But even as I am trying my very best to explain about the absoluteness of denying Self, most people will not realize what I mean. Many will tend to think that self-denial means simply to go to church twice a week, to wear clothing of a particular style, to participate in only specific types of activities, to refuse to eat some foods, or to attend only certain types of entertainment.

Self-denial may involve some of the above; but **true self-denial is simply doing what God directs instead of what you want to do.** And we will never know what God wants until we come to nothingness in love and wait before Him so that He can teach us how to hear and obey.

It is our inner attitude of heart which determines: "Above everything else, I want to follow Jesus!" Every other human activity must become secondary to the single burning desire to be God's true servant. This is why Jesus said in Luke 14:26: "If any man comes to me, and hate not his father, and mother, and wife, and children, and brethren, and sisters, yea, and his own life also, **he cannot be my disciple.**"

If there is anything in our life which takes precedence over our loving, listening to, and following Jesus—**then we cannot be His disciples.** As soon as we refuse to put Him first absolutely in our daily lives, we have ceased to be His disciple. This is the Narrow Way. **And most people will not hear this.** Unless we have waited on God, willing to let Him crucify out of us this carnal nature, we will continue to think that simply believing on Jesus intellectually, going to church, knowing the Bible, and doing good things will get us to Heaven.

But unless Jesus is absolutely first in our everyday life— unless we are walking in intimate fellowship with God and carrying out His will which He is telling us moment by moment from Heaven—then we proceed in a life of self-assertion, by-passing the way of self-denial and the cross.

We only hear God's voice as we have waited before Him through the years to learn the operations, the checks, and the guidances of the Holy Spirit. We only learn about being led of God as we actually obey Him and let Him lead us step by step. **If we do not wait sufficiently, we will go ahead unknowingly in fleshly self-assertion rather than in self-denial and will miss the Kingdom of God.**

God has so many wonderful lessons to teach us, but they are all to be learned along the road of the cross, the path one walks on the legs of "trust" and "obey". God wishes us to know this Way. He wants us to lose our lives for His sake and the Gospel's. Jesus came to teach us this way and to demonstrate it. This is what man has rejected. God has a plan for every life—a beautiful, marvelously exciting plan—but few have remained in His school long enough, quiet enough, faithful enough in prayer and witnessing in the Word; obedient enough so that He might teach us how He checks us in our conversation, in our behaviour, in our plans, and in our schedules.

If only we would be willing to consistently wait with joy upon God, He will refine us. There are fires to pass through as we wait which will burn out the dross and leave pure gold. But rarely will we stay in His hand long enough to be purified. It is true that when we are abiding in God's hand, no man can pluck us out; but we can get out of His hand simply by asserting Self. We get out of His hand by not praying and waiting upon God. We get out of His hand and into our own hands.

After so many experiences of disobedience following conversion, people are dulled to the voice of God, continuing in lives of self-assertion without even knowing it. They have the orthodoxy and the external pattern of acceptable Christianity, but there is no power of God operating through their life. There is no witness of the Holy Spirit. Often these individuals are the older people who have failed to mind God years ago. They have become hardened to the sweet voice of the Spirit and are only in a form of godliness. They are walking in the exterior life. But the Holy Spirit works through the interior life. Jesus said, "The Kingdom of God is within you."

I love all people and I love all churches. I have met wonderful people all through the United States and over the world. But God has called me to cry out to every church, every minister, and every layman that **we have been trying to have Christianity without the very first step of Christianity— and that is self-denial.** We cannot take one step after Jesus unless we deny Self and listen for God's guidance.

But we in the church have been trying to have Christianity without the leadership of the Holy Spirit. We have been going on in our own programs, in our own missionary ventures, in our own educational systems, in our building projects, in our visitation efforts. We have been trying to bring the Kingdom of God to life through our own efforts, our own talents, our own personalities, our own preaching, our own singing. Every leader in every church is precious, and I am not trying to find fault with anyone. But I must cry out to all our dear leaders that we in the professed church have lost the Kingdom of God. Dr. E. Stanley Jones said exactly that in his last book, "The Unshakable Kingdom and the Unchanging Person." *

Because we in the church have lost the Kingdom, we have been going on in the wilderness. We have been having the same program year after year. We are in a form. We sing, we pray, we testify a little, and we preach. It is monotony. Like the children of Israel, we go around and around, getting ever further from the land of Caanan.

But God wants to take us in a straight line to the promised land—which is simply walking in the Spirit, doing His will, waiting upon Him, losing all that He might be all. **We have been trying to do what God wants without doing what He says.**

Few people in all the ages have been willing to simply let Jesus lead them and be all to them. We in the church still want strings attached so that we might control to some measure. We have a little idea which direction we want things to

* Jones, E. Stanley, "The Unshakable Kingdom and the Unchanging Person," Abingdon Press, Nashville, Tennessee, 1972 (pp. 18, 21, 22, 72, and 73).

go. Wc want great crowds, a big Sunday School, an attractive building. We desire popularity. We want people to join our particular group. We want our special ideas to be accepted and acknowledged. Most every body of believers wants a little something for themselves, their church, their denomination, or their organization.

I have seldom experienced any body of believers praying in true prevailing supplication for God to send revival to any church outside of their own organization or form. Have you often heard reports of a Methodist Church joining as one person to pray for the local Church of God one mile away? Have you heard of the Nazarenes crying out for God to send a sweet awakening to the Friends? Our prayers are many times still very self-centered and self-assertive, because we are still manipulating our own goals, not God's goals.

God is seeking a people who will simply and totally be His —willing to be lowly, unnoticed, unrecognized, and unlauded by religious notables. The true power of God will operate through these lowly, contrite, self-emptied ones who know that they are undeserving of the least thing God has for them. He will wonderfully use these who have no plans of their own and no desires except to be vessels through which Jesus might be exalted.

This is the company of believers who are the true Church of God. Any lowly heart who is willing to die out to the earth and lose all for Jesus is the active member in the universal Church of Christ victorious. God's true Church is not a specific body of people who have called themselves by a certain name. It is not a particular religious order which prescribes to certain theological truths. The true Church of God is made up of every blood-washed sinner who remains lowly at the cross in self-denial, actually following Jesus under the cross. The Church of God is that body of believers which the Holy Spirit truly indwells; where Jesus is truly the Head: His mind is within them and the Holy Spirit is the Leader and Guide.

I fear that we leaders of the church have been trying to do the work of the Kingdom in our own skeleton, in our own ideologies, in our own structure of reason and beauty. Much of it is good and attractive, but it isn't born of the Spirit. One can have the earthly best, but if it doesn't thrust to every heart the divine imperative of self-denial and the cross, it isn't sufficient.

The Holy Spirit has revealed to me a very serious fact. He has shown me that the church today has become infected with the spiritual diseases of man's philosophies and carnal energies. Unless we bring to an end all of our best-intended attempts to work for God, confess our disobedience and sin, and return lowly, broken, and torn to His feet to be healed— we may possibly bring new converts into our assemblies and expand our churches, but every newborn we bring in will have the same diseases that we have. They will be brought into our fellowship and become infected with the viruses of self-assertion and respectable Christianity, never knowing that they are not walking with the Christ of Calvary. They will become crippled by self-assertion and blinded by an active carnal mind, never knowing that they are stumbling toward an eternal death.

Our job in the church is not to bring people into our fellowship. We cannot do it. Our assignment is to wait upon God. When He is then able to cleanse the church of those things which grieve Him and crush the lambs, then He will come through that holy and purified body of believers, move them to spiritual travail, and bring souls to a truly divine birth into the Kingdom. (Isaiah 66:8b—"For as soon as Zion travailed, she brought forth her children.") And when God brings them in they will be beautiful, healthy lambs. The glory of God will be in their souls, and there will be enough milk in the udders of the sheep to keep them alive and well (and the lambs feed only from the sheep—their milk the joy of the Lord pouring from obedient hearts).

We in the church have been trying to work out that which

was not our business to do. Our assignment is simply to wait on God, for He can do more in seconds than men can do in centuries. We have been trying to work out all the methods and get people in; we have tried to talk to them, persuade them, and change their lives.

But God simply wants us to become a people who will wait upon Him so that He can slay us and slay us and slay us in order that He can then have full control of us. He could do wonders for His glory if only He could find a body willing to undergo the divine surgery necessary to be truly used of Him.

The Lord wants us to die out to recognition, station, and popularity. We must come to the cheerful willingness to be on the bottom forever. God can only fully use the broken and humble. He can work through others to a measure, but His true presence and power of the Kingdom operates through the lowly: that which the world rejects and thinks foolish.

There is great glory here. There is great joy. Heaven is here in His hand. But the devil, carnality, and all of hell will not let you hear this. Even while you are reading this you will have to labor and cry and press in your heart to truly get hold of these sacred truths and begin to apply them to your life. We are in a ferocious battle against principalities, against powers, against the rulers of darkness of this world, and spiritual wickedness in high places. They steal any spiritual truth from you often before it can even reach your heart, unless you plead the blood of Jesus over your heart and mind, lifting the Shield of Faith over your soul. This exhortation would probably need to be shared a few hundred times to most congregations before they would begin to hear the urgency and seriousness of self-denial.

That is the real purpose of this book—to lovingly persuade people to really turn from themselves unto the living God and actually do His will. Not just follow God in form and in word, which is what many churches are now doing; but actually come to the basic simplicity of the Gospel of Jesus

Christ in self-denial, trust, and obedience. It's going to be an awful thing in Judgment if we have been in the church but missed the will of God; if we have been moral and upright, but have not waited on God that He might work through us His will.

In all of my ministry I have found very few individuals, let alone entire churches, who have been willing to humble themselves. But unless we actually come to nothingness and begin to walk with God, we are not actually the Church. **We are not in the Kingdom of God and we are not in the true Church of God unless we truly forsake all of our own ways and follow day by day the leadership of the Holy Spirit.** If we do not really do God's will—if we are not faithful and true as little children—we are stumbling blocks instead of stepping stones.

If we ministers in the church have not really minded God —walked in the Spirit by self-denial and obeyed in humility, not trying to know so much but simply coming to childlikeness —then we have taken the money of the church and deceived the flock. If we have not embraced the cross in the interior life, if we have not cried out in agony within our souls to do God's will, then we are going to be held accountable in Judgment (and right now God tells me, "I guide thee, direct thee, and tell thee what to do").

We are a thousand miles short of the will of God in most all churches. We have people on our boards and on our councils who are not walking with God under a cross. We have church leaders who are trying to maneuver the business of the body of Christ.

Jesus tells me in my heart that if we try to run the church with a carnal mind—if there is unsubmitted Self in our lives— we are as dangerous to that body as five rattlesnakes would be to a tiny child in his crib. It is that dangerous for one man or one woman in the church leadership to be carnal and not do God's will: it is that deadly to the lambs and the sinners who are watching the lives of those people.

You see, beloved, we must have a cleansing of all our precious church leaders from the very highest to the least. I love every church leader so very much; I love each one with all my heart. It takes love to tell the real truth in kindness and gentleness. But the Holy Spirit reveals to my heart that if I am in the church and have the slightest bit of carnality in my heart, then I am as dangerous to that body as rattle-snake venom. I will poison the body even when I am trying to help it. (All church leaders whose hearts are right with God will not resent this revelation; but all hearts not yielded wholly to God will be offended at it. Psalms 119:165.)

This is more serious than I can tell you, for rarely will a congregation rise any higher than its spiritual leader. We cannot lift anyone higher than the level on which we stand. If only we could convince our precious ministers of all our churches to really wait upon God and walk with Him so that His power could truly work through them. And if we have not waited on God until He can teach us ministers how to stop or go at His command; or to discern what the Holy Spirit wishes for our times together as a body of believers; then we are like teachers who do not know our ABC's. We may have the finest orthodoxy, but there is little power of God in us. The true love of God isn't pouring through us as it could and should.

It is this divine love which regulates the power of God. It is our love to God which determines our self-denial. We will seek His will and deny Self in proportion to our love for Jesus. What grieves my heart so badly is that many of our churches are disobedient and don't know it. Many of our precious people are living self-assertive lives of disobedience and haven't the slightest idea that they are doing it.

The world is dying for God's love. Sinners don't need our theologies and denominational ideas: they need the love of Jesus to make them know how wretched and empty their lives are. And this love cannot—I repeat: **cannot**—flow through a disobedient heart. I am not speaking of an earthly love, a mere refined human affection. I'm talking about the divine flow of God's love which pours like a mountain torrent through the crucified, yielded heart to every living person. This love contains no bitterness, no criticism, no harshness, no fault-finding, no murmuring. This love forgives all wrongs and overlooks all misunderstandings; it holds no grudges and makes no complaints; it is dead to all self-pity and alive to all praise. This is the love which makes men of all nations one in the Spirit.

And when you gather a few people together who love one another with this holy, pure, heavenly love—God will come down and make His abode among them. The power of the Holy Ghost will move through that body and sinners will be born into the Kingdom by the divine power of God. We know very little of such divine power. **We have lived so far from His perfect will that God has been unable to trust us with much of His presence.**

If the power which fell on Homer Pumphrey and me in August of 1942 in Circleville, Ohio would fall in any church or in any place, I know that all infidels and atheists would be saved in twenty-two seconds. The power would be so great that they would cry out, "Oh, God! Forgive me! I didn't know you were so great! Have mercy on me, Jesus!" Confession would leap right out of them. They couldn't help it.

This sacred event occured while Homer and I were in a hotel room in Circleville, Ohio. I made the statement, "I am convinced that very few people in all the world have everything that God wants them to have and are doing everything God wants them to do."

My precious brother took exception to my statement and replied, "Do you mean to tell me that these people are not doing all God wants them to do and don't have all He wants them to have?"—and he named over some of the renowned spiritual leaders of that day.

I answered him, "Homer, the Spirit is grieved." And when I said that, the power of God filled that room as a mighty

313

wind which lasted for three seconds. The glory of God was everywhere. It filled every little crack and crevice. It was the greatest power of God I have ever experienced. It was so powerful that Homer thought we were going to be translated. The words came right out of him, "What is God doing —is He calling apostles? What does He want me for—an armorbearer?" He hardly knew he was saying it. The words simply came out of him.

Over thirty years ago God descended on that room as a testimony of His presence to the fact that His Spirit has been grieved by almost all mortals in all the ages. He was giving witness with His mighty power that if only He could find a body of believers willing to lose all and come to nothingness, He would come through that body and lift Jesus to the world, and sinners would then be drawn to Him as on the day of Pentecost or even greater.

We have been attempting to lift Jesus by our own methods, our own preaching, our own personalities. But that is not the "lift" about which Jesus spoke in John 12:32 when He said: "And I, if I be lifted up from the earth, will draw all men unto me." Jesus was first placed on the cross and lifted up by cruel, carnal, wicked hands. The next lift will be by tender, gentle, loving, broken, obedient lives who have waited on God until all the carnal things are removed and the love of God flows freely among them. When God finds such a body, then He will come up through that body and lift Jesus to all the world in the might of the Kingdom of God.

When this spiritual lift of the divine Son of God occurs, all persons in that area will be drawn to God like to a magnet. They will not be able to resist this great moving power of God. This mighty drawing of Jesus could begin the Holy Ghost Revival to the World which I have been anticipating now for, over thirty years. This could be the "latter rain" (James 5:7) which will precede the return of Jesus. It is coming someday soon, whenever He can find a body willing to pay the price and truly follow Him daily in self-denial.

We have witnessed many marvelous things in Jesus, seeing a few saved here and there, and I am not trying to minimize what God has been doing anywhere on the earth. But what God **wants to do,** if only He could find a body yielded wholly to His will, is so tremendous that I am not able to get to it with words.

But we are not to seek to do something big for Jesus. We are not to try to work up a big revival or try to whip up a world-wide evangelistic campaign. The secret is this: as a body of believers we must all come to nothingness together. As Jesus permitted His body to be nailed on the cross as a sacrifice for sins, we in the living body of Christ must make the same sacrifice.

Can you hear it? Jesus gave Himself a sacrifice for us, so now the body should be willing to make the same sacrifice. **We must literally, as His body, in the interior life, go to the cross and die out to everything of earth: be willing to perish to all earthly achievements and the religious world.** And from this slain body God will bring the same power which raised Jesus from the dead and lift the resurrected Lord to the entire world.

This is the secret of all spiritual success in the church. But I preached many years before I knew that. This is what God is trying to cry through me to all churchdom: "We must die out to Self. We must lose all to find all. We must learn how to obey. We must go to the cross as Jesus went to the cross."

The absolute which we in the church must face is the imperative of the cross in the daily life of the believer. We have had enough preaching to last for centuries to come. We have enough devotional books to encourage us for years. There has been sufficient discussion and review of theologies and doctrines of holiness. **What is now needed is an actual life lived in obedience to the commands of Jesus.** We must stop talking "about" Christianity and begin letting Christ live through us.

He will not live through us as we think He ought. He has His own plans and His own unique desires for our lives. We will learn these plans only as we wait upon Him day after day and begin to learn how to be led of Him.

Most all men have wanted to squeeze God into certain limited molds and unchanging patterns. But when God creates, all of Nature obeys His will in an infinite variety of ways. Each tiny snowflake becomes a very special individual; each microscopic crystal forms slightly different from every other. Likewise, as He creates His Kingdom on earth, God will use infinite variety in leading His servants. No technique or applied methods could contain the unlimited inventiveness of our Heavenly Father as He leads His children to do His will. Men have always wanted rules to follow, when God has preferred to find humble followers who wanted to be ruled.

The Word tells us that "to as many as received Him, to them gave He the power to **become** the sons of God." We have too long camped at the foot of this glorious mountain of promise, assuming that, because we have "believed" on Jesus that we are fulfilling all the requirements of sonship. But another scripture tells us quite plainly that there is a difference in "the power to become" a son, and actually "being" a son. Paul reveals to us that the requirement of true sonship lies in "for as many as are led by the Spirit of God."

In order to be a true son of God, we must press on from conversion in order to be instructed in the mysteries of the Kingdom of God. To become a son is a lengthy process, and we must needs be about the business of "becoming." We need to be weaned from the patterns and inner proclivities of the earth to a heavenly vision and an eternal longing. We cannot permit ourselves to set our sights on certain patterns of religious achievment, on gifts, or on a particular goal of effectiveness within the accepted church structure. We must learn what it means simply to **walk with God.**

God's pattern for every man and woman has always been different; so we cannot look to any of His servants for a specific model of activity. However, we can look to Jesus for all instruction, finding in the Biblical record His teachings, His pattern of living, and His example in lowly servitude. Above all, we have His ringing cry: "A new commandment I give unto you . . . that ye love one another as I have loved you."

A lifetime would not suffice to meditate sufficiently upon the implications and practice of loving one another as He loved us. In fact, all eternity will probably never reach the limits of His love, which we are to embrace to the fullest of our limited capacities, by His grace and help. But this divine love is the binding adhesive between the numberless individuals making up His body on earth. His love flowing from one to another becomes the sinew and fiber which joins finger to hand, wrist to arm, and creates the living organism of His glorious Church.

God has sent this voice crying in the wilderness as a clarion call to true obedience to the Holy Spirit. As you are reading these final words you are choosing, or are approaching the choice, either to be a true follower of Jesus, or simply a believer in Christian principles. When Jesus was sent to earth, a great number believed the principles of God's revelations to the patriarchs and the prophets—but few, if any, were willing to acclaim Him boldly as the Messiah.

Very few have ever listened to God's men from the beginning. The religious leaders were unable to recognize Jesus, and He was the fulfillment of the revelation which they sincerely served. Most all Christian leaders, likewise, have failed to recognize God's servants. The established church persecuted Huss, Madam Guyon, Bunyan, Luther, Wesley, Finney, E. E. Byrum, and hundreds more. The Power of this earth has blinded our precious religious leaders so that they feel threatened by God's true servants. Even when one tries to point out the blindness to God's true servants of past religious leaders, today's leaders say, "Well, that was in the past. We have the revelation today. Our way is the true way. We are in the main stream of God's revelation."

(Very rarely has there been a church leader of any position or authority who has truly humbled himself and become submissive to the will of God. Every truly crucified church leader will not feel badly towards me for this declaration.)

In all my ministry I have loved every church. I have tried to encourage every minister and every layman. I have never talked about any denomination or any leader or any church. When I am in the pulpit God often comes through me in judgment to call the church back to true holiness and purity. But when I am alone, I never talk against the church or abuse the ministry.

Yet some church leaders think that I am a false prophet and that I am out to get church property. A number of religious leaders are afraid of me. They will often believe stories about us from people who have never heard us or known us, rather than persevere themselves to find out what we are really like. And it is a dangerous thing, beloved, to believe a lie.

It is the nature of a heart filled with divine love to believe the best of everyone. But Satan so fights this message of self-denial and the cross, that some church leaders have been willing to believe that I am out to cause division and start my own church; when all I am trying to do is what God has called me to do: and that is encourage every person to actually follow Jesus, and unite all believers around the world into a fellowship of divine love.

(It hurts my heart to hear the terrible things that people say about me; and yet God keeps me happy. I am rejoicing in my soul even though my heart is broken for the church. Jesus has told us that every true follower would be hated even as He was hated.)

318

Often the minister today is under considerable pressure from his denominational hierarchy to conform to certain patterns, schedules, training materials, and financial processes. I doubt if many laymen know a fraction of the pressures under which the precious ministers must labor today. They need our urgent prayer daily for Satan is trying to discourage them from being true and holy to their calling. Please hold up the hands of all true church leaders by praying for them, encouraging them with letters and words of appreciation, and by being faithful to all that God is calling you unto.

By His choice (for God has always chosen the foolish things of this world to confound the wise) I am one of His representatives on this earth, and because of this speak for Him when I ask: "Won't you, dear one, this very moment determine with all the strength of your heart, soul, mind, and body to truly follow Jesus day by day and second by second in self-denial and obedience, the Lord being your Helper?" I can guarantee that you will never experience greater fulfillment than in this lowly walk with Jesus.

If you were to hear the matchless voice of Jesus Himself audibly declare to you, "If you do not bear your cross and come after me, you cannot be my disciple . . ."—would you dare reply, "I know a better way"? And yet, that is what most persons have answered by the pattern of their lives since Jesus made known this minimum requirement of true discipleship two thousand years ago.

But I urge each of you, as you are about to complete this humble pilgrimage—do not simply lay this book aside as another story. Whenever the Gospel of Jesus Christ is presented by the Holy Spirit, those hearing must make a decision. You choose now either to truly come after Jesus, the Son of God, by denying Self to take up God's will daily and follow the Holy Spirit—or you choose, as many have decided through the ages, to reject the Way of the Cross.

The way of self-denial and the cross is not hard. Oh beloved, it is the very opposite! The way of the transgressor is hard. **Following after God's perfect will is the only way of complete inner fulfillment.** God would never mock his children by promising them the most consummate experience of Life, then deceive them into a dull and miserable existence. The great mystery hidden in the cross is that it is the door which opens to all life! This central truth of all living is so aptly captured in the marvelous hymn:

Jesus, I my cross have taken . . .
All to leave and follow thee;
Destitute, despised, forsaken,
Thou, from hence, my all shalt be:
Perish every fond ambition,
All I've sought or hoped, or known;
Yet how rich is my condition:
God and Heav'n are still my own!

—Henry F. Lyte, 1793-1847

This is a beginning for each of you reading this book— whether you are a Sunday School teacher, plumber, secretary, machinist, nurse, mechanic, psychologist, minister, layman, or high school student. You are either beginning on the upward path of seeking first God's will and His Kingdom; or you are beginning a darkening path towards self-desires which has already led millions and millions to heartbreak and eternal distruction.

Which beginning are you choosing as you turn this final page?

Important Notice to Each Reader of This Book

We trust this first reading of **A Voice in the Wilderness** has strengthened and challenged your heart. May we humbly suggest that you read through it carefully once again before sharing this copy with a loved one or a friend?

The primary purpose of sharing this pilgrimage is to alert the church to the absolute imperative of denying Self to obey the Lord Jesus. Because such an inner spiritual practice in daily life is so contrary to all the patterns of the earth, the Holy Spirit has revealed to Rev. Helm that most of us will need to re-read this book nine or ten times before this simple command from Jesus — to deny our own moment-by-moment desires in order to obey the promptings of the Holy Spirit — actually gets into our hearts and becomes a part of our interior lives.